Organization, Society and Politics

Also by Kevin Morrell

THE ETHICAL BUSINESS (*with K. Mellahi and G. Wood*)
THE REALITIES OF WORK (*forthcoming, with P. Blyton and M. Noon*)

Organization, Society and Politics

An Aristotelian Perspective

Kevin Morrell
Associate Professor of Governance, Warwick Business School,
University of Warwick

First published 2012 by
PALGRAVE MACMILLAN

Palgrave Macmillan in the UK is an imprint of Macmillan Publishers Limited, registered in England, company number 785998, of Houndmills, Basingstoke, Hampshire RG21 6XS.

Palgrave Macmillan in the US is a division of St Martin's Press LLC, 175 Fifth Avenue, New York, NY 10010.

Palgrave Macmillan is the global academic imprint of the above companies and has companies and representatives throughout the world.

Palgrave® and Macmillan® are registered trademarks in the United States, the United Kingdom, Europe and other countries

ISBN: 978-0-230-30446-8

This book is printed on paper suitable for recycling and made from fully managed and sustained forest sources. Logging, pulping and manufacturing processes are expected to conform to the environmental regulations of the country of origin.

A catalogue record for this book is available from the British Library.

A catalog record for this book is available from the Library of Congress.

10 9 8 7 6 5 4 3 2 1
21 20 19 18 17 16 15 14 13 12

Printed and bound in Great Britain by
CPI Antony Rowe, Chippenham and Eastbourne

For Sarah

Contents

Tables and Figures

Tables

Figures

Preface

This book applies Aristotle's practical philosophy to contemporary social concepts and problems. It is difficult to speak to a topic as broad as 'organizations, politics and society', or to claim ownership of 'an Aristotelian perspective'. The justification for this title follows in the introductory chapter and in the two opening chapters. As a courtesy to readers, this preface offers a general outline – ignoring Swift's advice on prefaces in *A Tale of a Tub*, first published in 1704:

> I have always looked upon it as a high point of indiscretion in monster mongers, and other retailers of strange sights, to hang out a fair large picture over the door, drawn after the life, with a most eloquent description underneath: this has saved me many a three-pence; my curiosity was fully satisfied, and I never offered to go in. (Swift, 2004: 60)

Swift's description of 'retailers of strange sights' seems relevant here. For some, seeing Aristotle stalk contemporary social concepts and problems will indeed be a strange sight, but this is central to the contribution. Reframing problems or concepts is often the first step to new insight, even if the source for re-presentation is an ancient one. More troubling is Swift's phrase 'monster mongers'. For a few, given Aristotle's toleration of slavery, his apparent misogyny and comfort with elites, calling directly on him may seem like monster mongering, and this is a barrier to re-presentation or reframing. These issues are given more discussion in the text than this preface allows, but the particular issue of sexism and language requires initial comment.

Sexism and language

At times Aristotle uses *anthrōpos* which can be translated either as man or mankind, or as human being or humanity (like the Latin 'homo'): for example, the *Nicomachean Ethics* (1181b15) describes politics as the philosophy of human affairs, *anthrōpeia philosophia* (Reeve, forthcoming). At other times, Aristotle uses *anēr* which is gendered and means manly or especially and prototypically male: like the Latin 'vir'. For example, the *Politics* (1276b16) describes the virtue of the good man, *agathos anēr* (Lindsay, 2000: 436). This book avoids gendered language, even if this deviates from implied translation of *anēr*. However, extracts follow the choice of translators, even if they use gendered language. A slight complexity on this point is that in Greek it is often possible to avoid using a noun or pronoun where English demands one, and it is conventional to use masculine forms to include the feminine (I am grateful to Richard Stalley for explaining this to me). Where translators use 'man', 'he' or 'his' I have not added '[*sic*]'.

Contents

The introduction claims provocatively that Aristotle discovered a social Fact. This is his description of a human being as *zōon politikon*: the kind of animal who naturally forms associations. Next come two chapters named after the title of the book which make the case for applying Aristotle in contemporary social science. The first, 'Organization, Society and Politics' argues that we can usefully revise our understanding of organization by considering it in terms of Aristotle's concept of *koinōnia*, a word that can be translated variously as sharing, community and association (Stalley, 2009). The next, 'An Aristotelian Perspective' makes the case for the continuing relevance of Aristotle's practical philosophy in the teeth of various objections.

Then, at the core of this book, is a discussion and application of Aristotle's practical philosophy based on the following four texts: *Politics*, *Nicomachean Ethics*, *Rhetoric* and *Poetics*. As others do, I argue for the interconnectedness of these texts; indeed it is this interconnectedness that is part of what still makes Aristotle's writings so compelling. However, to assist clarity and structure, each of these four texts is discussed in a separate, dedicated chapter, that is named after the respective text. Following each such 'discussion chapter' is an 'application chapter' showing where I have applied ideas from Aristotle's practical philosophy to understand contemporary problems in organization, society and politics.

Accordingly, the chapter following *Politics* outlines a way to understand the relationship between governance and the public good and incorporates case studies evaluating the administrations of four UK Prime Ministers: the MacMillan and Wilson governments, the legacy of Blair, and Cameron's notion of 'big society'. It also refers to the 2011 riots in the United Kingdom. The chapter following *Nicomachean Ethics* focuses on the nature of ethical decision making, and suggests that Aristotelian virtue ethics is more compatible with contemporary work in behavioural decision making than rational choice theories. The chapter following *Rhetoric* examines political leaders' speeches, and a particular form of argument – enthymeme – and shows how this is still relevant to understanding policy texts. The chapter following *Poetics* outlines an approach to teaching contemporary business school students about organizations drawing on Aristotle's notion of *mimēsis* (representation or imitation).

These applied chapters each make a case for the relevance of the corresponding text to the present day and in doing so they draw on my work published in the following journals: *Public Administration* (Morrell, 2006, 2009; Morrell and Harrington-Buhay, forthcoming), the *Journal of Business Ethics* (Morrell, 2004a,b; Morrell and Clark, 2009), the *Journal of Management Studies* (Morrell, 2008), *Human Relations* (Morrell and Hartley, 2006) and *Organization* (Morrell, forthcoming). The combination of discussion and application substantiates the more theoretical argument for the continuing value of Aristotle's ideas that is outlined in the introduction and the opening two chapters. The conclusion revisits the concept of public good and suggests a way to incorporate Aristotle's work with more contemporary insights from postcolonial studies, illustrating this with an analysis of the 1995 Property Rights forum in post-conflict Nicaragua (Morrell and Harrington, 2011).

The texts used

The primary source for all quotations from Aristotle is the revised Oxford translation of the complete works of Aristotle edited by Jonathan Barnes (1995). Where indicated, and only where the alternative translation seemed especially helpful or clearer, I have drawn on the following editions of the main texts referred to in this book. (This is indicated after an extract with the name of the translator.):

Aristotle (1997). *Poetics*. Translated by S. Butcher. New York: Dover Publications, Inc.
Aristotle (2009). *Politics*. Translated by E. Baker. Oxford: Oxford University Press.
Aristotle (2009). *Rhetoric*. Edited by Lee Honeycutt based on a translation by W. Rhys-Roberts. Retrieved 7 July 2009, from www.public. iastate.edu/~honeyl/Rhetoric/

I am also grateful to David Reeve for sharing with me his forthcoming translation of the sixth book of the *Nicomachean Ethics*.

Extracts from Aristotle are cited using the conventional system page, column, and line format established by Bekker – so, for example, when Aristotle gives us this phrase in the *Nicomachean Ethics*:

> one swallow does not make a summer, nor does one day; and so too one day, or a short time, does not make a man blessed and happy.

This can be found on page 1098, column a, lines 17–19, or more succinctly: (1098a17–19).

Acknowledgements

Nothing would be possible without the support of my family. For their time, and their comments, I thank: Surendra Arjoon, Jonathan Davies, Paul Edwards, Robin Holt, Kelvin Knight, Richard Kraut, Martin Parker, David Reeve, Richard Stalley and Scott Taylor. Thanks to Nicola Harrington-Buhay for her work supporting the case study of Nicaragua (discussed in the penultimate chapter). Thanks also to Virginia Thorp and Keri Dickens at Palgrave for their support and encouragement, and to Vidhya Jayaprakash for their help with the final stages of preparation of the manuscript. The book draws on work in several journal articles, the first two of which were written in 2002 and the most recent of which are forthcoming so thanks are due to the anonymous reviewers who helped me to improve arguments over that time, and the editors of those journals. In very small part it draws on essays written as an Undergraduate Philosophy student at Jesus College, Cambridge where my interest in Aristotle began.

Introduction

This book aims to demonstrate the continuing relevance of Aristotle to understanding contemporary organizations. As the title of this book suggests, the term 'organization' is understood broadly, so that it encompasses work organizations in both public and private sectors, and also a very wide variety of other social forms: from small voluntary associations and communities through to society as a whole. This is consistent with the use of organization in the comparatively new discipline of critical management studies (CMS), which challenges various hegemonies in relation to business and management. One such hegemony has been a narrow construction of 'organization' that limits its application to work, and concerns itself with the effectiveness of private corporations. Take, for instance, this parenthetic definition of organization which opens the first section of a popular text in organizational behaviour (this extract is from its twelfth edition):

> Let's begin by briefly defining the terms manager and organization – the place where managers work. (Robbins and Judge, 2007: 4)

In this text, as the following chapter argues, 'organization' means much more than the place where managers work. This is in large part because I use 'organization' in a way that tries to recapture and re-present what Aristotle identified as the basic imperative for association that we experience as social, or political, animals. This connects organization, society and politics, and is a far broader sense than organization is usually given, broader even perhaps than the sense it has in the literature on CMS.

Agonizing over the definition of terms is an activity for which academics are often pilloried. The clichéd answer of an academic asked for their opinion about 'x' is to begin, 'it depends on what you mean by "x"'. Yet definitions and the way in which we use language are extraordinarily important because such things carry power. The preface referred to my choice to translate Aristotle's *anēr* universally as 'human', rather than 'man' which potentially excludes or silences 'woman'. Perhaps somehow such a choice turns something that is, or that should be, remarkably abhorrent (privileging of one gender over the other), into something normal. In this way inequity, differences in power chances

1

and the arbitrary can become factual and sanitized by the formulaic gloss which academic definitions impose.

To draw attention to this choice (in a preface and introduction) could itself be taken not as an attempt at transparency, but as a kind of lip service, a rhetorical gesture masking deeper acts of privileging: like the choice by a middle-class, white male to write a book about the archetypal Dead White European Male. And yet this book is intended to be radical. Indeed it is arguably more radical by embracing such an uncompromising figure in the teeth of obvious and apparent problems such as Aristotle's sexism, his toleration of slavery and apparent demotion of individual liberty. The choice to engage with Aristotle's ideas certainly removes us from what Žižek (2002: 546) calls 'the benign universe of cultural studies chic [where] radicality ultimately amounts to an empty gesture that obliges no one to anything determinate'. This text holds up Aristotle's practical philosophy as a source for contemporary critique and emancipation and so is decidedly unchic, but (in Žižek's terms), the coordinates are clear. The starting point for this is to try to redefine organization construing it primarily as verb, rather than noun. Organization is not a place, but an activity (Cooper, 1990).

Robbins and Judge's construction of 'organization' as 'the place where managers work' invites a logical fallacy (*post hoc ergo propter hoc*): all managers work in organizations; therefore all organizations are places where managers work (and all organizations need to be 'managed'). But it is not just tendentious or flawed. To define organizations as places where managers work is, consciously or not, an act of positioning wedded to the interests of capital. It is an act of violence, excluding and silencing the worker, and also blind to other forms of association. This is common to other texts on organizational behaviour which often open with extraordinarily broad definitions of organization, then immediately abandon these as they focus on the (North American) capitalist firm. Then, in their remaining pages they salute a procession of powerful figures in hagiographic case studies.

The more generous understanding of 'organization' that CMS offers (and sustains) – as a wide, unspecified variety of social forms – makes it more likely that we identify and resist capitalist ideology in received accounts of cognate terms such as: work, effectiveness, team, common goal, and so on. A refusal to define organization so precisely or to sign up to apparent common sense challenges a discursive hegemony: an ordering of concepts, actors and relations expressed in statements which purportedly describe a state of affairs, but that in essence constitute them. It is important to challenge such hegemonies because they reproduce inequality and bolster class dominance (Gramsci, 1971).

This suggests that engaging with the definition of 'organization' is worthwhile, but how is it relevant to Aristotle, and to a project connecting organization with society and politics? Part of Aristotle's legacy has been to furnish the architects of any number of societies with definitions and categories that express positions of advantage and dominance, for instance the binaries: master/slave, man/woman, king/subject, citizen/barbarian. Even where the application of such categories rests on mistaken or insufficiently nuanced accounts of Aristotle, or perhaps on wilful misinterpretation, this still prompts the following question: why continue with something potentially contaminated, rather than seek for something new?

The answer I advocate in response to these questions is that Aristotle's approach to understanding the social world remains relevant because of his definition of human beings as a particular kind of animal, one that naturally organizes into groups. This is encapsulated in his most famous, usually misapplied, phrase that a human being is 'a political animal' *zōon politikon*. The reason this phrase is usually misapplied is that it is typically taken to be a statement about politics, and human beings' inherent desire to be involved in schemes or politicking. It is not just a statement about politics. Indeed, I would go as far as to say it is not even mainly a statement about politics. It is a biological statement reflecting Aristotle's way of differentiating humans from other animals. Notwithstanding that this definition itself could be taken as expressing hegemony, for me it seems so basic and powerful that it can help to reappraise radically the concept of organization, and related terms like society and politics. So much so, that in this text I describe Aristotle's definition of human beings as political animals as a social Fact. The more generous definition of organization discussed in the following chapter follows from a reformulation of this Fact, summarily that:

Organization as verb describes the activities of humans as political animals. As noun, 'organization' describes the groups and places within which such activities take place, but these groups and places result from acts of organization. As groups and places, these organizations in turn structure acts of organizing.

The first two sentences in this definition are discussed in detail in the following chapter. The third sentence in this definition of organization follows from Aristotle's brilliantly puzzling assertion that the city is prior to the individual and this is discussed in more detail in the chapter on *Politics*.

Now, obviously any claim to the status of Fact in the social sciences is provocative and so this intentional raising of a red flag needs some contextualization. To do this, briefly (if a little simplistically) Deleuze's (2004: 20–26) framework of relations between propositions in *Logic of Sense* can be used to describe the essential claims in this book. On Deleuze's terms, Aristotle's definition of humans as *zōon politikon* is an act of *designation* by him (it corresponds to a state of affairs); my claim in this book that this is a social Fact is an instance of *manifestation* (an expression of a belief). The corollary claims: that this framework offers advantages over other definitions, and that a particular definitional framework for 'organization' follows are *signification* (the implications of that belief).

This summary of Deleuze is a little simplistic because, as Deleuze says, designation, manifestation and signification are interrelated. An act of designation or signification implies manifestation because any proposition such as 'x' is a fact, or 'x' follows from 'y' is implicitly of the form, 'I' ('believe that "x" is a fact', or 'believe that "x" follows from "y"'). Notwithstanding the value of this nuance, when re-presenting the ideas of another, Deleuze's terms are useful to try to tease out differences between designation and manifestation. Here, this helps to show that whilst I claim that Aristotle was right in this most basic assertion, I am not (at least) saying it is a state of affairs, and also acknowledge that others will disagree. Capitalizing 'Fact' is an attempt to differentiate between these senses of designation and manifestation.

From this social Fact – a human being is *zōon politikon* – comes the possibility to destabilize dominant accounts of 'organization' because we can then invoke all manner of phenomena that we naturally recognize as social, but that are traditionally silenced by accounts of organizations that privilege capital. Organization becomes not just a place where managers work, but a diffuse category of social forms and, crucially, activities, encompassing politics, persuasion, ethics and aesthetics. Aristotle's work in practical philosophy speaks to all of these activities because he gives us this most basic definition of a human being.

A number of writers have worked with either Aristotle's *Politics* or *Ethics* to discuss contemporary problems. What this book does is different on two fronts. First it also seeks to draw on two of Aristotle's less frequently discussed works: *Rhetoric* and *Poetics*; and to explore relations across these four texts. Second, it applies each of these works in turn to study contemporary problems, and in particular through the lens of the comparatively new discipline of organization studies. This shows how Aristotle's work as a teacher, scientist and writer in pre-modern Greece can remain a source of inspiration, and of emancipation.

1
Organization, Society and Politics

'Organization' is a term that is used very widely here, consistent with its use in the leading journal in Critical Management Studies (CMS), itself titled *Organization*. A recent editorial in this journal embraces a generous usage conceptualizing 'organization' 'as noun and verb, accomplishment and process' (Parker, 2010: 5). Since 'organization' is so often used to refer to a place of work, or business, re-describing it in these broader terms is an act of politics. This is because the narrow and broader definitions of organization are expressions of inclusion and exclusion, of privilege and deprivation. Before elaborating on this and on the senses of organization as noun and as verb, it is helpful to restate the definition of organization that was developed in the introductory chapter, as an extension of the Fact that a human being is *zōon politikon*:

> Organization as verb describes the activities of humans as political animals. As noun, 'organization' describes the groups and places within which such activities take place, but these groups and places result from acts of organization. As groups and places, these organizations in turn structure acts of organizing.

To reframe 'organization' in far wider terms seems important in a time of global financial crisis. This is because we must revisit organization in order to challenge the occasional unspoken assumption that relations in society in general (the more generous sense of organization) and relations in certain kinds of firms (an impoverished sense of organization) are necessarily comparable, or even equivalent. If we understand 'organization' as the firm, as business, or as enterprise, we are never more than one move away from capitalism as a way of seeing. This can contaminate understanding of other social forms and relations.

Organization as noun

In the wider sense, as a noun and descriptive category, 'organization' can refer to a vast variety of social forms, not restricted to: corporations, public sector organizations, charities, societies, trades union and work associations, political parties, hospitals and schools, religions, sects and churches, sports teams and community groups, prisons, gangs, cults, terror cells, armies, even – perhaps more contentiously – families. Continuing with this sense of organization-as-noun, and being more generous still, we can challenge the implicit idea that organizations need to be in some senses permanent, or enduring. Then, for instance, we might begin to question whether audiences, mobs, groups of fans or crowds can also be understood as organizations. In the wake of the August 2011 riots across London, Birmingham, Manchester and elsewhere, the following chapter discusses whether we can interpret a riot as comprising organizations and involving acts of organization.

One explicit and intended consequence of these more generous uses of organization-as-noun is that this term does not just refer to a place of work. Subtlety and care about this point marks out some writers on organizational behaviour who emphasize 'work' in the titles of their texts (e.g. Watson, 2006; Wilson, 2010). Another consequence of leaving 'work' behind in the wake of a more generous definition of 'organization' is that the term is not restricted to groups that have definite boundaries, or that have explicit and formal criteria determining membership. Organizational members do not have to share the same goals, nor do they have to accept the same basis for authority. This is contrary to some of the most popular, and also potentially problematic, definitions of 'organization', which are not only often restricted to the world of work, but also tend to assume that by virtue of being in an organization, organizational members have common goals.

The members of an organization such as a sweatshop, criminal gang or even more ordinarily many workplace teams, do not need to be members voluntarily, but can be co-opted. They can remain at the core of an organization whose espoused or actual goals they despise, while desperately wishing for an alternative. They may choose to stay in an organization purely for some of the benefits that it affords them and not out of any notionally shared, normative purpose. Or, they may remain part of an organization not because of the goals that others within the organization have, but out of an impulse to belong and to associate.

The more generous uses of organization-as-noun do not commit us to pessimistic or cynical accounts of organization. More generous uses can be emancipatory, in the sense that they call into question an implied set of power relations. In doing so, they potentially challenge assumed hegemonies that are expressed in formal relationships such as that of employee–employer, supervisor–supervisee, manager–worker or conceptual categories such as leader–follower. Instead of a set of relationships under capitalism, the wider sense of organization-as-noun speaks more generally to other forms of association.

In this book I suggest that taking account of these broader senses of 'organization' can help us to consider the ways in which contemporary *society* is an – albeit far-removed – successor to the *polis* of Aristotle. By joining *Organization* and *Society* I want to explore the same kind of connection that Aristotle drew between a variety of social forms (he began with the family) and the *polis*. *Polis* is a word which has no ideal translation partly because our social world is structured so differently, but it is one that could defensibly be rendered as 'society'. For Aristotle, what different social forms (such as the family and the *polis*) shared was that they required, and were an expression of, *koinōnia*. This is to say, they entailed something social – a process that was held in common (Saxonhouse, 1982), or that involved a sense of community (Booth, 1994). In more general terms, Aristotle claims that humans as a species work together for *koinon sumpheron*, the common good. Stalley (2009: xxxvi–vii) identifies *koinōnia* as one of the key terms in *Politics* that is 'liable to be lost in translation'. He describes this, in a way that is comparable to Parker's analysis of organization (above) as a 'word family' comprising:

> ...the verb *koinōnein*, which means 'to share' or 'to participate' [the] noun *koinōnia*... literally a 'sharing' or 'participation', and is generally rendered in English as 'association', 'partnership', or 'community'...the adjective *koinos* which describes something which is shared or held in common. (xxxvii–viii)

These senses of *koinōnia* are common to typical definitions of 'organization', even in texts that focus exclusively on the world of work, and primarily on the organization as firm, business or enterprise. 'Organization' is:

> ...a structured social system consisting of groups and individuals working together to meet some agreed-upon objectives. (Greenberg, 2011: 33)

...a consciously coordinated social unit, composed of two or more people, that functions on a relatively continuous basis to achieve a common goal or set of goals. (Robbins and Judge, 2007: 5)

...a social arrangement for achieving controlled performance in pursuit of collective goals. (Huczynski and Buchanan, 2007: 8)

To make this initial connection between 'organization' and *'koinōnia'* perhaps leaves us with something that is not just broad, but also overly loose (this is how the definitions above could be described too). It also seems at first glance that taking Aristotle's idea of *koinōnia* as a basis for understanding organization leaves us vulnerable to the same criticisms of naïvety that can be levelled at definitions of work organizations (i.e. that they assume members have common goals). Yet there are subtle and important differences between Aristotle's notion of common purpose, and the idea of common goals. Aristotle does not see *koinōnia* in terms of market relations, instead it is about wider relations in a polity and *koinon sumpheron*. Indeed the considerations he brings to bear on *koinōnia* run in opposition to the logic of capitalism because they are about society and justice rather than the market:

A just political community can be judged to be one that serves the common advantage of all its members as contrasted with an unjust political community that serves only the private advantage of its ruling group. (Arnhart, 1994: 466)

As Arnhart shows, revisiting Aristotle's sense of what is 'common' does not just involve a broadening out from relations under capitalism, it is broader in the sense that Aristotle has a basic biological impulse in mind. This is far more fundamental and unifying than the very narrow sense of specific common goals that a work organization might have in the definitions above:

Human beings desire to live together even when they do not need mutual aid. They are brought together for the common advantage insofar as communal life satisfies their natural needs for moral and intellectual development. They also come together merely to preserve their lives because most human beings find a natural sweetness in simply being alive. (Arnhart, 1994: 466)

So a closer look at *koinōnia* reveals it to be not just subtly different, but also quite radically different from the connotations of an organization having common goals. Private sector firms have a common goal of maximizing returns for shareholders, but this is a world away from the 'natural sweetness in simply being alive'. *Koinōnia* suggests we can hold on to a broad, generous sense of organization, and at the same time drive an important wedge between the logic of capitalism and the human imperative to associate. At the same time this biological bedrock leaves us with an almost impossibly broad definition of 'organization'. Aristotle could perhaps be taken on this point to suggest that we can trace along an unbroken continuum of social forms beginning with an impulse to huddle together for warmth, and ending with abstract notions such as society or state.

Even if we allow this as an obvious oversimplification, the sheer variety of social forms gathered under the banner 'organization' suggests we are in danger of losing any analytical purchase. Notwithstanding some initial promising connections between 'organization' and '*koinōnia*', and the crucial advantage that this moves us away from narrow constructions of the firm, it is worth considering the basic question of whether we can define organization-as-noun more precisely. Since, on this generous usage at least, it is difficult to provide specific criteria for inclusion or exclusion in the general category of 'organization', one alternative and comparatively contemporary approach would be to advocate a definition that is based on Wittgenstein's concept of family resemblance (Mauws and Phillips, 1995; Wittgenstein, 1953). In other words, we could identify that there are identifiable commonalities across a set of social forms that can be called organizations, but concede that there is no set of necessary and sufficient conditions to determine classification.

This seems a sensible strategy, though it may be worth modifying slightly. A problem with this strategy is that even in the absence of necessary and sufficient conditions there do seem to be certain core or 'folk' truths expressed by the most popular definitions of organization (shared values, definite boundaries, common purpose, one source of authority, enduring identity, common rites of passage for members). A notable feature of Aristotle's approach to understanding concepts (in contrast to Socrates/Plato) is that across his practical philosophy he valued demotic, received opinion or *endoxa* (Haskins, 2004). This applies to evaluating arguments and determining truth, in the extract from the *Rhetoric* below, and also to judgements about politics, ethics and aesthetics in the subsequent extract from *Politics*:

> ...the true and the approximately true are apprehended by the same faculty...men have a sufficient natural instinct for what is true, and usually do arrive at the truth. (*Rhetoric*, 1355a14–16)

...the many, of whom each individual is not a good man, when they meet together may be better than the few good...just as a feast to which many contribute is better than a dinner provided out of a single purse...each individual...has a share of excellence and practical wisdom, and when they meet together, just as they become in a manner one man, who has many feet, and hands, and senses so to with regard to their character and thought. Hence the many are better judges than a single man of music and poetry. (*Politics*, 1281a43–1281b7)

Even if these folk truths about organizations are in some senses naïve, they do also seem to express something of the essence of the term or of ideal-typic organizations.

A supplementary definitional strategy to the family resemblance account would be to consider archetypes of organization, and then explore the extent to which other social forms diverged or converged with the typical features of these archetypes. These archetypes could be understood differently according to different disciplinary perspectives. So conventional management studies, and historically at least business ethics, concerns itself with private corporations, whereas critical management studies and sociology show more interest in informal organizations or in those who are marginalized by formal organizations. Combined with consideration of *koinōnia*, this may be a more useful way of making 'organization' tractable, even if we stop short of defining it with precision.

Organization as verb

Having considered the question of how to define organization as noun, it is worth briefly examining it as verb. Though this definitional section is much shorter, in a sense, the book is about organization as verb. This is because in Aristotle's work, ethics, politics, rhetoric and aesthetics are activities. As a verb and activity then, 'organization' is an expression and manifestation of power, with the tensions between freedom and organization lying at the heart of politics (Russell, 2010). The value of a generous definition of organization, which admittedly comes at the cost of precision, is that it allows greater examination of politics as an activity rather than as a discipline (though the two are interconnected). Joining 'organization' and 'society' is useful to turn our gaze away from assumptions of the market. By joining 'organization' and 'politics', this book advocates an approach to analysing organization that is characterized by an attempt to recognize and challenge forces of exclusion and privileging. In doing so, such a perspective needs to consider both structures and processes. This involves scrutinizing how different aspects of organization-as-noun (including definitional frameworks for organization) support exclusion and privilege: how they reify boundaries and membership status, how they mark out and prefer elites, how they connote belonging or exile, and how they silence and disenfranchise outsiders.

It also involves scrutinizing the activities of organization-as-verb: of how processes such as work, resistance, deliberation, collective action, sense-making/sense-giving can entrench, reproduce or destabilize inequalities. The collocation of organization and politics expresses 'an acknowledgement of individual and collective agency, in the active politics of constructing/organizing/deconstructing/regenerating/replacing' (Cooke, 2008: 913). This task is far harder if we rely on simple unitary definitions of organization that assume common goals or values, or a unitary 'authorising environment' (Moore, 1995).

To bring together the terms *Organization, Society* and *Politics* is something with which we might expect Aristotle to sympathize. For instance, he saw any attempt to distinguish between politics and ethics as deeply problematic, and indeed the transition from *Nicomachean Ethics* to *Politics* is difficult to pinpoint. A contemporary organizational theorist has also advocated blurring this distinction. The artificial and wrongheaded separation of these terms means that in effect we have a missing discipline when it comes to studying organizations. Whilst we have business ethics, there is no business politics:

> ...there is a rather tidy affinity between a narrow use of the word 'ethics' and a market managerial ideology that considers questions about persons to be legitimate but questions about political economy to be largely settled. So, in not asking questions of business politics, business ethics both justifies itself as properly concerned with 'ethics' and also avoids troubling the promanagerial hegemony of the wider discipline. (Parker, 2003: 189)

This identification of a missing discipline suggests the value of bringing organization and politics together, and it also reveals a fuller project for 'business ethics' – as an activity that does not just seek to shore up the ethical basis for corporate behaviour, but that considers the role of organizations in contributing to, or detracting from, societal well-being (Morrell and Clark, 2010).

More broadly still, this book contributes by re-presenting a number of contemporary concepts and problems, in such a way that the substance of what Aristotle writes can be drawn on critically. This re-presentation usefully contributes to current debates concerning critical theorists. This can inform discussions in a number of topic areas including: postcoloniality (Spivak, 1999); narrative (Genette, 1982); the basis for, and privileging of, authority (Lyotard, 1984); the situated nature of talk and action (Billig, 1987; Stubbs, 1983); inter-relations between knowledge and power, and the role of language in normalizing power relations (Fairclough, 1995; Foucault, 2002); repro-duction of hegemony (Gramsci, 1971); aesthetics as an explanatory framework for studying inequality (Bourdieu, 1993); and the basis for moral attributions in organizations and business (Mellahi, Morrell and Wood, 2010; Parker, 1998).

In an important sense then, it is through a re-imagining of the pur-pose of business ethics that the terms organization, society and politics are interconnected. Aristotle offers us a glimpse of a social philosophy where the concern of science for greater understanding is combined with, rather than defeated by, recognition that understanding the social is not only an act of science. This interconnectedness is redolent of a famous passage in *Howards End* where Forster's character Margaret describes:

> ... the building of the rainbow bridge that should connect the prose in us with the passion. Without it we are meaningless fragments, half monks, half beasts, unconnected arches that have never joined into a man. With it love is born, and alights on the highest curve, glowing against the grey, sober against the fire ... Live in fragments no longer. Only connect, and the beast and the monk, robbed of the isolation that is life to either, will die. (Forster, 2010: 297)

As the title of this book suggests, this imperative to connect is the impe-tus behind reframing organization in terms of Aristotle.

Only connect

For 2,000 years the influence of Aristotle on Western thought across many fields was both vast and definitive. Those writings of his which survived became core to fields as varied as: anthropology, biology, chemistry, drama, ethics, logic, literary criticism, physics, political theory, rhetoric and zoology. No other individual has had as much influence on the intellectual life of our species. The boundaries we now allocate to academic disciplines do not seem to make sense when we consider Aristotle's works. A rather prosaic explanation for this would be that there was not enough known in the ancient world to justify either having divisions between subject areas, or specialization among professional scholars. Even into the nineteenth century it was possible for Thomas Young (albeit a remarkable individual by any standards) to be a world- leader in research in several different disciplines: Egyptology, physics, optics, music, medicine and linguistics. Robinson (2006) describes Young as 'the last man [*sic*] who knew everything', and clearly one argument against disciplinary specialization in the ancient world was that one – sufficiently privileged – person could simultaneously know a considerable proportion of the existing academic literature across different fields.

Though this is certainly part of the explanation for the incredible breadth of his work, with Aristotle there is a compelling coherence to his writings which makes him, notwithstanding the anachronism, an interdisciplinary thinker (rather than someone who happened to be pre-disciplinary). An obvious premise for this book, and one which will make some feel uncomfortable, is that it is sensible to look to one figure for insight. Part of the justification for this with Aristotle is that his interdisciplinarity makes him uniquely suited to address the nature of questions relating to organization, society and politics. The purpose of this book is to demonstrate the continuing relevance of Aristotle's 'practical' philosophy: his approach to understanding politics and social forms as expressed primarily in works such as the *Politics, Rhetoric, Nicomachean Ethics*, and *Poetics*. Aristotle is still influential in, or indeed central to, contemporary debate in these respective areas. And yet these writings cannot be considered entirely separate from his studies in anthropology, biology and physics, even though the latter in particular have been surpassed by modern science, or by his logic, which still exercises contemporary philosophers.

Take, for instance, the basic Fact which underpins this book and the reframing of 'organization' in a way that connects the term with 'society' and 'politics', and distances it from the market. Aristotle's most famous phrase that a human being is *zōon politikon* is an assertion of extraordinary consequence. From it follows the connection between politics and ethics:

> ...it is a peculiarity of man, in comparison with other animals, that he alone possesses a perception of good and evil, of the just and

the unjust, and other similar qualities; and it is association in these things which makes a family and a city. (*Politics*, 1253a7–18)

Though *zōon politikon* is almost always translated as a human being is 'a' political animal, it can make more sense in some contexts to translate this as a human being is 'the' political animal (Masters, 1990: 210), since it follows from a theory of biological classification (Arnhart, 1994). For Aristotle, human beings are archetypically different from those other 'gregarious animals' (such as bees) because the other gregarious animals do not reason through speech (Bartky, 2002). From this ability to exercise reason follows activities such as politics, and organization, and also ethics, rhetoric and aesthetics.

The Fact that a human is *zōon politikon* is of extraordinary consequence in helping understand Aristotle's worldview. This is not just because it expresses his approach as a biologist, and not just because it makes clear the connection Aristotle sees between ethics and politics, but it simultaneously ties in to Aristotle's logic. This most basic taxonomy coheres with the theory of definitions in a classificatory scheme in book 5 of *Categories* (2a13–4b19). There is debate as to the interpretation of *Categories* (De Haas, 2001), but it is generally taken to ascribe membership to things using a five-fold hierarchical system: genus, species, difference, properties and accidents. The first two elements in this hierarchy, genus and species, represent the binomial nomenclature of the Linnaen system. Modern humans are of the genus *homo* and species *sapiens*. For Aristotle the thing that makes any species unique is its 'difference'. What makes humans a unique species, the 'difference', is their ability to reason. 'Properties' such as the ability to communicate or laughter are direct consequences of this essential difference (Ayers, 1981). 'Accidents' refer to contingencies that allow for differentiation between individuals but do not compromise the essential substance, such as physical appearance (Suppe, 2001).

In Aristotle's terms, if we continue to try to define 'organization' (as noun), we can identify that many of the features of particular organizations – such as things that relate to their constituency, character and history are matters of contingency or *nomos* (convention) and accordingly accidents. Yet more fundamentally, once we consider organization-as-verb, the factors that lead us to organize and form groups are more readily understood as matters of *phusis* (nature). A human is *zōon politikon* by nature (*phusei*), and by extension, organizations are political, social forms by nature.

The question as to what applies 'by nature' is an important one and it is also discussed later, because it has a bearing on how to interpret Aristotle's views on slavery and the subjugation of women (Heath, 2008). 'By nature' does not mean that any one kind of organization must exist of necessity. Importantly, when it comes to his practical philosophy (particularly the works *Politics*, *Nicomachean Ethics*, *Rhetoric* and *Poetics*), 'by nature' does not take on the same sense as it does in Aristotle's *Physics*. Aristotle has been criticized for being less than clear on the distinction between uses of nature in for instance physics and ethics (Annas, 1996); but, it is apparent that the kind of scientific claims that Aristotle makes about the social world are not comparable to those he makes in his works on biology, physics or logic. It is important to understand this because questions relating to science and certainty underpin whether we find Aristotle's project across his practical philosophy plausible. If we have a nuanced understanding of such things, we can develop his project 'only connect' in our own era.

Science and certainty

Aristotle was careful to draw a distinction between different kinds of science in terms of the degree to which they allowed certainty. The extract below shows this but initially, and notwithstanding the qualifications elsewhere, it is important to underline here that he refers specifically to an educated 'man'. Education, in Aristotle's times was for the male elite:

> ...it is the mark of an educated man to look for precision in each class of things just so far as the nature of the subject admits; it is evidently equally foolish to accept probable reasoning from a mathematician and to demand from a rhetorician demonstrative proofs. (*Ethics*, 1094b24–7)

There are a number of ways of interpreting this statement, and consequently a number of ways in which we might react to Aristotle's project. Since this statement is so pivotal to understanding the continuing relevance of Aristotle's practical philosophy, and the logical basis for this book, it is worth examining these in some detail. Each view of science and certainty represents a different set of epistemological and ontological commitments which either support or reject the claim to the social Fact underpinning this book: that a human being is *zōon politikon*.

Within the contemporary social sciences, debate about the absence of a dominant *paradigm* (Kuhn, 1970) (common epistemological assumptions about methods and phenomena) and the desirability or dangers of following the standard science model can be understood exactly on Aristotle's terms: namely a question as to the extent to which organization studies allows for precision, and the kind of scientific consensus necessary to make progress. In organization studies, debate about this is sometimes referred to as the paradigm debate or paradigm wars (Hasard and Kelemen, 2002; Pfeffer, 1993, 1997; Van Maanen, 1995; Weick, 1999); an intra-disciplinary echo of the cross-disciplinary, so-called science wars (Flyvbjerg, 2001). There are parallel debates in politics and sociology about the nature and status of replication research, where replication – normatively the principal vehicle for theory testing in the Popperian model of science – is scarce (Abbott, 2007; Firebaugh, 2007; King, 1995). The lack of consensus has some curious results; alongside the valorization of replication research, as a 'must' (Amir and Sharon, 1991) and 'indispensable' (Eden, 2002), is an apparent unwillingness actually to carry out such research, and a rejection of such tests as unpalatable. Efforts to carry out replications result in 'a vague sense of disrespect', where replications are 'second-class citizens' (Hendrick, 1991: 42). This is revealed in the attitudes of some journal editors, who have (anonymously) commented on replications as 'boring' and stated that readers aren't interested in them because they 'don't reflect cutting edge stuff' (Neuliep and Crandall, 1991: 88).

This is one example of a lack of consensus across many of the social sciences that makes it difficult for scholars to conduct research in a programmatic way. This ongoing question results in an uncertainty as to the status, both ontological and cultural, of social research. This arises in part from the broad challenges of carrying out social science research, and absence of a paradigm, but also because many of the social sciences are both comparatively new and also address interdisciplinary problems. As a result, speaking generally, there is deep-rooted status anxiety amongst social science researchers, and a consequent problem with professional identity. This can compromise the simultaneous pursuit of both *epistēmē* (scientific knowledge), and *phronēsis* (practical wisdom) that is required in the less precise sciences. 'Modeling economic theory on physics required economists to reject practical reasoning, and instead adopt theoretical reasoning as its primary mode of thinking about the economy' (Clark, 2010: 680). Though it is, as I have said, something of a generalization, there are many contemporary manifestations of this status anxiety in the practice of research across the social sciences. One such manifestation is the curious status of replication research, another is the phenomenon of 'evidence-based' policy. Derived from evidence-based medicine (Sackett et al., 1996), this approach to social research brushes aside a host of differences between medicine and policy studies – an instance not of physics envy, but physician envy (Morrell, 2008, in press).

In the wake of *postmodernism*, greater scepticism about claims to precision and certainty has also come about because of a recognition of the limits of scientific methods, and scepticism about the claims of science to be value-free, progressive or objective (Allen, 2003; Potter, 1996; Thorpe, 2001). Though rejecting such a schema for social science opens up possibilities, it also risks leaving a space that is filled either with uncertainty and Angst, or a toleration that is at once all-encompassing and relativist. In organization studies, and discussion of business ethics, Walton (1993) argues that despite its strengths – 'postmodernism has nailed the coffin on the "physics approach" to ethics' (ibid.: 298) – it brings with it dangers '[b]y making toleration in ethics a nearly supreme virtue, postmodernism risks turning a compromising society into a compromised society' (ibid.: 297). Postmodernism is also associated with a rejection of earlier authority figures, such as the Dead White European Males of whom Aristotle is a forebear. Though as Rasmussen suggests (1993: 274) it is a mistake to see Lyotard as 'chief representative of postmodernism', he does provide a brilliant summary definition or framing of postmodernism in terms of 'incredulity towards grand narratives' (Lyotard, 1984: xxiv). Aristotelianism is arguably the most intellectually influential Grand Narrative of them all.

The uneasy status of social science, and postmodernism pose questions for any project 'only connect', inspired by Aristotle. For instance, just how sensible is it to seek scientific explanation across different disciplines – not only in the social sciences, but in the humanities? Can it be a defence to identify Aristotle as pre-modern or ancient and does this in any way exempt or distance him from the criticisms levelled at modernity or fantasies of Enlightenment? Or, is it possible that the original tenets of his thinking are in some way compatible with certain characteristics of postmodern thought? The reference to his premodernity can certainly be helpful at least rhetorically (Duska, 1993); but if we are seeking to apply his work to contemporary organizations, society and politics, it is preferable to evaluate Aristotle on the strength of that work rather than seek to interpret it largely in terms of his context. More promisingly there do seem points of sympathy between Aristotle and postmodern/postcolonial critique. In comparison with his contemporary Plato, Aristotle is not as heavily burdened with transcendental commitments and his attention to the world immediately around him could seem a defence, though his method is closely associated with empiricism. Virtues are context-bound and 'tradition-constituted' (Fives, 2008: 169), unlike Utilitarian or Kantian precepts (MacIntyre, 1984a, b, 1988). Also, Aristotle does value demotic opinion which could be interpreted as narrative with a small 'n'. In addition to the broad charges and questions postmodernism raises, there are three further perspectives we might take on the relationship between Aristotle's account of science and certainty.

From a *radical-constructivist* stance, one might say that the lack of any possibility of precision explains why Aristotle's works of practical philosophy can remain relevant: they are not genuinely works of science. Constructivism has some additional nuances in debate on Aristotelian ethics (Lara, 2008), but here is used more broadly to indicate a belief that the social world is not 'knowable' in the same way as the natural world, and that it does not exist independently of our perceptions, discourse and judgements. A radical-constructivist stance would imply that we bring the social world into being by the way we frame it, whether these constructions are based on Aristotelian precepts or on more chic figures, each could be equally relevant, and both are equally incapable of grasping certainty.

In so far as a constructivist stance opposes a positivist perspective on social science, it is a view with which I have some sympathy. However, despite protestations by its advocates, it also frequently seems like a recipe for despair. This is because, though they are not equivalent, constructivism can be a short step to the kind of relativism that would appear to relegate disciplines such as ethics and political studies to the status of non-science, posing problems for any claims to engaged scholarship (see Flyvbjerg, 2001: 25–37). On this line, questions about the optimal system of government, the nature of happiness, or moral conduct, or the desired form and purpose of rhetoric or drama are irresolvable. This suggests that any seminal discussion of these can remain relevant because we do not make any kind of progress in a Popperian (conjecture-refutation) or Comtean (postivist) sense (Comte, 1853; Popper, 1959, 1962). There is, in Forster's terms, no 'rainbow bridge' connecting different ways of engaging with the world unless we project this for ourselves, and if we do it remains an illusion.

A different account of the relationship between science and certainty would be to maintain that these works do indeed constitute a kind of science but that the explanatory scope of this kind of science is perpetually limited given the nature of the objects (more accurately, 'subjects') of interest. This is the account of *phronetic social science* which Flyvbjerg (2001) advocates (though his account of *phronēsis* is rather different from Aristotle's). Aristotle's practical philosophy remains a good working explanation, or at least a stable basis for exploration, precisely because there are certain constancies to the organization of social forms. At the same time, the need perpetually to consider context in social science research, and the complexity of social phenomena, means a phronetic social science will never afford the kind of law-like explanations that natural scientists identify. This seems very close to the position which Aristotle advocates in the *Nicomachean Ethics* (1094b12–16):

> Our discussion will be adequate if it has as much clearness as the subject-matter admits of; for precision is not to be sought for alike in all discussions...fine and just actions, which political science investigates, exhibit much variety and fluctuation, so that they may be thought to exist only by convention and not by nature.

One benefit of this is that it suggests that, although using Aristotle commits us to some form of empirical engagement with the world, we need not commit to a naïve realism that would be associated with empiricism. When using Aristotle, we can employ a softer or more critical version of realism: that the social world has a reality independent of its own, but access to that reality is problematic (Sayer, 1992). However making this move is not that simple or straightforward because Aristotle apparently goes on to express Truths about organization, society and politics in more strident terms than we would associate with critical realism. He describes the unfolding of man's *phusis* which finds expression in the city-state, or *polis*, as a thing in nature:

> ...the state is by nature clearly prior to the family and to the individual...the individual when isolated, is not self-sufficing; and therefore he is like a part in relation to the whole. But he who is unable to live in society, or who has no need because he is sufficient for himself, must be either a beast or a god; he is no part of a state. A social instinct is implanted in all men by nature. (*Politics*, 1253a19–30)

In passing, to show the fluency between the terms politics and society in Aristotle, Barker translates 'live in society' (above) as 'share in the benefits of political association'. I will return to this passage later, and to a concept of Aristotle's which still strikes me as extraordinary and fascinating: that the city is prior to the individual. Here though, to continue the discussion about science and certainty, I want to comment on the idea that the *polis* exists 'by nature'.

In what is at first reading quite a puzzling interpretation of this famous passage, Ambler (1985: 179) suggests that 'Aristotle's opening declaration of the naturalness of the city is made for reasons other than because it is simply true'. In other words, Ambler argues, the reference to the city existing by nature is an invitation to philosophical investigation of the city. It expresses a more complex truth than would be implied by any attempt to read literally across from Aristotle's *Physics* (where nature is closer to necessity) to his *Politics* (see also Lindsay, 1992). Given the breadth of the term organization as used in this book, Ambler's call for nuance and a non-literal reading is helpful. It allows, for instance, that a variety of social forms, over and above what we might take to be Aristotle's version of the ideal *polis*, can exist 'by nature'.

A third perspective on the nature of science in Aristotle's practical philosophy can be derived from the Foucauldian (2002) concept of 'Episteme' (capitalized to avoid confusion with the form of scientific knowledge that is *epistēmē*). Epistemes represent, 'the underlying codes of a culture that govern its language, its logic, its schemas of perception, its values, its techniques' (O'Leary and Chia, 2007: 393). Epistemes are implicit and internalized structures for sense-making; the logics that govern what constitutes legitimate knowledge, and that structure inference and action in social settings. This perspective suggests that Aristotle's work remains influential because it has had such impact on subsequent thought that certain topics have been constructed and then defined in terms of what he and his followers or critics have written. This is not realism because the idea of an Episteme is to question a correspondence account of truth (between Aristotle's ideas and the contemporary social), but to see any such truths as constructed. However it is not radical-constructivism either because Epistemes are social structures.

To summarize the last few paragraphs, radical constructivism is a sceptical perspective that rejects the possibility of a social science, and would render not just this book but many others irrelevant. The second position (phronetic social science and a critical or soft realism) embraces the possibility of a social science but understands social science to be necessarily different. In this sense it vindicates the position of Aristotle in his call for different possibilities for precision. The third position (Epistemes) is a soft constructivist stance which concedes that some discussion of Aristotle remains necessary and relevant, but suggests that the explanation for its continuing relevance is a contingent one – a matter of *nomos* rather than *phusis*.

Other perspectives (anywhere between perhaps solipsism and hard realism) are possible but these three seem informative to me. Each of them in different ways is an explanation for the continuing influence of Aristotle, but clearly it is the second one with which this book is in most sympathy. This follows from the belief that not only does Aristotle remain influential, but also that what he says remains relevant. To develop this in more detail, Chapter 2 examines the case for an Aristotelian perspective.

2
An Aristotelian Perspective

This chapter offers additional justification for, and some necessary context to, the title for this book. In doing so, it begins to discuss the nature of Aristotle's practical philosophy and argue for its continuing relevance to the study of organization, society and politics. The chapter concludes with an outline of the remainder of the book. To begin, I want to address directly the question of how Aristotle's work remains relevant, and in doing so to consider some of the problems with calling on a long dead philosopher.

'Recruiting' Aristotle

In *A Tale of a Tub*, which was the source for the opening quote in the preface, Swift (2004: 25) ironically praises one of Aristotle's works as:

> ...that wonderful piece *De Interpretatione*, which has the faculty of teaching its readers to find out a meaning in everything but itself

Admittedly, like a lot of Aristotle's work, *De Interpretatione* (a treatise on language and logic) is not easy to read. Swift's joke though is not really at Aristotle's expense. Instead, he is taking a swipe at his own contemporaries: eighteenth-century scholars who apparently believed that insight or erudition could be accomplished by reference to Aristotle, 'like commentators on the Revelations, who proceed prophets without understanding a syllable of the text' (ibid.). Swift's remarks remain uncomfortable reading for present day social scientists since we may find ourselves being guilty of, or being unfairly criticized for, analogous practices.

Given contemporary tastes and fashion, and beliefs (occasionally misplaced) about progress within a discipline, it is arguably not especially impressive to invoke an ancient philosopher, even one as venerated as Aristotle. Indeed, for some thinkers, the very fact that Aristotle is venerated is itself grounds for suspicion. Even so, a common rhetorical function that referencing serves is to recruit figures of authority to bolster an argument. Normatively, references can help readers to trace and evaluate a line of thought, but they can also have an empty, ritualistic function that helps maintain a pretence about a certain kind of knowledge (Chia and Holt, 2008); or that displays allegiances, or seeks to procure approval. This way of using Aristotle, often at the beginning of a work, and in a cursory manner has the unfortunate effect of affording him the status of a secular prophet rather than a philosopher whose work is still relevant.

As one example of this kind of 'recruiting', Aristotle has recently been held out as a pioneer of 'evidence-based policy/management':

> ...few seemed to have recalled the long tradition of evidence-based activity (as broadly defined) in government...Where did Aristotle's knowledge come from? He conducted studies of different governance structures in various city-states, including their constitutions, to determine which features would lead to desirable political consequences. He published this in the *Politics*. (Shillabeer, Buss, and Rousseau, 2011: 6)

A non-trivial point to make about the quote above is that *Politics* (like the other main works discussed here) was not 'published' by Aristotle (Bobonich, 2006). The grounds for recruiting Aristotle here seem to rely on equating the *Constitution of Athens* with what evidence-based advocates call a 'systematic review' of the literature (Morrell, 2008). This is at the same time amusing (because the *Constitution of Athens* is nothing like a systematic review), and also disturbing (because the *Constitution of Athens* is nothing like a systematic review). One could argue that an 'evidence-based approach' to politics is almost the opposite of what follows from Aristotle's work on politics and ethics, because Aristotle says it is foolish to seek precision in matters that do not allow it (as the Chapter 1 argues in some detail).

It is perhaps a little unfair to single these authors out since this seems a perennial problem with people writing about Aristotle. Writing in the nineteenth century, and more graciously than I have just done,

Poste wistfully regrets in the preface to his book on the logical works of Aristotle (the *Organon*) that:

> ... it does not appear that the pages of the Organon are often turned over by very diligent hands. Nor is this very difficult to be accounted for, if we consider their obscurity – a quality, indeed, which they share with most of Aristotle's productions. (Poste, 1850: iii)

Other people have recruited Aristotle in a similar fashion, and some others seem to have misunderstood him. A recent example is a clutch of writers who suggest Aristotle's account of *phronēsis* refers to procedural or tacit knowledge, or some kind of intuition or unconscious facility (Flyvbjerg, 2001; Gunder, 2010). More generally, an array of different beliefs and positions has been attributed to Aristotle, and these beliefs are certainly incoherent as a set. They are also, in my opinion, in some cases limited or mistaken because they try to carry too much across from Aristotle. For example, Aristotle has been described anachronistically as someone who would now be, 'a pragmatic organization theorist' (Argyle, 2002: 366); or more contentiously, as, 'pro-business and pro-profit' (Collins, 1987: 567; see also Hadreas, 2002). There are others who call on Aristotle's account of ethics to suggest that he is saying something that can be straightforwardly applied to 'business'; for instance who imply the private firm (even a large multinational corporation) is an analogue or metaphor, or even contemporary example of the *polis* (Hartman, 2004). To me this seems mistaken because Aristotle has little to say (directly) about 'business' ethics, and the *polis* is a different animal to the contemporary firm under capitalism because its central concern is justice, rather than profit. The *polis* represents an association of all the parts of a society, not only those who can vote – or, by extension who are members of a corporation (as an aside, Aristotle, being born in Stagira, could not himself have voted in Athens). The *polis* emerges 'by nature' rather than under a form of capitalism. In contrast however, to those who try to carry too much across from Aristotle, it is possible to leave too much behind. So, to suggest that the *polis* is so different that we cannot learn anything useful for contemporary society also seems misguided. For me, the Fact that a human being is *zōon politikon* confounds this.

The uncomfortable sense we might have that reference to Aristotle is not always for the sake of necessity but serves a rhetorical, 'recruiting' purpose is perhaps not helped by an idiosyncratic form of referencing. This (as outlined in the preface) is based on a nineteenth-century edition of Aristotle's work by Immanuel Bekker, a German philologist. Those familiar with it will know that in this system, references to Aristotle are in a standard alphanumeric form: a page number, column letter, and line number. So his explanation of what causes shooting stars in *Meteorology* begins at 341b (the first line of column b, page 341) and ends at 342b25 (line 25 of column b, page 342). This convention serves a useful purpose in allowing people to compare and find relevant passages across different subsequent translations and editions of Aristotle's work. This is helpful because many of the terms Aristotle uses do not really have exact English equivalents – *arête* might be translated as 'virtue', or as 'excellence'; *eudaimonia* as 'flourishing' or (sometimes misleadingly) as 'happiness', and so on. As the Chapter 1 outlines, *koinōnia*, which is perhaps the central Aristotelian term in this book, can be translated by different writers as a number of things that we might want to hold onto as separate concepts, for instance: association, community, partnership (Stalley, 2009); or – as I advocate – organization. At the same time as being useful, the Bekker convention can reinforce the suspicion in readers that by including reference to Aristotle, authors are seeking to invoke a special kind of authority. Statements from Aristotle are passed down and seem to arrive in a different, 'holier' way than those from other scholars.

In this book I argue that what Aristotle writes can be drawn on critically, and in a way that speaks to contemporary debates in critical theories of organization. So it is relevant for discussing topics such as: business politics/ethics, postcoloniality, narrative, authority, discourse, knowledge/power, hegemony and aesthetics. However, the problem of 'recruiting' Aristotle is a serious one and the Bekker convention is only one aspect of a wider issue which rightfully draws particular antipathy and scepticism of (speaking a little loosely) postmodern critics. If postmodernism is to mean any one thing (which would itself be an incoherence), it is to challenge veneration or traditional and assumed authority (Lyotard, 1984). Both postmodern critics' scepticism and Swift's scepticism would extend towards those who feel that an academic project should contain some reference to Aristotle if only to follow convention, or to create the impression that one is being thorough and comprehensive. These uses are just as troubling as calling on Aristotle to invent a history and heritage for a new empire, as the authors promoting evidence-based management cited earlier try to do. Such factors play a role in ensuring Aristotle remains influential in the sense that he is still cited. Notwithstanding that he died two and a half thousand years ago, in the unfortunate language which scholars in the United Kingdom often have to deploy, Aristotle's 'impact' remains such that recent editions of his work would be 'returnable' for an assessment exercise. Yet being able to demonstrate impact in terms of citations is not in itself a good reason for recruiting Aristotle, or indeed for recruiting anyone. Scholarship is constrained if we treat Aristotle as an obligatory passage point (Latour, 2007), rather than as a continuing source of inspiration for the task of critique.

For Aristotle's work to inform understanding of our society and politics we first need to confront a number of things that are uncomfortable about his account of how the city-state should be governed. Aristotle is often held to believe some people are naturally slaves (the corollary is that some are naturally masters). He apparently advocates the exclusion and subjugation of women, and he regards what we might perhaps think of as an ideal democracy as being deviant (Morrell, 2008). He can be recruited as a defender of the powerful, the rich and of elites, and his views are in tension with the prevailing Western intellectual climate of liberalism. Nussbaum (2001a: xx) describes his 'first and most striking defect' as 'the absence...of any sense of universal human dignity, a fortiori of the idea that the worth and dignity of human beings is equal'.

Individual freedom, equality and universal suffrage are either underplayed or absent in his vision of a city-state governed by a male elite who share 'a single moral perspective and have enough wealth to live at leisure and hold political office without pay' (Kraut, 2002: vii). At the same time Aristotle's political conservatism would seem to make him resistant to the kinds of revolutionary change, or radical redistributive political designs that might bring about fairness. Notwithstanding Goldstein's (2001) argument that the *Politics* provides an operational theory of revolution, a prize virtue for Aristotle is political stability, and this means he is – with reference to the institutions of the state – ultra-conservative.

To what we might consider an enlightened, contemporary social theorist, all of these sentiments are offensive, and Aristotle would seem a prime and necessary target of more recent philosophers and social theorists. He could be dismissed as an architect of grand narratives (contra Lyotard, 1984), as naïve about the relationship between power and knowledge (contra Foucault, 1991, 2002), as simplistic and fundamentally misguided about the roles of categories and reason (contra Deleuze, 1990), or as someone responsible for a now long obsolete construction of 'the social' (contra Latour, 2007). Most sweepingly, perhaps, he is the archetypal Dead White European Male. There are responses to these sorts of challenges. For instance, as argued in the Chapter 1, a starting point may be to emphasize that Aristotle is a pre-modern rather than a champion of modernity or the Enlightenment. This means that when we read him we have to do so mindful of changes in context and the history of ideas. Or we could simply acknowledge that Aristotle remains a source of inspiration for radical libertarian and radical communitarian thinkers alike (Long, 1996). Still at heart they prompt us to ask why should this (or any) commentary seek to defend Aristotle?

Without even contesting whether these criticisms of Aristotle are fair, it is worth noting, to our collective shame, that it would require very little work to turn the most offensive aspects of Aristotle's political philosophy into a description of the way our post-Enlightenment world is structured. Patriarchy, global capitalism, and the legacy of colonialism combine in such a way that our supposedly modern society realizes and entrenches principles of misogyny, slavery and racism. There is mass poverty and, for many, the continual spectre of starvation, which they only escape through experiencing a far more vicious and unequal form of slavery than the kind Aristotle describes. Women are subjugated as assets of all kinds are governed by a white male elite. We live in a world that has been dominated for hundreds of years by purportedly civilized Western democracies, but these are, as Derrida suggests, more like beasts than sovereigns:

> ...the most powerful sovereign states which, making international right and bending it to their interests, propose and in fact produce limitations on the sovereignty of the weakest states...Those powerful states that always give, and give themselves, reasons to justify themselves, but are not necessarily right, have reason of the less powerful; they then unleash themselves like cruel, savage, beasts, or beast full of rage. (Derrida, 2009: 281)

Indeed, if we were to base global governance on even the most ill-informed, simplistic and uncharitable accounts of Aristotle's description of an ideal system of rule, then radical reform would be needed to address these inequalities. Offensive as the idea of slavery is to us, Aristotle describes an almost symbiotic relationship between master and slave, one that is constituted through proximity, and defined relationally:

> ...the master ought to be the source of such excellence in the slave, and not a mere possessor of the art of mastership which trains the

slave in his functions. That is why they are mistaken who forbid us to converse with slaves and say that we employ command only. (*Politics*, 1260b6–8)

In a later extract that undercuts any simplistic reading of his toleration of slavery, Aristotle also states that no one is a slave by nature, 'liberty should always be held out to them [slaves] as the reward of their services' (*Politics*, 1330a34).

In contrast, as Spivak (1999) identifies, a consequence of contemporary capitalism is that in many modern consumer–producer relations, there is no such dyad, not even one with such asymmetric power chances (Morrell and Jayawardhena, 2010). There is no 'other', instead, there is a powerful party, and a silenced one – a complete absence of interrelation and no possibility of liberty. The 'subaltern' is entirely disenfranchised and has no chance of establishing a proximate relationship with her contemporary master.

Rich contemporary societies quite obviously exist, which exploit invisible labor living in poverty. This labor is politically disenfranchised and has no social–cultural voice of its own. There are more peasants than knowledge workers, and there are more illiterate impoverished women than feminist professionals; but the peasants and illiterate women are silenced and the others have a voice. (Letiche, 2010: 263)

The master–slave relationship Aristotle describes is of a basically different kind to the one produced in many settings by global capital, or by contemporary forms of management which echo practices underpinning industrial-scale slavery:

...modern managerial practices were to be found in the operation of the ante-bellum plantations...Taylorism can be seen in the application of scientific method, the selection of the best person for the job, and the monitoring of performance. The principles of classical management can be seen in the division of labour, the development of sophisticated organizational rules, a chain of command, a distinction (just) between line and staff esprit de corps, analyses of the appropriate span of control, debates about unity of command (related to the separation of ownership and control), and attempts to instil discipline. (Cooke, 2003: 1906)

Now, it would be a curious defence of Aristotle's political philosophy to start by pointing to examples of 'worse' forms of slavery than the 'ideal' kind he outlines. Slavery, it seems to me anyway, is a categorical bad, and opposition to slavery should also be unqualified. This makes Aristotle's defence and toleration of slavery one of the biggest challenges to adopting an Aristotelian perspective. Lindsay (1994: 128) nicely summarizes the most typical interpretations of this defence:

> Aristotle's defense of slavery... is generally read to be either (1) specious, due to his own enslavement to Greek prejudice or his simply nodding; or (2) intentionally specious, as part of a rhetorical enterprise that begins from common opinion in order to elevate it; or (3) a defensible position that nonetheless would, if effected, improve markedly the slavery practiced in his day.

Assuming that we do not instantly follow one of these conventional lines, there are more sophisticated counterarguments and defences to the charges made against Aristotle on slavery (Dobbs, 1994; Frank, 2004), and misogyny (Dobbs, 1996; Nichols, 1992; Swanson, 1992). For instance some readings rest on finding Aristotle's defence of slavery 'deliberately defective' (Lindsay, 1994: 131; identifying and sympathizing with Shulsky, 1991). Clearly there are nuances and qualifications to be made in Aristotle's discussions of slaves, of women and of other disenfranchised groups, and there are inconsistencies in the texts (which, again, it is worth remembering that he never intended to be published). Aristotle seems at times to contradict himself, or place varying emphasis on the inevitability of these categories, or on the potential for emancipation, or the legitimate basis for the dominance of the superior.

There is undeniably a need to appreciate the context for his assertions (Heath, 2004): when the societies that were available for him to observe employed slaves, and subordinated women, and where for him even to suggest the possibility of emancipation and equality for both would have been comparatively radical. As Lindsay (1994) suggests above, some writers recuperate Aristotle by suggesting that some of his assertions about these topics are ironic, or intentionally difficult to follow – in some sense a puzzle to be solved by his readers (more accurately his students, since these were notes for lectures). It may be he could not commit to paper what his exact feelings on the topic were (Levy, 1990). We can also consider whether Aristotle is at times describing and trying to explain systems of power relations as a biologist, rather than imagining or advocating changes to these relations, as a contemporary social theorist might. At the same time as recognizing the value of his biological perspective, we could also acknowledge that the basis for many of his assertions was a flawed account of biology. So at times he seems to use similar logic to later racists, to apologists for slavery, and to misogynists.

These features of text and context are real, but it seems to me at least that there remain serious problems with Aristotle's political philosophy. Trying to recuperate Aristotle on some of these points seems to be the academic equivalent of trying to push water uphill.

It does not seem justifiable to suggest that lacking the ability to read him in the original Greek inevitably makes one blind to instances of irony, or unable to recognize occasions where he makes deliberate error (assuming this even happens in Aristotle). As Gaskill (2002: 207) amusingly points out, 'none of us are native speakers of ancient Greek'. Clearly too, as scholars such as Nussbaum (1976) show, reading Aristotle as well as is humanly possible is extraordinarily difficult. It requires, as she shows us by setting such high standards, an extraordinary appreciation for textual provenance, and the ability to detect nuances across different editions of some of his texts. One has to be awake to every subtlety in translation, cognizant of insertions, deletions and plain errors by subsequent editors, and aware of the controversies surrounding the array of positions attributed to Aristotle.

Sometimes these are fine-grained nuances and points of difference, at other times there seem to be vast chasms between diametrically opposed interpretations. Additionally, we largely work with texts that were never intended for publication. It is clearly mistaken to say, as Flynn does, that on issues relating to slavery and misogyny Aristotle's views were 'unreflectively adopted from Greek culture' (Flynn, 2008: 363). Allowing for all this, at times it seems very hard to avoid what seems like an obvious reading of him as an 'outright misogynist', to use Ball's phrase describing some feminist critiques of Aristotle (Ball, 2004: 23). Regrettably, it seems to me, this description, at least at times, does fit. This is true even if it relies partly on caricature or oversimplification, or fails to take full account of important nuances (such as the distinction between private and public life) that do not simply relegate women to the household (Swanson, 1992).

There are, and again it is important to qualify this with an 'it seems to me', clearly passages that are racist and misogynist in the texts discussed here. For instance, in his discussion of good characters in drama in the *Poetics* (1454a19–22) Aristotle writes:

... goodness is possible in every type of personage, even in a woman or a slave, though the one is perhaps an inferior, and the other a wholly worthless being.

He goes on to say that in order to evoke sympathy, character qualities must be appropriate and that for this reason a woman should not be 'manly, or clever' (1454a23). It is not difficult to couple these assertions in the *Poetics* with the defence of slavery in *Politics* (however we choose to contextualize that defence) and then conclude that whatever insights Aristotle may have are tainted, if not fatally compromised. The interconnectedness of Aristotle's works is one aspect of his philosophy that many find appealing and it is also part of the justification here for considering the continuing relevance of his practical philosophy. Proclaiming the value of this interconnectedness also makes it harder to cherry pick without appearing incoherent, or worse still as somehow advocating some things which are offensive. Overarching these specific offences is the more general, seemingly inescapable conclusion that Aristotle's vision of the ideal contemplative life is only open to a few. Furthermore it seems that this is a situation Aristotle regards as acceptable since he does not devote any time to imagining radically different societies.

Yet, at the same time, writers from a number of different traditions who acknowledge these serious problems with Aristotle have embraced him. Libertarians such as Sen (1985, 1992, 1999) and Nussbaum (1988, 1999) can draw inspiration from his idea of what it is to be human: to live as a creative social being that defines itself in terms of an ability to realize potential, or capabilities, rather than current attributes or assets (see Crocker, 1992 and Mathias and Teresa, 2006 for reviews; and also Sayer, 2011). The attraction of this is similarly powerful for those writing in a Marxist tradition – who are also motivated by a concern for the realization of human potential, which they see as otherwise frustrated under capitalism (MacIntyre, 1984a; see also Knight, 2007: 104–24 for a review). Communitarians can welcome Aristotle as the first, and greatest, advocate of constitutionalism, what Goodman and Talisse (2007: 7) describe as his 'great theme' (see also Biondi, 2010).

We need not buy into all aspects of Aristotle's philosophy to recognize the value of considering connections between disciplines such as ethics, politics and aesthetics. Neither do we need to accept his reality for our own, or treat parts of his work that are descriptive as though they are ideal visions for our own society. If we share his appreciation for the law and for constitutions, this does not mean we have to share his laws or his constitution. In an important sense too, we can appreciate aspects of Aristotle's method without holding onto some of his most fundamental and basic mistakes, which in my view are the product of context-bound and therefore inexorably limited applications of that method.

This suggests that if we can see continuing merit in some of Aristotle's works and in the work of those who have been inspired by his writing, he can rightly remain of contemporary relevance. This need not commit us to adopting his system wholesale, or agreeing with any of the more troubling aspects of his political philosophy. Equally, it need not mean we have to disregard differences between his context and ours, or that we fail to take account of work subsequent to his. However, even if we can set some distance between ourselves and – what seem to me to be – the more offensive aspects of Aristotle's philosophy, there remains another, perhaps more basic problem. To claim continuing relevance for Aristotle involves making considerable assumptions.

These assumptions are all in one way or another vulnerable to a position based on *knowledge-relativism*: the view that there is no absolute, universal or transcendent knowledge of the social world. Knowledge-relativism denies there are social facts, and a fortiori would rule out what I have described as the social Fact: a human being is *zōon politikon*. Knowledge-relativism suggests that any work is the product of a particular perspective. This perspective is in turn produced by a set of contextual conditions rooted in class, culture, language and history.

Applying this to Aristotle, knowledge-relativism suggests that any claims that he made to understand society were local to his time and place, and are not portable. Though he is by no means a relativist, Lukacs (1971: 111) asserts this when he says, 'it is as idle to imagine that in Plato we can find a precursor to Kant...as it is to undertake the task of erecting a philosophy on Aristotle'.

The basic charge of relativism is familiar enough, and it is fair to say that to embrace it in full would seem to represent a threat to any attempt at scholarship. Even so, there are different aspects to relativism and although these are interrelated, it is helpful to try to disentangle them, because that paves the way for the clearest statement of the book's purpose, and the justification for its ambitious title.

Three aspects to relativism

First, to suggest Aristotle is of contemporary relevance, we would have to believe there are enough salient features common to his context, and to the present, to allow his claims about organization, politics and society to warrant continued consideration.

Sitting in front of my mass-produced desktop computer, it seems easy to identify with a relativist perspective and reject transferring Aristotle's claims to knowledge of our social world. There are any number of potential counterfactuals from history, for example: Christianity, Islam, the ascendancy and decline of numerous empires, the Renaissance, the discovery of new civilizations, communism, global capitalism and multinational corporations, the changing face of war, the imperative for oil, environmental pollution, mass media and mass transportation, the nuclear age, the internet and social networking. Each of these revolutionary changes continues to influence our contemporary society and each of them is also associated with social forms that have distinctive and differentiating characteristics, and that were unprecedented. They also involve particular ways of organizing that would have been alien to Aristotle's context. Stalley (2009: xxxvi) suggests:

> ...we have to enter imaginatively into the world of the Greek *polis* while at the same time seeking to relate it to the world of the modern state in which we live. But it is precisely because it enables us to see the problems of our own day from a very different perspective that reading the *Politics* can be so valuable.

This is an attractive idea, and clearly true to an extent, yet it is also clear that such stark essential difference raises challenges as well as opportunities for contrastive insight. Relying on the idea of contrast and difference in itself is unsatisfying. After all, many things could offer a different perspective and ultimately, to be able to learn something, we have to identify sufficient similarity. To do this briefly, many similarities can come from revisiting the idea of organization as noun and verb. As noun, many organizations associated with government bear comparison with Greek ones, supporting both noble (rule of law) and base (privileging a male elite) aspects of our society. As verb, ancient Greece remains the source of ideas for understanding social and cultural activities central to Aristotelian philosophy and to human experience: rhetoric, politics, ethics and aesthetics. As is suggested in the Introduction and throughout, Aristotle's claim that a human being is 'a', or 'the', political animal lies at the crux of this.

Second, in addition to sufficient contextual similarity, we would have to believe that as human beings we have important features and characteristics in common with the citizens of ancient Greece. Darwinian evolutionary theory suggests that basic biological changes in species that are globally dispersed would occur very gradually, and over a timescale far longer than has elapsed since 300 BCE. In a biological sense, and assuming that there is truth in Aristotle's category, this would suggest that we are *zōon politikon* in the same way that the ancient Greeks were *zōon politikon*. However, although speciation may be very gradual, there is debate about the extent to which we may have changed in terms of our capacity for consciousness, and the extent to which there have been changes in our intellectual and cultural evolution over that same period. To continue to work with Aristotle we would have to deny *cultural relativism* because we are products not simply of our genes (units of biological inheritance) but also of 'memes' (units of cultural inheritance).

The term memes, coined by the biologist Richard Dawkins (1976), is a metaphor deliberately modelled on genetic aspects of replication, heredity and variance. Blackmore defined the difference as follows:

> The gene is an instruction for building proteins, stored in a cell and passed on by reproduction. The meme is an instruction for producing behaviour, stored in a brain and passed on to other brains by imitation. (Blackmore, 1996, no page; see also Blackmore, 1999)

The importance of imitation as a vehicle for learning can be understood in terms of memes, and is discussed in a little more detail in the chapter on the *Poetics*. Here though, it is enough to draw on and deploy this concept to understand the threat posed by cultural relativism, by asking, 'are the cultural experiences, beliefs, memories and sensitivities of the ancient Greeks – those things which we might perhaps think of as making them human – sufficiently similar to our own to allow for comparisons with our experiences?' Konstan's (2006) view is that even something as fundamental as emotion in ancient Greece was partly a product of the cultural and historical setting of the *polis*. Considering a contemporary expression of emotion (Munch's *The Scream*) he extrapolates:

> The emphasis on expression corresponds, then, not only to an interest in the communicative function of the emotions but also to a Romantic conception of the self as an internal and private locus of feeling, which is exposed particularly in moments of intense passion – a view of the self that was receptive as well to the hermeneutics of Freud [and] the Cartesian emphasis on expression again coincided with the view of the self or soul as a distinct internal domain ... Aristotle's cognitively-based account of the emotions may

be seen as the analytic counterpart to the contemporary cultural disposition to view the emotions as responses to stimuli in the environment, as opposed to self-subsisting inner states that are recognized through their corporeal manifestations. (Konstan, 2006: 29–31)

If we accept his thesis (that the fundamental role and basis of emotion has changed) it does not simply challenge the particular relevance of three of the works discussed in some detail here: *Rhetoric* (which in part deals with appeals to emotion), *Ethics* (which sees moral reasoning as integrated with the emotions) and *Poetics* (which places emphasis on the role of art in swaying emotions). Instead it would seem to pose a greater challenge, namely that there is a radical separation between the basic, lived experience of Aristotle's contemporaries and our own society. Again briefly, a simple response to this challenge can come from considering the enduring appeal of Greek culture. Homer, Horace, Sophocles, Euripides, Aeschylus, Aesop and others all still have something to say to us about emotion. They can all still invoke pity and fear, the two central emotions in Aristotle's theory of the aesthetic.

Third, we would have to believe that even though a substantial portion of Aristotle's work has been surpassed or superseded, that which survives contemporary scrutiny (by Aristotle's own standards) still offers the possibility of fresh insight into contemporary phenomena of interest: in short, that his work is more than being simply of historical interest, or a milestone on the way to later, superior ideas. Given the approach taken in this book, which focuses on specific texts in Aristotle's practical philosophy, this is a more fundamental challenge than might first appear. Instead of simply suggesting that later commentators' interpretations of Aristotle are useful, I want to make a stronger claim: that even in the study of contemporary organizations and politics, we do not need simply to allow for the continuing relevance of Aristotle, but that we can acknowledge that several of his original texts bear serious, direct consideration.

There has been a vast amount written about Aristotle and exponentially more that has been directly influenced by his work. Advocating a return to these original works could seem to be neglecting centuries of subsequent scholarship, or more contemporary insights immediately relevant to considering 'organizations': such as the distinction between practices and institutions (MacIntyre, 1984a; Moore, 2005). This approach also raises two attendant difficulties, and numerous other questions. The first difficulty is settling on the exact status of these texts: What of the writings of Aristotle that we know are lost?

Do the surviving texts reflect one person's work or those of subsequent scholars? Is their apparent coherence partly a function of editing or other work post hoc? Would Aristotle himself have seen these works as accurately reflecting his views? The second difficulty is deciding how to read these texts: Is it possible to rely exclusively on translation and translated terms? Can we concentrate only on certain elements, or given the clear imperative towards a system by Aristotle, do we always need to consider this work as a whole? If his theoretical philosophy or his biology is flawed, does that jeopardize his practical philosophy? It also raises concerns highlighted in the Preface and Introduction about the reliance on 'holy' or at least potentially unchallenged texts, and the dangers of recruiting Aristotle.

This book grapples with these questions, and the three kinds of relativism, throughout but it is essentially committed to the idea that Aristotelian thought is no 'burial ground'. It is, 'what it can and should be – a source of genuine knowledge and a reliable guide for the perplexed' (Ball, 2004: 24). To demonstrate this the following chapters introduce and then apply in turn the following four Aristotelian texts: *Politics, Rhetoric, Nicomachean Ethics* and *Poetics*.

3
The *Politics*

This chapter introduces Aristotle's work on politics, more specifically the text *Politics*. This might sound tautologous were it not for the fact that there are many aspects of Aristotle's politics covered in other works, for instance the *Rhetoric* and the *Nicomachean Ethics*. Accordingly this chapter begins by situating *Politics* in relation to other ideas in Aristotle before summarizing and then reviewing some of the main arguments in the text. It concludes with a consideration of the continuing relevance of *Politics* from a contemporary perspective on organizations, society and politics.

Aristotle's *Politics* in the context of his other work

The categorization of a human being as *zōon politikon*, which I provocatively described as Fact, is one instance of the interconnectedness Aristotle's *Politics* displays in relation to his work in biology and also his logic and his ethics. Aristotle's writing reflects the concerns and habits of a biologist, and he approaches seemingly every topic with his mind on aetiology and dissection. This applies to the *Politics*, just as it does to his discussion of rhetoric, aesthetics and ethics, even though he is careful to describe these aspects of practical philosophy as not amenable to scientific proof.

Aristotle is fascinated with how parts are connected to the whole, and frequently uses biological metaphors to express relationships between what we might think of as quite abstract concepts, such as family and society. For Aristotle, the kind of association which is necessary for political groups to form is an extension of a biological union between male and female. In the following passage at the opening of *Politics* he offers an explanation for states and communities in terms of procreation and an imperative common to all life:

> He who thus considers things in their first growth and origin, whether a state or anything else, will obtain the clearest view of them. In the first place there must be a union of those who cannot exist without each other; namely, of male and female, that the race may continue (and this is a union which is formed, not of choice, but because, in common with other animals and with plants, mankind have a natural desire to leave behind them an image of themselves). (*Politics*, 1252a24–30)

Later in the same book of *Politics* (book II) he continues:

> ...the family is the association established by nature for the supply of mens everyday wants...when several families are united, and the association aims at something more than a supply of daily needs, the first society to be formed into the village...when several villagers are united in a single complete community, large enough to be nearly all quite self-sufficing, the state comes into existence, originating in the bare needs of life, and continuing in existence at the sake of the good life. (Politics, 1252b13–30)

It is through association that humans form families, then villages and communities, and finally the state (here I use state, city-state or city interchangeably as approximations to the *polis*). It is appropriate to acknowledge there is no contemporary equivalent to the *polis*, a city-state which Aristotle did not think could be as large as 100,000 citizens (*Ethics*, 1170b30–32), though this does not stop us following Aristotle's argument. Aristotle states that it is through association that a human being is both part of the city, and then in turn, the city is integral to helping humans to flourish – to pursue the good life. It is because of this imperative of association that as well as depending on his biology, what I call the social Fact of a human being as *zōon politikon* connects with his ethics. Aristotle also suggests in this passage, in what can appear something of a paradox, or an anachronism, that:

> ...the state is by nature clearly prior to the family and to the individual since the whole is of necessity prior to the part; for example if the whole body be destroyed, there will be no foot or hand,

except homonymously, as we might speak of a stone hand. (*Politics*, 1253a19–22)

This seems to contradict his assertion that the association necessary for the state to form is an extension of a basic and primordial biological union, but this is because it is only through association that human beings can realize their potential – only in the *polis* can human beings flourish. Without association, humans are less than they could, or should be. Putting this even more strongly, the implication of the state being prior is that a human being can not be fully human unless they are part of the *polis* (Stalley, 2009).

To accept Aristotle's apparently anachronistic statement – that the state is prior to the individual – places us at odds with much contemporary work in organization studies, and also with the focus of two key social science disciplines: economics and psychology. This is an advantage here because out of the social sciences that are conventionally taken as informing organization studies (politics, anthropology, sociology and social psychology being the main others), these two are the ones that have most been put to work in support of what I have called an impoverished sense of organization: a focus on relations in the firm under capitalism. More broadly, Aristotle's emphasis on association, and his definition of the individual in terms of society, contrasts with the prevailing intellectual climate of liberalism, and with what Collins describes as the 'liberalist reverence for individual freedom':

Liberal justice assumes that the individual is of higher dignity or sanctity than the community; in preferring open markets to sumptuary laws, it judges free exchange and prosperity to be superior to cultural and religious habits that may impede them; in insisting that there can be no taxation without representation, it identifies individual Labour and the enjoyment of its fruits, as compared to need or membership in a certain community, as the true ground of property. (Collins, 2006: 15)

Though liberal thinkers have embraced Aristotle, it is perhaps easier to see from an assertion that the state is 'by nature clearly prior to the family and individual' how his political philosophy can appeal to communitarians. But, an alternative way of interpreting this prioritization of the state is to see it as a statement about the possibilities for self-actualization that can only be afforded to individuals through organization. The person separated from the state is like 'an isolated piece at draughts' (*Politics*, 1253a5): the game is prior to the piece because it is only through the game that an individual piece finds meaning. So this statement about priority need not be translated immediately into a statement about preferences (as somehow in favour of the state, with individual rights or liberty being a secondary consideration). Instead, as Kraut makes clear, these are defined relationally:

> To say that we have a *polis*-nature means that the closer a *polis* comes to being what it should be, the more worthwhile it is to be an active citizen, and the closer we come to leading good lives. (Kraut, 2002: 253)

Questions about the governance of the city are also intimately connected to Aristotle's discussion of virtues. The crowning virtue of magnanimity or great-souledness described in the *Nicomachean Ethics* finds expression in statesmanship (Arnhart, 1983), and the effect of the great-souled man [*sic*] on the city (Howland, 2002); 'not every citizen is a good man, but only the statesman and those who have or may have, alone or in conjunction with others, the conduct of public affairs' (*Politics*, 1278b1–5).

A number of consequences follow from connecting Aristotle's work in *Politics* with his approach to biology. The first is that many of his views seem strikingly modern. For instance Arnhart (1994, 1995) shows how readily they can be linked with Darwinian social theory. Also, the idea that natural (in the sense of biological) tendencies govern social behaviour is close to some tenets of evolutionary psychology. This has an unfortunate aspect though, since one problem attributed to Aristotle, and also to Darwinian explanations of politics, is that these can be used to justify inequity. If such things as slavery or patriarchy are seen as a product of biological imperatives, and natural laws of selection, replication and adaptation, they may be seen as inevitable and therefore excusable. Sewell's (2004) critique of evolutionary psychology, and its basis in the, at times questionable, science of primate studies, speaks to these same concerns:

> Beneath this apparently noble appeal to rationality and objectivity lies a necessarily conservative ideology – a thinly veiled appeal for the status quo where the least disruptive and, therefore, most stable social order is one that inherently favours domination of the majority by a minority of aggressive males. (ibid.: 938)

This link between the natural (biological) and the social is a problem for any contemporary writer advocating serious consideration of Aristotle's political philosophy, because one of the most fundamental but also difficult assertions in *Politics* is that the state exists by nature. Since Aristotle's analysis of cities and their constitutions would have suggested to him that all civilizations had relied on some form of slavery, the assertion that states exist by nature would seem to commit him to the idea that slavery also exists by nature. Similarly, since women were disadvantaged and excluded from political office in almost all ancient civilizations, this too would seem to be something 'natural'. This position could quickly take us into very bad company: eugenic and racist arguments are often given some spurious biological basis. Interestingly though, Aristotle does not take slavery as a social fact, or a universal, but acknowledges that some believe:

> ...that the rule of a master over slaves is contrary to nature, and that the distinction between slave and freeman exists by convention only, and not by nature; and being an interference with nature is there unjust. (*Politics*, 1253b20)

As mentioned earlier, he feels that liberty should always be held out as a possible for every slave and later he says that some noble men would never be slaves and some base men would always be slaves: 'It is clear, then, that some men are by nature free, and others slaves... some are slaves everywhere, others nowhere' (*Politics*, 1255a1–30). Additionally, though some passages in *Politics* do seem to us to be racist, it is important to note this is not based on visible characteristics, but on moral character, 'the beauty of the body is seen whereas the beauty of the soul is not seen' (*Politics*, 1254b39).

In the passage above (*Politics*, 1253b20), Aristotle draws on a distinction that I discussed in Chapter 1, between *phusis* (nature) and *nomos* (convention or custom). But Aristotle has a quite careful and subtle way of talking about nature that is more important to appreciate when it comes to his practical philosophy as opposed to his natural philosophy, in say, his *Physics* and *Metaphysics* (Frank, 2004). In *Physics* he acknowledges that something that exists by nature is not the same as something that is necessary, instead it describes a regularity or pattern, 'tendency... towards the same end, if there is no impediment' (*Physics*, 199b15). So Aristotle's use of 'by nature' is different from a phrase that we might use, such as law of nature, or state of nature (Kraut, 1996). He explicitly differentiates nature from necessity, moving on to the next section of the Physics by saying, 'As regards what is of necessity...' and he does this too in the *Metaphysics* beginning book 4 with a definition: 'We call nature...' (1014b15) and book 5 with another definition: 'We call the necessary...' (1015a20). Defences to charges against Aristotle as an apologist for slavery and misogyny often turn on a distinction between nature and necessity:

> Aristotle's account of slavery in Politics I, accordingly, serves not to describe and set apart a domain that is pre- or nonpolitical, but to warn his audience of free citizens of their vulnerability, not only to accident and force but, more importantly, to the power of acting in shaping their political destinies. (Frank, 2004: 95; also Kraut, 1996)

Similarly, Arnhart (1994: 464n) suggests:

> Some of Aristotle's readers have scorned his biological naturalism because he seems to use it to justify the exploitation of women and slaves. Some scholars, however, have noticed ambiguities in what Aristotle says about women and slaves that suggest subtle criticisms of how they were treated in ancient Greece.

It is worth noting that the most popular defence of Aristotle's toleration of slavery (a relativist defence) – that he was a product of his age – is a partial explanation, if not as Frank maintains a mistaken one (Frank, 2004). Aristotle denies the justice of slavery following military conquest, which puts him at odds with his contemporary society (Kraut, 2002), and indeed with many later advocates of slavery, such as – for most of its history – the Catholic church. At the same time defenders of Aristotle must concede that he makes some clearly offensive statements, 'the male is by nature superior, and the female inferior; and the one rules, and the other is ruled; this principle, of necessity extends to all mankind' (*Politics*, 1254b10).

The main arguments within the *Politics*

Politics gives us 'the classic statement of the preliberal view of political authority' (Collins, 2006: 2). It is an appropriate starting point for modern discussions of democracy, citizenship, the nature of society, public good, and civic virtue; topics that remain central considerations in political philosophy and public administration (Kraut, 2002).

In book I of *Politics*, Aristotle sets out the biological basis for linking politics with ethics, and asserts that the city-state is a community of men who associate for some common good (*koinon sumpheron*); indeed, as the highest form of association, they aim at the highest or noblest good – *eudaimonia*. Aristotle also asserts in book I that the city-state exists by nature, and that a human being is *zōon politikon* by nature. Book II considers different perfect states proposed by others (for instance Socrates and Plato) and ancient governments (Sparta, Crete, Carthage). The beginning of book III discusses the ontological status and agency of the state, which is defined in terms of its citizens as a 'composite' (1274b33–1275b21). Aristotle then investigates the nature of a (good) citizen (1275b23ff.) before proposing a theoretical framework for different forms of government (1278b6ff.). This then introduces a quasi-empirical discussion about different forms of government, and the extent to which they can be stable, and can support governance of a stable state. This discussion must, to a large extent, have been informed by the *Constitution of Athens* (Fritz and Kapp, 1974). It is continued in books IV to VI. For contemporary readers, the most notable arguments in these books concern Aristotle's identification of the benefits and limitations of different forms of democracy. Summarily, he favours elements of democracy but advocates mixing of different forms of government (polity), and constitutionalism, to avoid different forms of tyranny (including tyranny by democracy). The final two books (VII and VIII) of the *Politics*, which are typically considered to have been written earlier, set out an (unfinished) description of an ideal state and devote time to considering the role of education.

Applying Aristotle's *Politics*

As the brief summary above suggests, there are a great many themes in *Politics*, and many of them would be relevant to this book – which seeks to reframe 'organization' in such a way as to establish connections across the terms 'organization, society and politics'. A choice needs to be made however about which topic(s) to focus on, and in making this choice I want to concentrate on an idea where I have found myself drawn to an Aristotelian perspective in relation to what might be called, broadly, 'governance'. This is the concept of the public good (*koinon sumpheron*).

The public good

We can trace the origins of Aristotle's interest in the public good, like so many other aspects of his work, directly to his work in biology and in studying animals. I suggested in the introduction that it is conceivable that in another universe, on an alternative earth there could have been a thinker as influential as Aristotle but whose ideas were based on a fundamentally different starting assumption. Instead of believing that human beings were simply another kind of animal, such a thinker could have understood humans as an alternative kind of being altogether. Yet Aristotle's account is strikingly modern in this regard. He discusses animals in terms of their modes of living and actions. Some are gregarious, while others solitary, and of those who are gregarious, some are social and others independent:

> Social creatures are such as have one common object in view; and this property is not common to all who are gregarious. Such social creatures are man, the bee, the ant and the crane. (*History of Animals*, 487b34–488a10)

Interestingly, Arnhart translates 'social' in this passage as 'political' and this would seem justifiable in the sense that the distinguishing characteristic of all of Aristotle's political animals is that they cooperate for some common work or function:

> Human beings are more political, however, than these animals because of the uniquely human capacity for speech (*logos*)…Through speech human beings can deliberate about the 'common advantage' (*koinon sumpheron*) as the criterion of justice. A just political community can be judged to be one that serves the common advantage of all its members. (Arnhart, 1994: 466)

Several writers have suggested Aristotle's framework of virtues and common good, and his account of the governance of the *polis*, can be transferred to understand firms or managers. Most promising among these is Moore's (2005) suggestion of an additional nuance to Aristotelian virtue ethics. This is to make a distinction (drawing on MacIntyre, 1979, 1984a, 1988, 1999b) between practices and institutions, and two kinds of goods: internal (such as affiliation among members), and external (like profit) (see also, Moore and Beadle, 2006; also Sison, 2008, ch. 3). Moore argues that firms, even under capitalism, can be virtuous (develop corporate character) if they achieve 'balance': they can promote the pursuit of worthy internal goods, and can resist potentially corrupting external goods and negative influences from other institutions.

A fuller discussion on the practice/institution distinction is beyond the scope of this book (see Knight, in press, for a recent discussion); because I advocate returning to the original texts. It is also not clear to me how MacIntyre can be applied in this way (i.e. a defence of the possibility of a virtuous capitalist firm). Briefly, the difficulty as I see it with Moore's account of 'balance' is it includes a concession to capitalism. This may be empirically 'real', and in that sense reflect the attention to the contemporary social context in MacIntyre's practical philosophy, but it also takes us away from the more radical implications of Aristotle's account of virtue and the *polis*. To seek accommodation or balance under capitalism takes us further from the MacIntyre of *After Virtue* who believes conflict is 'at the heart of social structure' (discussed in Knight: 106–26). For Aristotle, the *polis* exists for the sake of the good life and this consists in worthwhile activity by its citizens. The goal of the city and the constitution of virtue lies in the activity itself, rather than in some separate product: there is no 'balancing' in the sense of striving for a middle ground (like there is in pursuit of a mean), the pursuit of flourishing is unadulterated. It is a target aimed for rather than a consideration to be balanced.

Hartman and others (e.g. Flynn, 2008) rely on a slightly bolder and more straightforward application of Aristotle, making a *polis*/firm equivalence:

> Aristotle would approve of our focus on the organization. He takes the notion of community so seriously as essential to ethics that he claims that politics is the culmination of ethics. Today, when organizations seem to be overtaking nation states as the primary form of association and identification, and corporate culture is such a powerful determinant of behavior, he might well say that the culmination of ethics is organization theory. (Hartman, 2008: 261)

There is truth in this, although (contra Parker, 2003) it implies a separation of politics and ethics which Aristotle would not recognize. At the same time, it does not really help us to understand the contemporary firm, or the limitations of capitalism as an ideology if we oversimplify Aristotle's framework that connects what it is to be human with an account of virtue and with organization as *koinōnia*. It seems to leave us either with: (i) contestable suppositions such as 'good ethics is good business' – what Hartman goes on to advocate, 'Firms that succeed by providing goods and services valuable to their customers are doing something morally good, and something good from the perspective of their bottom line'; or (ii) banalities that could be distilled from any widely accepted normative framework (it is wrong to lie, cheat, steal, kill and so on). A subtler approach is taken by Solomon who at once defends the transferability of Aristotelian considerations of virtue (caring, consideration and *eunoia*), at the same time as promoting a much more inclusive construction of 'business ethics':

> ...mutual respect, caring and compassion is what we all in fact expect and demand in our various jobs and positions. To be sure, it is unfortunate that so many managers and employees and even executives do not get that respect, do not care or show compassion as they should, in part because of the brutally competitive and chauvinist images in which they conceive of what they do. But once we start insisting that the ethics of business is not simply confined to 'business' but begin by examining the very nature of the good life and living well in a business society, those conceptions are bound to change. (Solomon, 1998: 531).

There is scope, as Solomon does here and elsewhere (1993, 1994), to understand the contemporary firm as a community, or importantly as different kinds of community, 'good and bad, successful and unsuccessful, benign and evil' (Solomon, 1998: 274; see also Koehn, 1995, 1998).

However, it can also be helpful to see where the comparisons between the *polis* in Aristotle's *Politics* and the contemporary firm break down. This happens quite quickly if we emphasize that Aristotle's account of common good depends on a logic that runs counter to capitalism. Solomon acknowledges this at one level, but in order to keep a close parallel between *polis* and firm he proposes two arguments that are discordant. The first argument is that the pursuit of profit is not supremely important, '[p]rofits may be "the bottom line", but that should be read as a ground for doing what the corporation is doing rather than the ultimate purpose to which all corporate and individual activities should be driven' (Solomon, 1994: 275). The second argument is that for firms to be profitable they have to behave ethically, to play the long game rather than go for quick, zero sum wins, 'virtually any business and every institution thrives (or not) on the basis of repeated exchanges' (ibid.: 280). This is a source of incoherence, as Boatright (1995) identifies in a review of Solomon's (1993) *Ethics and Excellence*, because there is a difference between (i) revealing an ethical foundation for business, and (ii) advocating an ethical approach to business:

> If the virtues in business are derived from business as it is practiced...then there is no way...to criticize these virtues and the actions that follow from them. On the other hand, if we derive these virtues from a conception of business as it ought to be...then what is the justification for that conception and not some other? (Boatright, 1995: 358)

It seems unlikely that capitalism typically fosters the virtues associated with *koinōnia*, because (as argued in Chapter 2), the common good rests ultimately on notions of justice in society rather than on profit in the firm: standard economic theory says much about freedom and the market, but little about justice (Van Staveren, 2001). Polanyi (1957: 53–4) expresses this as a dichotomy, saying, Aristotle in, 'denouncing the principle of production for gain, "as not natural to man"' proposed 'the divorcedness of a separate economic motive from...social relations' (in Booth, 1994: 655). Betz argues:

> There is no social, economic or political institution which can exist if the participants in it unrestrainedly lie, cheat, steal, injure, threaten or physically endanger one another. This is the settled, agreed on, taken for granted kind of morality which business requires as much as other elementary social institutions. We do not want and will not tolerate locker-theft in our factories or in our schools. We cannot accept lying from clerks in our retail stores or from social workers in our welfare departments. There will be no getting one's way by bullying violence either in our church meetings or in our stockholders' meetings. (Betz, 1998: 697)

Betz goes on to suggest that because of this basic, settled view on moral behaviour, and contrary to some cynics, '[h]andshakes cement deals, the word of the representatives of two businesses bind their principals to perform and there need not, normally, be recourse to courts or legislatures to compel performance'. On this view, it is only when we have recourse to complex, unsettled problems in business ethics that questions about politics – and the missing discipline that Parker (2003) identifies of 'business politics' – will feature.

A case could be made for this, but more is lost than gained in applying the *Politics* in this way. Betz's taken-for-granted 'handshake' morality contains truth but if we are to discuss such fundamental precepts, and downplay the pull of the profit motive, any major religion could be appropriated as a normative model of conduct in business (we can't do business if we lie, steal, harm etc.). Again in terms of fundamental precepts, Aristotle's notion of *koinōnia* can be applied to all manner of institutions (and practices), not just the firm, but 'chess clubs, laboratories, universities and hospitals' (MacIntyre, 1984a: 194).

In considering notions of community and common good, we need to revisit one of the limitations of a generous definition of organization, which is the problem of collapsing 'state' and 'business'. It is because of this emphasis on justice that Aristotle has been so influential in politics. One criticism of contemporary liberal perspectives on politics and organizations (and with which Aristotle would decidedly not agree) is that the super-structure of the state is often understood as an extension of the private corporation. Biondi (2010: 94), in a review article, argues:

> Many people – especially those in stable, liberal, democratic countries – take for granted the purpose, nature, and scope of the superstructure under which they live and how it differs from other types of associations [with] liberal neutralism as advocating a state on a business model, which lacks the necessary conception of the common good needed to justify and sustain a political society.

Biondi argues that 'Aristotle's theory gets liberalism out of this bind' precisely because it resists a conflation of state with business. Chapter 4 illustrates the value of preserving a focus on state rather than business when it comes to considerations of *koinōn sumpheron*. This theme is also revisited in the conclusion.

4
The Public Good

This chapter applies Aristotle's work on politics to contribute to debate on a long-standing topic of interest in the study of organizations, society and politics, namely the notion of the public good (*koinōn sumpheron*, public good, common good and public interest are treated as synonymous here). This is an interdisciplinary theme and it links to our understanding of ethical life, since the good citizen and state are defined relationally for Aristotle. This chapter begins with a theoretical account of public good and discusses the question of what constitutes good governance. This is informed by three case studies from British Politics: the Profumo affair, which precipitated Prime Minister Harold MacMillan's resignation and succession by Alec Douglas-Home; the legacy of Tony Blair's 'New Labour' government; and the idea of 'big society' associated with Prime Minister David Cameron.

The public good

At least since Plato's *Gorgias* and *Republic*, and Aristotle's *Politics*, the relationship between (i) the exercise of power and (ii) outcomes for society has been of perennial interest. In contemporary academic discourse, questions about the former relate to 'governance'. Questions about the latter can be described as concerning 'the public good'.

There has been a great deal written about 'governance' and 'the public good'. Although these terms are used in different literatures, they are not defined consistently or precisely. The rhetorical flexibility in the term governance and in the phrase the public good confers certain benefits. It allows us to reference in a summary way broad sets of ideas, problems and relationships at interlocking levels of analysis (Karllson, 2000). However, when trying to apply these terms to a particular problem or domain, this rhetorical flexibility is limiting. In such cases greater specificity and precision is called for, even at the cost of limiting the reach of such phrases that – because of their generality – have an immediate appeal at various levels of analysis and to various constituencies (Frederickson, 1991). The way these terms are discussed here offers a theoretical contribution to some long-standing debates in management, public administration, economics and political science (Perry and Rainey, 1982; Roxbee Cox, 1973; Samuelson, 1954).

To contribute to these debates requires an initial statement as to how and where this chapter stands in relation to well-established ideas. Existing work on public good can be described in terms of three perspectives on the relationship between the exercise of power (governance) and societal outcomes. First, this relationship raises a series of practical and pragmatic questions to do with the 'how' of organizing the public sphere. These 'how' questions concern management, control and measurement: in short, a *cybernetic* (in the specific sense of 'steering') perspective (e.g. Chaudhuri, Graziano and Maitra, 2006; Jones and Goldberg, 1982). The first half of this chapter introduces and discusses definition of the term governance from this perspective. Second, evaluating the effects of power on society involves assessing configurations of outcomes (ends), but it also involves assessing the ways in which particular outcomes are encouraged or prohibited (means). These are ideologically charged, ethical questions: an *axiological* perspective (e.g. Bentham, 1781; Ross, 1980). Third, political administrations lay claim to the effective management of public services and this forms the justification for the ownership of power. Democratic governments try to balance political with economic costs and face an imperative to persuade constituents that revenue is being spent effectively (Ezzamel, 2001) and that they demonstrate good government. One role of the academic community is to subject the claims those in power make to scrutiny: a perspective of *critique* (e.g. Bache, 2003; Jann, 2003; Starkey, 1995). These perspectives are different rather than distinct, for instance 'how' questions in administration are also ideologically charged (and are open to scrutiny and critique). Although these overlap, for the sake of clarity, they are discussed in separate sections below.

A cybernetic perspective on governance and the public good

Governance

The origin of 'governance' lies in the Greek term *kybernēsis*: piloting. 'Governance' has contemporary connotations of steering or stewardship and different writers acknowledge this core sense (Jessop, 1998; Starkey, 1995). However, there is great variation in terms of how governance is deployed in different disciplines. This can be inferred superficially by considering the different disciplines in which governance is a core term: socioeconomics (Campbell, Hollingsworth and Lindberg, 1991; Crouch, 2006; Hollingsworth and Boyer, 1997; Hollingsworth, Schmitter and Streeck, 1994); development studies (Hyden and Bratton, 1992; Leftwich, 1994); organization studies (Jones, Hesterly and Borgatti, 1997; Starkey, 1995); globalization studies and international relations (Kooiman, 1993; Rosenau and Czempiel, 1992; Senarclens, 1998); political science (Pierre, 1998; Pierre and Peters, 2000); public administration (Hood, 1991; Rhodes, 2000) and the study of social policy and policy implementation (Daly, 2003; Gaudin, 1998; Rhodes, 1997).

'Governance' also features as a discrete analytical concept with particular connotations. Outside the field of public administration, and over the last decade or so, debates surrounding 'governance' have been most prominent within the burgeoning literature on corporate social responsibility (CSR) and business ethics. The widespread and long-lasting recriminations that accompanied Enron, Tyco, Worldcom and other corporate scandals are routinely thought of as failures in 'corporate governance' (Daily, Dalton and Cannella, 2003; Sundaramurthy and Lewis, 2003). This also applies to an extent to the global financial crisis (Sun, Stewart and Pollard, 2011).

Across, and within, these different literatures, 'governance' has no agreed definition. It has been described as a 'vague', 'pre-theoretical' 'buzzword' (Jessop, 1998). Lynn, Heinrich and Hill (2001: 5) point to a 'breadth and ambiguity of definitions', Bache (Bache, 2003: 301) states 'its use often lacks definitional clarity', and Rhodes (1997: 15) says it has 'too many meanings to be useful'. Others describe governance more cynically, as a 'very fashionable' 'neologism' (Pollit and Bouckaert, 2004: 10), or 'political catchword' (Pierre and Peters, 2000: 50). This means its 'usage has been both loose and universalising' (Daly, 2003). Jann (2003: 113) suggests governance is 'an all-purpose political concept', which resonates with Bevir, Rhodes and Weller's (2003: 14) description of it as an 'elastic' term.

Difficulties defining governance translate into problems with operationalization and analysis. For example, despite substantial research over time in the field of corporate governance, Daily, Dalton and Cannella (2003: 371, original emphasis) suggest, 'we know where *not to* look for relationships attendant with corporate structures and mechanisms, perhaps even more so than we know where *to* look'. There are typically subtle, and at times more dramatic differences in the way in which the root term governance is understood and operationalized. Though governance is occasionally portrayed as systemic or cultural (Starbuck, 2003) much research operationalizes it in rather narrow terms of control:

> Corporate governance regulates the ownership and control of organ-izations... It sets the legal terms and conditions for the allocation of property rights among stakeholders, structuring their relationships and influencing their incentives, and hence, willingness to work together. (Konzelmann et al., 2006: 542)

Though studying governance in this sense is vital, it is also limited because a narrow construction of control misses the broader 'big' questions relating to the control of power, which lie at the heart of Aristotle's *Politics*. Control is a core theme in contemporary organizational theory and CMS, but the focus here is usually on what is sometimes called 'soft' power, with a consequent emphasis on cultural and social technologies of control (Delbridge and Ezzamel, 2005; Knights and McCabe, 1999). In contrast to these (Foucault-inspired) accounts, the corporate governance literature understands control in terms that would be more familiar to Aristotle. They focus on the actions of powerful individuals, for instance the chief executive, chairman and board members, and on the firm's equivalents to a constitution such as codes of conduct (Deakin and Konzelmann, 2003; Jones and Goldberg, 1982; Mayers, Shivdasani and Smith, 1997). Naturally these have far less force than the constitutions in *Politics*, which is a less frequently discussed limitation to comparisons between firm and *polis*.

The assumptive paradigm underpinning the corporate governance literature is agency theory – a prioritization of individual choice, typically construed as self-interested, rational and utility maximising. The agency bias reflects a legal/economic perspective on choice, rather than an approach consistent with Aristotle's account of deliberation and *phronēsis*. The effects of this bias have been far-reaching, also influencing assessments of accountability in non-profit organizations, and provoking debate as to the role of the academy by directly or indirectly influencing the moral climate for organizational life (Donaldson, 2005; Ghoshal, 2005). In much corporate governance literature, this bias is expressed in a focus on ownership in its narrowest 'corporate' sense: that is to say on interpreting the organization as an agent and an aggregation of agents. This is very different from the sense of the *polis* as a composite where individual and *polis* are understood relationally and where it is impossible for a human being to be fully human outside the *polis*.

The emphasis on individual agents and on the body corporate forecloses a range of alternative answers to what Starkey identified as 'the essential governance question', 'the nature of power, its "ownership", exercise and limits' (Starkey, 1995: 838–9). These broader issues are of particular relevance when considering the contribution of an administration to the public good in society.

Governance and public sector work

A number of writers identify basic differences between private and public sector work in terms of their association with government, the links to core public services, a civic ethic and the underlying authorizing environment (Kelman, 2005; Moore, 1995; Morrell, 2006a; Pettigrew, 2005). It is perhaps surprising then that the way corporate governance is understood is so readily comparable across both sectors; where outcomes are governed by the interplay between individual agents' choices, systems of private contracts and a regulatory backdrop of constraints and impositions (Mayers, Shivdasani and Smith, 1997). In US healthcare for instance, 'governance' is often reduced to analyses of the structure of governing boards of hospitals, and particularly the influence and representation of clinical groups (Kocher, Kumar and Subramanian, 1998; Lister and Herzog, 2000; Saleh et al., 2002). This has been paralleled to some extent in the focus for healthcare reform in the United Kingdom, with the creation of new organizational forms in the NHS and systems of incentives. 'Foundation Trusts' were defined in law as 'public benefit corporations', and were determined by their accountability requirements and their requirement for representation by 'local communities and front line staff', with autonomy linked to financial performance (HMSO, 2003). The effects of privatization of public services go far beyond a simple change in ownership but, as in the case of the Scottish Executive's (SE) programme of prison privatization, they are often justified by a narrow consideration of incentives and costs. In the case of the SE's programme this was insensitive to contextual factors and notions of the wider public, a failure 'to capture social costs or benefits' or even acknowledge basic limiting assumptions about cost over time (Cooper and Taylor, 2005: 500).

More fundamental and far-reaching assessments of corporate governance allow space for nuanced and context-sensitive accounts (Jackson and Carter, 1995; Starkey, 1995). In methodological terms, this allows for approaches that differ from the standard cross-sectional or quasi-longitudinal designs using financial data and other performance measures. Instead, through more in-depth qualitative study over time (e.g. Pettigrew and McNulty, 1995), the latter approaches allow more scope to study interaction, process and structures (Roberts, 2001). This added interpretive scope is, arguably, more apposite when considering society at large given the complex accountability requirements of public sector officials and leaders, and the formal political environment that authorizes the work of public sector organizations.

Instead of focusing exclusively on issues such as associations between board composition and outcome variables – the narrow sense of 'corporate' governance – to evaluate the fuller impact of corporations, the delivery of public services, or the effectiveness of administrations, we must interrogate the wider institutional framework for exercising power. One clear and ready to hand framework for understanding this is in terms of archetypal modes for configuring service delivery: networks, markets and hierarchies (Rhodes, 1997; Sbragia, 2000). This offers a corrective or compensating account of structure in contrast to approaches that construe ownership in pure agency terms, or that focus exclusively on soft power. It redirects attention to the wider regime, which provides the ultimate logic for the exercise and nature of power (Starkey, 1995: 839).

Across the public sector, often the most far-reaching and contentious reforms are ones that affect governance modes. Attempts at marketization produce conflicts and tension cross-nationally and in different parts of the sector, for instance 'choice', voucher schemes, capitation (payment per client treated or served), internal markets, the 'purchaser/provider split', privatization, the commodification of 'science' (Cooper and Taylor, 2005; Gibbons et al., 2004; Harrison and Wood, 1999; Hyde and Davies, 2004; Kazancigil, 1998; Morrell, 2006b; Mrotek, 2001). More broadly, the transnational phenomenon of new public management, and managerialism, can be understood as an explicit attempt to replace hierarchic modes with market-based initiatives, and to replace administration with management (Ballas and Tsoukas, 2004; Shergold, 1997). In the private sector, markets govern the allocation of resources. However there is considerable debate in the public sector as to the appropriate governance mode for resource allocation: hierarchies may be inefficient but they may also preserve equity and a sense of principle; markets may reproduce and pattern inequalities, but competition can encourage efficiency gains; networks may be difficult to scrutinize and regulate, but establishing partnerships and trust may offset some of the costs and risks associated with markets – benefits associated with 'relational' governance (Akbar and Venkatraman, 1995; Poppo and Zenger, 2002).

There are, undeniably, difficulties in relying on reference to these modes, and in relying on such a high level of abstraction. There are many different variations on 'market', 'hierarchy' and 'network' depending on the type of government, the socio-political context, the type of good or resource being allocated, institutional histories and identity, professional jurisdiction and so on. Hollingsworth and Boyer (1997) differentiate between clans, clubs and communities who on this model would all fall under the rather crude category of network. As well as acknowledging the absence of a definitive type, it is important to note that these modes coexist. For instance, markets rely on a legislative framework (a hierarchical mode) and are rarely perfect, hence trade often depends on some prior connection (a network mode). Hierarchies can be undermined by favouritism (a network mode) or some forms of bargaining (a market mode). Nonetheless there is a stable, surface appeal to these types – albeit at a high level of abstraction. Markets can be contrasted in principle with the hierarchical modes of organizing stereotypically associated with the public sector. Network modes describe relations between agents that are in principle more local and less impersonal than the rules of hierarchy or the profit motive. Having proposed this as a resolution to the problem of defining governance, the next section discusses an approach to defining the public good, initially differentiating this from the cognate though potentially confusable term 'public goods'. This is intended as a contribution to the axiological perspective on governance as set out in the introduction of this chapter.

An axiological perspective on governance and the public good

Public goods

In economics, public goods are understood as non-rivalrous (one person's consumption does not reduce the benefit of another's consumption) and non-excludable (when one person consumes, it is impossible to prevent another consuming) (Hudson and Jones, 2005). In a paper, 'conventionally considered as the foundation of modern public goods theory' (Pickhardt, 2005: 283), Samuelson (1954: 387) defined a public good more eloquently as one that 'all enjoy in common in the sense that each individual's consumption of such a good leads to no subtraction from any other individual's consumption of that good'. Strictly, these conditions imply that no market can exist for such goods and accordingly governments have to fund the protection or provision of such goods through taxation. However this definition is very demanding and it is difficult to identify goods that totally satisfy both conditions. Accordingly, the phrase public good is often used more loosely to describe goods and services that are largely or ideally non-rivalrous and non-excludable, and which resist or challenge the power of the market rather than rendering it wholly unworkable. As an illustration, Marquand (2004: 32–3) identifies the following, which he carefully describes as 'goods of the public domain':

> ... fair trials, welcoming public spaces, free public libraries, subsidized opera, mutual building societies, safe food, the broadcasts of the BBC world service, the lobbying of Amnesty International, clean water, impartial public administration, disinterested scholarship, blood donors, magistrates, the minimum wage, the Pennine way and the rulings of the Health and Safety Executive.

Some of these lie closer to the strictest definition of a public good than others. For instance, as a global broadcaster, access to the BBC world service is non-rivalrous. However, this 'good' is not absolutely non-excludable. Access (as with libraries) depends on cultural capital (Bourdieu, 1993), that is the ability to speak whichever language is being broadcast, and also on material resources – a radio or access to the internet. These nuances undermine the homogeneity implied in 'public'. Welcoming public spaces are non-excludable in the sense they are open to all. They are only non-rivalrous up to a point however, since they would have limited capacity, and be less welcoming when crowded. Subsidized opera is neither non-rivalrous nor non-excludable since there is a limit on attendance and those unable to afford tickets are excluded. Some public goods (sometimes called pure public goods) are simply 'there': for instance fresh air. Governments do not fund provision of these though they may need to regulate externalities that potentially compromise these goods, pollution being an obvious example. In Marquand's list, clean water comes close to the category of pure public good, though ensuring cleanliness requires intervention, and utility companies are often from the private sector. So too does the Pennine Way, though that has to be maintained, and was created in the first place.

Each of these qualifiers illustrates how the non-rivalrous and non-excludability criteria are limiting. Instead we often rely on a tacit understanding of what constitutes a public good and Marquand's list, and his carefully chosen phrase denotes a series of goods one would associate with 'the public domain'. In providing references to diverse goods he offers insight into a reasonably stable category, and a resolution to the problem of the strictness of the definition of public goods. Resisting the illusory appeal of necessary and sufficient conditions (non-rivalrousness and non-excludability) allows a more nuanced and flexible approach to defining goods that are in some senses public. It is an approach where we can point to examples and express category membership using a relational, type-definitional framework, much in the same way we colloquially understand terms like 'table' or 'game' without being able to offer necessary and sufficient conditions (Mauws and Phillips, 1995; Wittgenstein, 1953). This is not to say there will always be consensus as to what goods lie in the public domain, but Marquand's list is a working solution because all the goods on the list are non-excludable and non-rivalrous to some degree.

The public good

When we speak of the public good this is a shorthand signal for shared benefit at a societal level (Shergold, 1997). This abstract (philosophical / political) sense should not be reduced to the established specific (economic) sense of a public good (above). There is some conceptual overlap: other things being equal, the fair and efficient provision of public goods contributes to the public good, and the unfair, inefficient provision of public goods harms the public good. However, the public good, and public interest, or 'abstract devotion to the public good' (Tullock, 1984: 89), are ultimate, 'meta'-categories for evaluating change or buttressing appeals to particular courses of action (Patashnik, 2003; Roxbee Cox, 1973). In this sense they provide an overarching normative framework (Shapiro and Rynes, 2005).

The currently fashionable, though rather vague, term 'public value' is a recent attempt to explicate the public good (Stoker, 2006). The originator of the term, Moore (1995) proposes that creating 'public value' can be a guiding principle for decision making in the same way that private sector practitioners can invoke a prime directive of maximizing 'shareholder value'. Public value is proposed as the means by which practitioners in the public sector gain similar clarity and consensus as to their basic remit. Such clarity of purpose could overcome some of the difficulties occasioned by working in a more complex regulatory and 'authorizing environment' than the private sector. Whereas (Moore argues) private sector managers have a comparatively clear and well-rehearsed end goal – to maximize shareholder value – it is harder to describe the ultimate purpose for public sector managers partly because public sector managers have more complex accountability requirements. As public servants funded from taxation and responsible for discharging policy, they are answerable to a wider and more variegated constituency than the faceless 'shareholders' of private industry. Moore seeks to address both these challenges (lack of clear, overriding purpose; complex accountability requirements) by imaginatively outlining an account of 'public value', and proposing it as a parallel end goal. Just as managers in the private sector try to 'add value' (increase the worth of the company to shareholders), public sector managers can try to 'create public value' (benefit society).

To illustrate his argument, Moore uses inspiring vignettes that show how problems in public administration have been addressed creatively. The first of these, which opens his book, is a public librarian's response to coping with increased numbers of what Moore describes as 'latchkey' children. The creative response involves the librarian seeking ways in which to work with this constituency, rather than using the situation instrumentally to argue for extra funding, or responding officiously and banning the 'latchkey' children. By involving the children in activities and providing them with additional resources at little extra cost (by changing staff rosters for instance), the librarian enhances the value their library creates in that community.

This is one of the most celebrated and discussed cases in the book, yet it is important to note that it is fictitious. Moore describes it thus, '[t]he case...is a hypothetical one, stimulated by a discussion in my hometown' (Moore, 1995: 318). This important detail is omitted from the actual text and only explained in an endnote. Bizarrely, and troublingly, this tale and an equally fictitious tale of 'the' sanitation commissioner have been referred to in the academic literature (in a review of the book) as 'descriptions' and 'cases' (Kniss, 1998). The imaginary librarian has been put forward as an example of how to implement public value by the National Health Service for Innovation and Improvement (Coomber, 2007). Her 'work' is referred to by the Young Foundation in an analysis of New Labour policy where Davis (2005b) describes her as a 'solitary, smart professional'. A *New Statesman* article in 2004 (written, incidentally, by someone at Moore's own institution) described the librarian as Moore's 'favourite example' of someone who 'builds public value' (Crabtree, 2004). The concluding passages of *Creating Public Value* also treat works of fiction and empirical cases as identical. In recapping the 'managers whose problems we have faced', Moore (1995: 293) lists the 'reflective librarian' (fictitious) and 'hard-driving sanitation commissioner' (fictitious) alongside 'bold leaders', 'enterprising heads' and 'determined operational strategists' (based on empirical data). The cases are inspirational and thought provoking, but this carefree approach to method is a real cause for concern.

There are also a number of theoretical limitations with this account. Moore does not at any point specifically define what is meant by the term 'public value'. As well as the absence of a clear and unequivocal definition, he does not refer to any underpinning theoretical framework or make firm links to an established body of ideas. He offers no theoretical propositions to test or develop 'public value', and no hypotheses or guidance on how to examine the term empirically. In these important senses, his account falls short in providing us with a theory of public value. It is certainly problematic for instance that the central term 'public value' lacks definitional clarity. Kincaid (1997: 257–8) argues that as a consequence, it 'can be applied equally well to agency survival and even aggrandizement'. He continues, 'the author needs to fall back, in the end, on moral exhortations to government managers who might misappropriate the lessons'. As well as these intrinsic theoretical limitations, one central premise in the argument for 'public value' is questionable. Moore suggests public sector managers lack a clear remit equivalent to that of shareholder value in the private sector. But, 'value' or 'shareholder value' in private sector firms is not straightforward. Whilst there is a superficial coherence or gloss in the phrase 'shareholder value', in practice, value is contested (Ezzamel and Burns, 2005). Accordingly, the suggestion that public sector managers should look to shareholder value as a comparatively clear remit is somewhat simplistic. Though 'public value' has an initial appeal, these concerns mean it is also rather thin. When trying to use it analytically, 'public value' can become as slippery as the catch-all term governance, and perhaps in different ways these two terms remain insensitive to analyses of power.

In one sense this is because the constituent element 'public' is contested (Frederickson, 1991). This theme is revisited and discussed in more detail in the concluding chapter. Here, I propose to set aside the question of how to define the public directly, and instead address what constitutes the good for the public. More particularly, I want to propose a basis for evaluating the exercise of political power. This can inform appraisal of the relative merits and demerits of different modes of governance and their relation to the public good. Perry and Rainey (1988: 184) suggest there are 'multiple, sometimes conflicting conceptions of the public interest'. A number of such senses can be detected in

Pickhardt's (2005) recent wide-ranging review of some of the relevant historical and economic literature: the benevolence of the governing elite, adherence to the principle of justice, a system of government that combines efficiency with fairness, *Gemeinsinn* or a sense of community, and the altruistic behaviour of citizens both individually and as a collective. At different levels of analysis each of these could feature in an evaluation of societal outcomes and feature in debates about the superiority of markets, hierarchies and networks as governance modes. The actions of an individual public servant, the policy of a public sector group or organization, the national policy of a government ministry or agency, the impact of a firm or the actions of a transnational body such as the United Nations or European Union could all harm or benefit the 'public' depending on how that is constituted (Mok, 2002). Following Pickhardt, at a societal level, assessment of public interest could be a matter of a portfolio of different performance indicators, for instance: income differentials, access to core services, educational attainment, levels of crime and violence, electoral turnout, levels of blood and organ donation, etc.

However, any approach reliant on performance indicators faces difficulties since consideration of the public good invokes axiological (fundamental, ethical) questions and not simply technical or cybernetic ones. For instance, how would one decide on the relative weighting of these indicators other than with recourse to some normative principles (could they even be commensurate)? Theorists are likely to arrive at different accounts of the good if they begin from different starting assumptions. For instance, Nozick (1974) argues that if individual liberty is sacralized there is a compelling case for free market principles (something of an elision if one concedes that markets are not 'free' but are themselves generative social structures dependent on order, and constitutive of control). Alternatively if concerns of the good are at a societal level and concern justice, there is a case for subordinating the principle of liberty for all (Rawls, 1971).

Differences such as those reflected in Nozick's and Rawls' divergent accounts of the good for society underline that at their heart, questions about the public good remain axiological. To try to define this more precisely, virtue ethics can be used to develop an account of the good. This offers two direct advantages. First, it offers some clarification and is therefore itself more open to critique and interrogation than vaguer formulations of the public interest or public good (such as 'public value'). Second, in methodological terms, it offers a description of the control of power that is neither agency centric nor predicated solely on soft power, but which considers how actions are situated and constituted with reference to context over time. In combination with the proposed account of governance modes above, a virtue ethic account of the good offers space to develop a powerful approach to evaluating the normative claims about the configuration of public services: a perspective of critique. This includes greater sensitivity to context and an improved account of the relations between power and society.

A perspective of critique on governance and the public good

Virtue ethics

In Aristotle's account of the good, the aim of analysis is to move beyond a list of good things, to an overarching conception of what is the good. Aristotle:

> ...believes that the right place to start an inquiry into well-being is to take note of the multiplicity of good things, and then to move beyond a mere listing of them. (Kraut, 2002: 51)

Aristotle argues that there are many things which are deemed to be good. Further, he argues that although these are diverse, they are also interconnected. To develop a systematic account of the good, he suggests we need to understand the way in which these are related as well as to develop a hierarchy of good things. He suggests that different activities 'aim' at different good things, 'the end of the medical art is health, that of shipbuilding a vessel, that of strategy victory, that of economics wealth' (*Nicomachean Ethics*, 1094a7–8). These can be understood as *proximate* ends, which is to say each of these ends is in themselves subordinate to other activities and ends. Health is not an end in itself, but it enables other activities; a ship is used for other activities which have their own ends; victory may be a precondition for peace, which is necessary for political administrations to pursue other ends; wealth may enable development; and so on.

The concept of virtue is also discussed in the chapter on the *Nicomachean Ethics*. Here though this particular approach to understanding the good is worth mentioning because it hints at the scope to move beyond Marquand's list of goods of the public domain (fair trials, safe food, clean water, etc). Marquand's list indicates an entrenched diversity in considering outcomes for society. This has benefits, but also forecloses a more broad-ranging assessment of the extent to which a political administration contributes to good in society. To pursue the goal of an overarching conception of the good is to open up the space within which a more broad-ranging assessment is possible. A coherent account of the public good does not simply speak to the cybernetic or axiological perspectives on the relationship between governance and the public good. It is a precondition for critique because this avoids the rather thin analytical senses of terms such as 'public value', which can serve as rhetorical cover for instrumental and self-serving rationalizing since it is so loosely defined (to say this is not to doubt the intentions or integrity of the term's inventor, Mark Moore). In contrast, in Aristotle's account of virtue there is a well-trodden account of what the good means in political thought.

Virtue ethics can be traced back farther than Socrates/Plato and Aristotle, though they offer the seminal accounts. Two of their most famous works (*Republic* and *Politics* respectively) also address the most suitable ways in which society should be organized (Ross, 1980). As well as having historical relevance, virtue ethics has contemporary appeal: Copp and Sobel (2004) offer a recent review of work in virtue ethics. It is a different tradition to the more abstract and impartial modes of Utilitarian or Kantian ethics, and rejects ethical master principles because it draws attention to the individual as a moral agent, and to their context in the widest sense (Arnold, Audi and Zwolinski, 2010). It can be thought of as a narrative ethic since it considers the implications of actions in terms of an agent's environment and personal history, as well as the future implications of that action on the agent's moral worth or character. Virtue ethics prioritizes the cultivation of *arête*: virtue, or moral excellence, through following good habits and acting in accordance with the pursuit of the good. Evaluation of someone's character and moral excellence can only really be done at the end of their life, though it is a constant struggle to meet standards of excellence. In the sense that virtue is only ultimately assessed on one's death bed, it is a teleological account (Morrell, 2004a). As illustrated below, when this approach is applied to evaluating governance and the public good, this encourages us to evaluate the exercise of power over time.

Aristotle suggests that there is an ultimate good at which all activity aims: a final end, or *telos*. This ultimate good for mankind is *eudaimonia*, 'activity of soul exhibiting virtue [*arête*]'. *Eudaimonia* is sometimes rendered as flourishing: activity where we pursue those things that make us distinctively human. Evaluation of whether one has successfully aimed at *eudaimonia* is finally realized only at the end of one's life.

Aristotle describes politics as a 'science' whose end is 'the good for man' (*Nicomachean Ethics*, 1094b6–7). A benefit of considering the connection between Aristotle's virtue ethics and contemporary accounts of the public good is that Aristotle's account of ethical behaviour can be applied not only to individuals but to institutions too, 'though it is worth while to attain the end merely for one man, it is finer...to attain it for a nation or for city states' (*Nicomachean Ethics*, 1094b9–11). In relation to the public good, the implication of this analysis is that political administrations exist to create the conditions within which citizens can live the good life. They provide, or regulate the provision of, public goods, but these are only proximate ends. The role of politics is to achieve excellent administration, and an environment in which citizens can flourish. Furthermore, since the state and individual are defined relationally, the actions of the state should also exhibit virtue. This analysis suggests that one can evaluate the claims or legacy of an administration in relation to the public good by assessing: (i) how it controls power over time; (ii) how it itself exhibits virtue; and (iii) how it creates the conditions within which citizens can live the good life. This offers a simple but powerful mode of critique, one that is rooted in a coherent account of the public good.

Illustration

Some illustrations may be helpful here. First, let us consider the legacy of the UK Conservative governments 1957–64. The UK Prime Minister Harold MacMillan and his successor Alec Douglas-Home formed cabinets that were remarkable cliques. MacMillan exhibited what would now seem astonishing nepotism when he gave government posts to 35 family members, employing 7 of them in his cabinet (Marr, 2007). Both he and Douglas-Home displayed a fondness for including Old Etonians in their cabinets. These crude versions of network governance – by old school tie and nepotism – were jarringly out of synch with the liberalization of the early 1960s. This entrenched an elitism that heightened the impact of the Profumo affair, and the legacy of this Conservative era is hypocrisy, deceit and scandal: vices antithetical to the public good (this case is discussed in greater detail in Morrell, 2009).

With reference to the simple analytical framework proposed above, these governments failed to contribute to the public good in each regard. The way they controlled power over time was through reliance on nepotism and cliques (crude forms of network governance). This meant they were out of touch with their citizenry at a time of liberalization. These vices meant they ruled as an isolated and distant elite, in contrast to two core ideals underpinning the virtuous *polis*: a common education for all and masses and the elite ruling together (Kraut, 2002). In undermining confidence in the institutions of the state, and being so demonstrably unrepresentative, they damaged the link between government and civil society. The gulf between the ruled and the ruling elite was prejudicial to pursuit of the good life.

Second, more recently, in evaluating the Blair era of government, we could draw some parallels between his style of 'sofa government' and the cosy networks enjoyed by MacMillan and Douglas-Home. The more distinctive strands in this New Labour administration were the arrogation of powers to number 10 and the influence of unelected advisors. Blair's government eroded civil liberties: curtailing freedom of speech and the right to protest, establishing DNA databases and affording police the power to swab people by force, persisting with an ID card agenda, curtailing rights to trial by jury, extending the rights of the state to detain people without trial (Porter, 2006). His government also pursued a war that was morally and legally questionable in the face of unparalleled public opposition.

These measures, the 'sofa government' tag, and the pursuit of war describe a particular way in which power is controlled over time: a presidential style inconsistent with the UK model of democracy or with Aristotle's view of the plurality (the mass and elite ruling together). Each of the measures that curb liberty, and the war itself, was largely justified with reference to the threat of terrorism. Guarding against a terrorist threat should be a proximate end, something governments 'aim' at in a number of ways: including an enlightened foreign policy. The only reason for doing this is so citizens can pursue the good life. If this is compromised by curtailing liberty and creating a climate of fear, and by increasing the power and influence of the state, then an administration is not aiming at *eudaimonia*, but totalitarianism.

Third, to bring things (at the time of writing) up to date, we can consider Prime Minister Cameron's idea of 'Big Society' in the context of riots and looting in 2011 in some of the UK major cities: London, Birmingham, Manchester, Bristol and elsewhere. Big Society was given prominence in the Conservative Party's manifesto, titled 'Invitation to Join the Government of Great Britain'. Were it not for events such as these riots, which illustrate deep divisions between sections of UK society, one could be accused of flippancy by pointing out that the mass of the populace are not really able to join the government of Great Britain. We do not own ministerial cars, claim parliamentary expenses or have flats in central London. Vanishingly few people in Britain have the educational opportunities that David Cameron and many of his cabinet colleagues did while they were being educated at elite public schools such as Eton – where fees are currently £30,000 per year (Eton College, 2011), and where, in February 2011, nine government ministers (eleven including whips) were educated (Chakraborty, 2011). It would be more apposite, given the parliamentary expenses scandal, and the recession, to invite the government to join Great Britain.

Faced with a crisis in society of mass revolt, or as it is currently being framed, mass criminality, the Cameron (coalition) government's response has not been to seek for solutions from Big Society, 'we will not succeed in building the Big Society…unless we stop government trying to direct everything from the centre'. Instead the Prime Minister, cabinet, Home Secretary, and our politicians as a whole, have (at the time of writing) been unanimous in advocating severe punishment by the state – removing offenders from society on the (self-fulfilling prophecy) grounds that such people have no place in our society. If we wanted to describe the rioters in the same terms the vast majority of the mainstream media and UK politicians have done, we could recall Aristotle's assertion that 'he who is unable to live in society…must be either a beast or a god; he is no part of a state' (*Politics*, 1253a19–30). But these rioters or looters clearly are part of our state. They are part of the electorate, and their behaviour is a product of a form of government and education. Diagnosis and treatment are not helped by the language of Big Society which is extraordinarily clumsy and patronizing, 'our society is broken, but together we can mend it' (Conservative Party, 2010: 35). This formulation reflects divisions between the powerless in society and our political class: who apparently believe a message about society has to be made so simple that even the masses can understand it, hence a society can be 'broken'.

The reflex assessments of mass disorder are similarly clumsy. Rioters, or as they are currently (at the time of writing) being framed, looters, have frequently been described by Westminster politicians, including Prime Minister Cameron, as 'mindless' and engaging in 'acts of criminality'. But criminality implies intent, so it cannot be described as mindless. If these were mindless acts, we would not be justified in punishing the rioters, something which Aristotle makes clear in the *Nicomachean Ethics* and which is discussed in detail here in the corresponding chapter. It is also clear these riots, or more carefully smaller groups who took part in and created some of these riots, were on occasion extremely well-coordinated and their actions were often directed. A rioting mob (which in UK law has to be 12 or more people), though temporary, has – almost by definition – a greater sense of coordination, purpose and common goal, in short more mindfulness than many capitalist firms. (It is tempting to draw further parallels between looting mobs and the acquisition and self-interest we associate with some private sector firms but space constrains.) To riot is to break very intentionally with social conventions and so requires a particular kind of coordination, though it is not 'managed' in the way a firm is. A more radical but also careful defining of organization informed by Aristotle can help analysis here. Notwithstanding common purpose, direction (in some cases) and coordination, these riots are certainly not the *koinōnia* which Aristotle identifies as sharing in a collective goal. This is because he has in mind a good for society, rather than a consideration of what is good for a particular organization under a particular mode of capitalism. Criminality can be organized and directed to ends, but these acts are not intrinsically virtuous.

Politicians have again, almost universally, said that these riots have had nothing to do with politics or protest. Yet, the riots did not take place in prosperous areas like Henley or Harpenden, but in areas of deprivation and long-term, intergenerational unemployment. Strikingly, this disorder seemed to have been as much defined by age as by class. Past and present governments, and families, are responsible for failing these young people. So too are the innumerable hymns our media dedicate to capitalism and which emphasize a material construction of happiness based on acquisition and consumption. Rather than an emotive or comforting dismissal (mindless criminals, no part of society), we should remember that political administrations must be evaluated as to whether they create conditions that allow their citizenry to flourish. In these terms it is easier to understand how phenomena such as rioting are not borne of mindless criminality but spawned from inequality. Lack of material goods may lead to theft, but, as the Archbishop of Canterbury identified in an interview in 2009, this is not necessarily owing to a lack of goods per se, it may reflect comparative inequality:

> When people suffer from material poverty and deprivation…they don't just suffer the lack of a few things, they suffer a lack of confidence; a lack of a sense of having a stake in the society around them. They feel that they've fallen off the edge and that they are dispensable. (Church Urban Fund, 2011)

Conclusion

Notwithstanding that the ethical is always the political, and vice versa, this chapter has tried to draw sparingly on Aristotle's account of the good in the *Nicomachean Ethics*. It remains however a basis for a more coherent definition of the public good, and consequently a better vehicle for critique than vaguer formulations such as 'public value'. One more particular problem with virtue ethics is that it can be hard to define which virtues are appropriate, and also what order of precedence they should take. For example, should compassion be more important than prudence? It can be difficult to 'read off' a course of action on the basis of a virtue account, but resolving issues is partly a matter of considering the context.

Part of the appeal of a virtue account is that it offers scope for local and contextualized accounts of worthy action. This is in accord with narrative constructions of behaviour and sense-making, but a marked contrast to the grand, impersonal systems of (say) Kant and Bentham. The emphasis on sensitivity to context has made some contemporary scholars more sympathetic to virtue ethics in preference to accounts that presuppose absolute standards of the good. This is partly because universal assumptions can become dogma and close off the potential for sophisticated dialogue about moral problems. (MacIntyre, 1984a)

One boon of the virtue ethic account in the context of this chapter is that it is possible to describe each of the governance modes discussed earlier in terms of associated virtues. Each governance mode can be understood as the context for the control of power within which different characteristics are prized. This leads to a multilayered account of the governance mode/virtue ethics nexus. Simplifying somewhat for the sake of illustration, in market-mode virtuous organizations compete successfully, while virtuous individuals are entrepreneurial; in hierarchy-mode, virtuous organizations have 'good' (unambiguous, appropriate, comprehensive) procedures, virtuous individuals follow these without prejudice; in network-mode virtuous organizations are collaborators, virtuous individuals develop and sustain effective relationships. In addition however, we must consider the limitations of these abstract descriptions of the control of power. This account of the public good, based on virtue, does not incorporate Kantian maxims or other principles. Hence it would seem, a narrow attribution of 'virtue' could be assigned to administrations or individuals who committed atrocities. A wonderfully competitive market could exist for something that should not be marketized – the fair and universal provision of healthcare may be an example (Morrell, 2006a). Hierarchies could have watertight procedures and rules, but these in themselves may be inequitable or authoritarian.

Aristotle does have a response to this. The modes for controlling power (markets, hierarchies, networks) are proximate, and they can only ever aim at other ends. An efficient market or well-ordered hierarchy are in themselves no good things. They only become virtuous if they enable other ends to be pursued (and by extension, the ultimate end of *eudaimonia*). Hence virtue refers to actions in accordance with the good, which would preclude atrocities, inequities or a basic incoherence between the mode of power (perhaps markets) and the domain over which power is exercised (perhaps healthcare provision or education).

It is questionable whether this analysis resolves a basic problem with an unqualified account of virtue: some principles certainly seem necessary to check perverse readings of virtue by an administration. Kantian principles, such as a 'duty of care', feature – at least normatively – in many parts of the public sector (Timmins, 1995). Indeed they are closely associated with some of the virtues associated with ideal bureaucracies: impartiality, equal treatment for all (du Gay, 2000). However, there are problems with relying on the presence of what might be an apparent given, such as a 'duty of care'. Resources are finite and it may be impossible to satisfy Kantian imperatives in an under-funded service. In Aristotle's terms, the proximate ends of rationing in one public service may be clear, but, it may be hard to see whether this jeopardizes or enhances the possibility of an administration pursuing the public good across a portfolio of services. Challenging though this issue is, it illustrates another two benefits that a virtue account of the public good has over Kantian norms. Whereas one can 'aim' at virtue because there is the possibility of choosing the least worst option, Kantian principles may offer no room for compromise. Additionally, Kantian norms are imperatives: insensitive to contextual contingencies.

5
The *Rhetoric*

As with the other texts in Aristotle's practical philosophy, *Rhetoric* needs to be understood in the context of a number of his other works. Accordingly this chapter begins by situating the *Rhetoric* in relation to these, before summarizing and then reviewing some of the main arguments in the text. It concludes with a consideration of how Aristotle's rhetoric has been applied by more contemporary writers on organizations, society and politics.

Aristotle's *Rhetoric* in the context of his other work

As well as ethics and politics being so closely interrelated, Aristotle also links closely considerations of ethics and rhetoric, something that at least to modern readers might appear curious (Duska, 1993). Rhetoric has a pejorative sense in ordinary usage as 'mere words' (Fairclough, 1995: viii), but retains the second, different sense with which Aristotle's work is associated, namely as a discipline concerned with how content is organized and a form of science that deals with argument and persuasion (Dryzek, 2010). Notwithstanding Plato's *Gorgias* and *Phaedrus*, Aristotle's discussion of rhetoric is the principal ancient treatment of the topic, and it remains extraordinarily influential and relevant. This is true even if for some writers it is influential and relevant only because it serves as a departure point, or basis for contrast.

In similar terms with which he differentiates practical sciences (such as politics and ethics) from those that allow greater precision (logic) in the *Nicomachean Ethics*, Aristotle describes rhetoric in the following way:

> ... rhetoric is a combination of the sciences of logic and of ethics; and it is partly like dialectic, partly like sophistical reasoning. But the more

we try to make either dialectic or rhetoric not, what they really are, practical faculties, but sciences, the more we shall inadvertently be destroying their true nature; for we shall be refashioning them and shall be passing into the region of sciences dealing with definite subjects. (*Rhetoric*, 1359b9–16)

Rhetoric for Aristotle is both an art and a science, and arguments involve not just the exercise of logic, but also appeals to emotion. It would be a mistake however to interpret appeals to emotion, or emotional responses to arguments, as in some way independent of reason. Typically today, we often think of appeals to rational argument and to emotion as somehow separate. In terms of a crude cultural shorthand, this could be expressed as the difference between the 'head' and the 'heart', or perhaps the logical ordered world of 'Vulcans', and that of 'Humans' (Sharp, Woodman and Hovenden, 2005). One of Aristotle's key contributions to understanding social action, and an insight that seems to have been overlooked by much subsequent post-Cartesian culture, is that emotion and reason are fundamentally intertwined and so such dichotomies between head and heart are flawed.

In a sense, a lot of the more contemporary literature on decision making, which calls into question rational choice paradigms, is recapturing this emphasis on emotion (this literature is discussed in more detail in the chapter on ethics). An implication of some behavioural analysis of decision processes is that rationality can be understood as something retrospectively imposed to describe decision processes that involve emotion, heuristics, impulse or habit. Aristotle's account of rhetoric is not simply acknowledging that these coexist, but involves a more subtle account of their intertwining and interdependency:

Aristotle's theory of rhetoric presupposes his theory of the emotions. For Aristotle, the emotions are open to the appraisal of reason. Such appraisal of emotion is possible because the emotions are partially constituted by beliefs. (O'Neill, 2002: 165)

The point about rhetoric providing grounds for belief is made very clearly in the *Rhetoric* where, unlike the connotations we have of the word rhetoric today, Aristotle sees it as an appropriate means of arriving at proof (allowing that, given the nature of the subject as both art and science, absolute precision is unattainable). Instruction in the art of rhetoric is, in a sense, a way of levelling the playing field, so that determinations in the *polis*, such as those relating to justice or politics, are based on the appropriate grounds.

> Rhetoric is useful because things that are true and things that are just have a natural tendency to prevail over their opposites, so that if the decisions of judges are not what they ought to be, the defeat must be due to the speakers themselves, and they must be blamed accordingly...if another man argues unfairly, we on our part may be able to confute him. (*Rhetoric*, 1355a20–34)

In the same passage, Aristotle also clearly says, 'we must not make people believe what is wrong' and so he clearly demarcates the study of 'rhetoric' from 'sophistry', which may clarify some confusion relating to critiques of Aristotle's project (as nicely explained by Holt, 2006: 1674).

Yet considerations of logic and rationality, and judgements in the courts, are married in *Rhetoric* with considerations of emotion. Chia and Holt (2008: 479, original emphasis) identify that, 'For Aristotle, the authority of any knowledge claim was a function of rational demonstration *and* affective persuasion, not simply logic alone.' It is because of the connection between reason and emotion, and the view of rhetoric as being both art and science that one can connect Aristotle's views on rhetoric and ethics with those of his psychology. Again his views are strikingly in sympathy with modern science so that (contra Descartes and countless theologians) Aristotle in *On The Soul* rejects the assertion that the soul and the body are separate, 'the affections of soul...are inseparable from the natural matter of animals' (403b16–20), where an animal refers also to man. He also does this in *Metaphysics*, where he says soul and body 'refer to the same thing' (1043a36). The Greek *psuchē* is usually translated as soul, but can also be mind (hence the root of psychology); though it is important to emphasize that for Aristotle all creatures had a soul, including insects (411b19). Rather than a Cartesian mind–body dualism, or what is sometimes disparagingly called a 'container model' of mind, Aristotle sees the soul as 'enmattered' (*On the Soul*, 403a25). As Olshewsky (1976: 401, original emphasis) expresses it:

> ...for Aristotle life is not *put into* the body as some separate entity from outside. It is rather formed *out of* the body into the peculiar shape and function for which that body has the capacity [Plato] sees a soul as an esoteric something which infuses an alien entity and thus gives it life in some mysterious way [Aristotle] sees a soul as the

completion of a body in which resides the capacity for life by its very nature.

Chia and Holt trace some interesting connections between Aristotle's rhetoric and his theory of mind (2008: 479):

> Aristotle also commends the rhetorical effort as being something directly engaged with; an ongoing ability to deliberate in public without recourse to established designs or models... Implicit in Aristotle's recognition of the complicity between logic and affective response is an awareness of the more basic knowledge associated with an ability to 'get on' in conversational scenarios – to demonstrate publicly a capacity to embroil others in the immediate and emerging reality of a day-by-day life without recourse to detached reflection and representation.

A view of the soul as the form of the body, or its actuality (with the body as potentiality), allows that 'one does not have to attempt an identification of mental events with physical events in order to integrate the physical with the mental world... a greater sophistication than is perhaps common even now' (Barnes, 1995: 194).

Given its important role in relation to issues such deliberation, rhetoric is connected to both politics and ethics. It is not simply because of the content of the discipline that we can draw connections across rhetoric, politics and ethics. It is also because of the nature of rhetoric as 'an offshoot of dialectic and also of ethical studies. Ethical studies may fairly be called political' (*Rhetoric*, 1356a25–6) (see Schofield, 2006: 306).

The main arguments within the *Rhetoric*

Bocatto and de Toledo (2008: 24) suggest that classic Aristotelian rhetoric:

> ... proposes that a speech consists of different parts: the presentation of the individual in terms of the ethos (i.e. credibility), the logos (i.e. the content matter or the informative part of the argumentation) and the pathos (i.e. the impact on the audience).

These three aspects are indeed central to the text of rhetoric, and comprise the three main forms of rhetorical 'proof'. Proof is understood in a different sense than is implied by logical proof since rhetoric is an art or skill that brings something into being (it relates to *technē*) rather than a science (*epistēmē*). *Rhetoric* also outlines how there are three main kinds of rhetorical style (or more accurately oratory) that are suitable depending on the audience and the kind of address (Molina and Spicer, 2004). These are (in a kind of chronological order) forensic or judicial oratory, which is of particular relevance in the courts, this kind of oratory is concerned with retrospectively establishing facts to underpin deliberations relating to guilt or innocence. Then there is epideictic or ceremonial oratory, which is more oriented to present considerations, and related to the determination of beauty and virtue – Graff (2001) describes this as closer to a written style of rhetoric. Finally, deliberative oratory is of particular relevance to political debate, since this kind of oratory is about future choices, 'the central means by which the *polis* is able to confront the contingent and pursue the expedient' (Timmerman, 2002: 77).

As well as these tripartite classifications, which bear the Aristotelian hallmarks of dissection and sharp definition, the *Rhetoric* is best known for two ideas in particular: *topos* and *enthymeme* (Gross and Dascal, 2001). However, precise definition on these points is not straightforward. Dyck (2002: 106) amusingly suggests that among readers of *Rhetoric*:

> Most agree that two of the crucial terms of the *Rhetoric* are *topos* and *enthymeme*, that the relation between them is important, and that the explication of neither is clear.

The following chapter goes into considerable detail about the device or family of devices known as enthymeme. Prior to that it is useful to identify some contemporary applications of Aristotle's rhetoric.

Contemporary applications of Aristotle's *Rhetoric*

Management studies, perhaps more so than many contemporary practical sciences, displays a fascination with language (see Green, 2004 for a review). This can be partly understood as the legacy of twentieth-century philosophy, but it is also a consequence of more recent applied forms of study, which share a concern with the way language is situated, occasioned and deployed as a resource (Fairclough, 1995; Potter and Wetherell, 1997; Stubbs, 1983). These approaches can be traced in part to the ancient study of rhetoric, but central to the linguistic turn is the idea that as a practice language is of fundamental social importance: the grounding of all activity (Wittgenstein, 1953), which forms one basis for

exercising power (Foucault, 2002). As such, the role of language is central in the study of management (Alvesson and Karreman, 2000; Green,
2004; Oswick, Keenoy and Grant, 2000). It is relevant in understanding: how new practices are disseminated and interpreted (Abrahamson
and Fairchild, 1999; Green, 2004); how actions and expectations are
legitimized and authored (Benjamin and Goclaw, 2005; Chreim, 2005;
Mueller and Carter, 2005); how people make sense of social phenomena
(Barry and Elmes, 1997; Boje, 1991; Weick, 1995); and how the practice of management is carried out (Alvesson and Sveningsson, 2003;
Minzberg, 1973; Watson, 1995).

Different approaches to examining language critically are sometimes
grouped under the broad banner of discourse analysis. As Alvesson and
Karreman identify (2000: 1145), often such catch-words can be 'a smoke-
screen for an unclear and ambivalent view on language'. One value of
retaining an emphasis on rhetoric is that it is anchored in a long tradition of studying arguments initially in oratory but also in texts.

The role of language is also central in understanding the relationship
between the study of management and management itself. For example, in describing the legacy of 'bad management theories', Ghoshal
argues that a 'gloomy vision' of human nature has been propagated
within business schools. Inspired by amoral, instrumentalist accounts
of behaviour and motivation, this has shaped the thinking and practice of managers and, 'actively freed... students from any sense of moral
responsibility' (Ghoshal, 2005: 76). Similarly Ferraro, Pfeffer and Sutton
explain the influence of 'economics language' on management studies
in terms of the broader phenomenon of the self-fulfilling prophecy, or
'Pygmalion effect' – a process where labels and descriptors shape norms,
expectations and actions (Ferraro, Pfeffer and Sutton, 2005; Merton,
1948). In each of these instances there is an interplay between the theories and labels used to describe social phenomena, and the effect of the
use of such descriptors, a 'double hermeneutic' (Giddens, 1984).

From a contemporary perspective on rhetoric and 'discourse', a
limitation in *Rhetoric* is that it underplays the relationship between
knowledge production and power: the constitutive aspect to language
(McLaughlin, 2001). It would not be accurate to say this is wholly absent
in Aristotle, since rhetoric is partly *technē* – an activity that brings something into being – and he attaches importance to the performative
aspect of rhetoric. Yet the idea that language constructs reality would
presumably be unfamiliar to Aristotle, or at least unwelcome given his
preoccupation with taxonomies and classification. A recent example
of interrelations between knowledge and power is given in Foucault's

analysis of a discursive practice (Foucault, 2002), where knowledge is seen as constructed in a context and reflecting the practices and functions of a particular community, rather than having a transcendental status. The practices of a given community are situated and evolve as the community develops ways of representing truths and legitimizing their own authority (Locke, 2001). Since these truths are constructed, there is a basic interrelation between claims to authority and expert knowledge, and the exercise of power. Appeals to scientific progress in public administration or management can be seen in this light since they can sanction the exercise of power, and because they appear to reference independent and transcendent ideals (Foucault, 2002: 196–208). However, such appeals can also be interpreted as moves in a language game (Mauws and Phillips, 1995). In other words, rather than referring to an objective standard of truth, they become seen as part of a local, situated way of talking. 'The meaning of words is specified by rules of intelligibility embedded in the institutional context' (Astley and Zammuto, 1992: 444). Such moves often serve as self-evident means of legitimation (Lyotard, 1984: 41–7).

Bauer, McAdams and Pals (2006: 84–5) locate Aristotle's work on narrative within a broad tradition of sense-making within the social sciences:

> People make sense of their lives by creating life stories. People use narratives to try to derive some measure of unity and purpose out of what may otherwise seem to be an incomprehensible array of life events and experiences... The process of constructing life stories takes place in everyday life, as people participate in activities, talk about them with others, think about other's perspectives on them, and reflect on how all these things fit together – on and on, day in and day out, appropriating new experiences and revising old stories slowly over time... Life stories, like stories generally, make use of characters, plots, themes, tones, and other narrative elements to convey meaning. Themes – or recurrent, goal-directed sequences in life narratives – go a long way in establishing meaning.

This is helpful in suggesting some points of affinity, or crossover, between studies of aesthetics and rhetoric in the present day. In the next chapter I try to show how, using some of the techniques and principles within Aristotle's *Rhetoric*, it is possible to provide criticisms of contemporary policy documents. This is done with reference to a government White Paper (in the United Kingdom, White Papers pave the way for legislation and often set out the case for reforming a public service). For this to be a classically Aristotelian project, such an analysis would involve evaluating arguments within a policy document in order to make clearer the extent to which such a document provides an adequate basis for belief. The more contemporary study of rhetoric, 'new rhetoric', suggests that this kind of pure Aristotelian project would be naïve and would advocate instead that one should consider discursive aspects to rhetoric: ways in which a given document were situated and occasioned. It is naïve to think otherwise because to focus on texts in themselves assumes that they have an independent reality, or are perhaps only amenable to one 'master' interpretation, as if they exist in a vacuum. But, to take the example of a White Paper, White Papers do not populate a white space, they only make sense in a particular context, and different constituencies will make sense of any particular White Paper in different ways.

To differentiate this 'new rhetoric' from Aristotle's view, one might say that new rhetoric understands an audience not as recipients but as interlocutors (Tindale, 2006). This is an important nuance since it is by interpreting and appreciating rhetoric-as-discourse that we can have a more sophisticated understanding of power relations, for instance recognizing that the very possibility of communication presupposes some common norms, a 'community of minds' (Perelman and Olbrechts-Tyteca, 1969). New rhetoric allows that a text can construct truth (rather than simply mask or reveal it), and also that interpretation(s) can construct truth(s). Both these things seem self-evident, perhaps particularly when we consider political documents, but they are underplayed in Aristotle's *Rhetoric*. This is perhaps ironic given that Aristotle's own texts have been taken to mean so many different things, and indeed created different worlds. The following chapter takes account of some of these aspects of new rhetoric but remains faithful to Aristotle's approach. To do this, it examines and analyses the role of aphorisms in speeches (talk), and *enthymeme* in policy documents (texts).

6
Talk and Texts

This chapter demonstrates the continuing relevance of Aristotle's work on rhetoric to show how across both 'talk' and 'texts' many of the themes and devices Aristotle identifies are still relevant in understanding contemporary attempts to persuade. Rhetoric can be identified and analysed in two media: talk and texts. Under the general topic of 'talk' this is illustrated by the analysis of political speeches. Under 'texts' the chapter looks at documents setting out policy. One way we can recapture Aristotle's sense of interdisciplinarity in the study of politics and of contemporary organizations is through examining rhetoric. This is a phenomenon where, notwithstanding advances in our understanding of language, the most ancient and influential writings on the subject sit quite comfortably beside recent research.

Rhetoric in talk

In contemporary analyses of rhetoric and conversation or 'talk', talk is understood as local to a particular context and often in terms of an institutional frame of reference. We are aware of this most obviously when we encounter highly formalized encounters with institutions, such as in medical or legal discourse, or perhaps in instances of management jargon. However, even in everyday settings conversations can be analysed as being highly stylized and conventional. Even these kinds of talk (at a restaurant or in the supermarket) are occasioned (characterized by sequences and turn-taking) and situated (take place in a particular social milieu) (Huisman, 2001; Okamoto and Smith-Lovin, 2001). Everyday conversations are highly complex social encounters, where things we would ordinarily never actively consider, such as knowing when it is one's turn to speak, are evidence of extremely sophisticated and learned skills or tacit conventions. These applied forms of rhetoric have enhanced the study of political rhetoric, so for example the idea of turn-taking has been used to analyse analogous processes in such instances as the following: in political speeches to understand audience responses like booing or applause (Atkinson, 1984, 1985; Clayman, 1993, 1995; Greatbatch and Clark, 2003); or in the use of aphorisms in political speeches (Morrell, 2006a); in other phenomena, such as the effect of advertising (Proctor et al., 2002); as well as in organizational behaviour in situ (Huisman, 2001).

One theme common to both talk and texts is the use of rhetorical devices or formats: for example Atkinson (1984) shows how public speakers use various techniques to cue a response such as laughter. There is sense in considering formats because we know that as well as speakers having to consider whether a joke is funny, that is the actual content, in order to provoke laughter they also need to know-how to 'set it up' or 'cue' a response. The use of rhetorical formats makes the audience aware when it is safe and expected of them to applaud or laugh – there are parallels in *Rhetoric* in Aristotle's attention to rhythm and his suggestion that closing sentences should end with a long syllable (Fortenbaugh, 2005). The most common rhetorical format for jokes is 'puzzle – solution': a speaker explicitly or implicitly poses a problem or conundrum and then resolves it. Repetition for emphasis and lists as well as the use of contrasts can also cue a reaction.

As a brief example below are two extracts from President Obama's presidential nomination acceptance speech at the Democratic National Convention in Denver (*New York Times*, 2008). The first (fairly straightforward 'puzzle-solution') was followed by laughter, the second (a more complex combination of listing, repetition and contrast) by applause. Drawing on an important idea within conversation analysis, well-scripted speeches use such formats in order to let audiences know it is 'their turn'.

Puzzle-Solution

Now, I don't believe that Senator McCain doesn't care what's going on in the lives of Americans; I just think he doesn't know.

Lists, Repetition and Contrast

The men and women who serve in our battlefields may be Democrats and Republicans and Independents, but they have fought together, and bled together, and some died together under the same proud flag. They have not served a red America or a blue America; they have served the United States of America.

The second extract is appropriately very powerful, combining lists (*parallelism*) of three (Democrats, Republicans, Independents; fought, bled, died; red, blue, United States), with repetition of words at the end of successive clauses (*epistrophe*) (together, America). This is particularly effective because of the climax 'United States of America' (*gradatio*), which is heightened by contrast (*antithesis*) (they have not served...they have served).

Whereas a typological approach to analysing aphorisms treats them as isolated fragments, placing greater emphasis on the context within which they are deployed offers a processual perspective. Together this typology and the analysis of these speeches enhance understanding of leaders' rhetoric. As Aristotle acknowledged (*Rhetoric*, 1345a), any such endeavour has ethical implications, but the following sections develop an approach that is (i) self-contained, (ii) original and (iii) useful – without discounting the problem of how such a framework might be deployed.

Aphorism

Aphorisms are phrases designed to make an impact. If aphorisms are well designed, and appropriately communicated, they can be powerful summaries that create a memorable impression, 'a single allusion condenses much that needs to be read, or perhaps unravelled into the threads that connect it to the larger problems it signifies' (Merrow, 2003: 288). They are a feature of language across all media, and share some of the properties of utterances, since they are complete units that are brief and have clear boundaries (Aronoff and Miller, 2001). Aphorisms also share similarities with sayings, such as adages, saws and proverbs, in the sense their wording is fixed. However, whereas aphorisms are often employed to prompt thought, central to these other forms is a notion of familiarity (Davis, 1999). Though it is difficult to separate aphorisms from other similar forms known as 'paroemias' (Gándara, 2004), it is worth differentiating between the aphorism as an ideal-typic category, and writing or speech that we might label aphoristic. Prose that is aphoristic is stylized and crafted but more flexibly employed in argument, since its meaning is not yet fixed; notwithstanding that an example of aphoristic prose over time could become labelled an aphorism.

As well as considering the formal qualities of aphorisms, it is useful to investigate how they are employed. In general terms, writers have used aphoristic phrasing to good effect in philosophy (Mill, 1859/1985; Nietzsche, 1886/1973; Wittgenstein, 1921/2001), drama (Shakespeare, Wilde, Shaw) and spiritual texts such as *The Prophet* (Gibran, 1923/1996). Within the tradition of Zen Buddhism, short pithy sayings or puzzles are used as a way to ward off worldly distractions as a potential route to enlightenment (Reps, 1991). Taking these different uses of aphorism as a single class, one can identify a common type of effect, which is to encourage *aesthetic engagement*: an experience that is extra-mundane, whether it involves reflection, or association with a fictional or non-worldly phenomenon.

In addition, it is worth acknowledging one other well-established function of aphorism, namely where it constitutes or references a *guide to action*. There has been a long tradition of such writing, beginning perhaps with the analects of Confucius in the fifth century BC. These were a series of maxims designed to offer advice on negotiating through life and business (Confucius, fifth century BC/1996). Other works designed to offer guidance are renowned for their aphoristic style, a feature that means their impact endures. Sun Tzu's *Art of War* has a pithy approach that offers advice to would-be generals, but its writings have also been used as guidance in other settings (Sun Tzu, fourth century BC/1971). More contemporary writers have used aphorisms to communicate powerful ideas on statecraft or to give guidance on life. These include: Kenko, a fourteenth-century Japanese poet (Kenko, fourteenth century/1998); Gracián, a seventeenth-century Jesuit priest (Gracián, 1637/1994); La Rochefoucauld (1665/1959); and Machiavelli (1532/1984).

Both modes of use (aesthetic engagement or guide to action) may be desirable, depending on the circumstances. The work an aphorism does can also change over time. For example, leaders in organizations can use pithy phrases to summarize a vision, capture a mood or set the tone for change (Conger, 1991). These can provide a social 'script' (Gioia, 1986; Gioia and Poole, 1984), summarizing shared cultural knowledge (Morrell, 2004) and thus enhancing scope to orient organizational members' actions – the guide to action mode. Over time however, such phrases may become slogans, where use echoes an underlying idea or philosophy and serves as a shibboleth, reinforcing group membership – in other words closer to the mode of aesthetic engagement. There are other possible trajectories, but throughout history, political leaders have used aphorisms as part of their rhetorical repertoire to persuade and influence and thereby exercise power.

Analysing aphorism

The brief introduction to the potential power of aphorisms suggests that recognizing them as a rhetorical device opens up opportunities for critique and scrutiny, most obviously in the study of leaders' rhetoric. Since some leaders employ specialist writers for key speeches, the boundaries between 'text' and 'talk' blur: for politicians, key 'speeches' are often first texts that have been meticulously crafted, revised and edited. This suggests that in seeking to analyse aphorisms in leaders' speeches, it is appropriate to draw on understanding of aphorism in other media. Though exemplar cases are necessarily idealistic, they can also draw out common themes to aid analysis. To explore this, I studied 20 writers widely recognized as having crafted memorable phrases. One aphorism from each was chosen as representative of their style (the method for this is outlined in more detail in Morrell, 2006).

There are a number of ways of making sense of linguistic phenomena, and consequently a number of ways of analysing them. This chapter, consistent with the emphasis in Aristotle's *Rhetoric* on persuasion and assisting deliberation, concerns the effects of aphorism on the reader/listener, not simply their intrinsic qualities. This represents a move away from analysing these texts in terms of their content, and towards seeing them in terms of how content is organized. If aphorisms are understood as prompting a response (albeit internal), it makes sense to use analytical techniques that address interaction and the way discourse is organized, instead of techniques that address content/thematic elements (Bligh, Kohles and Meindl, 2004), or purely visual/presentational issues (Awamleh and Gardner, 1999). This approach is also more in keeping with the twentieth-century philosophical traditions of viewing language as situated, and meaning as relationally constructed (Foucault, 2002; Kenny, 1973; Wittgenstein, 2001).

Considering the effects of aphorism then, Atkinson (1984) and Heritage and Greatbatch (1986) identify a number of techniques used by public speakers, informed by the study of conversation analysis (CA). Of these, five (position-taking, headline-punchline, puzzle-solution, contrast, listing) seem particularly suited to analysing aphorisms (Den Hartog and Verburg, 1997). Earlier in the chapter I gave two examples of common rhetorical formats (puzzle-solution and listing). Here, to recap these and introduce briefly examples of each technique, the following illustrates them using a speech by former Prime Minister Blair at the New Labour party conference in 1999 (Blair, 1999).

Headline-Punchline

To 2 million people given a pay rise through the minimum wage. [Headline]
Tory pledge 1: we'll cut it. [Punchline]

Puzzle-Solution

What threatens the nation-state today is not change, [Puzzle]
but the refusal to change in a world opening up, becoming ever more
  interdependent. [Solution]

Contrast

10 years ago, a fifteen-year-old probably couldn't work a computer. (A)
Now he's in danger of living on it.   (B)

Listing

These forces of change driving the future:
Don't stop at national boundaries.   (A)
Don't respect tradition.   (B)
They wait for no-one and no nation. (C)
They are universal.   (D)

Position-taking

Today at the frontier of the new Millennium I set out for you how,
  as a nation, we renew British strength and confidence for the 21st
  century.

Sometimes formats are combined, so for example in the following
extract two three-part lists are combined with a puzzle-solution. The
first list (which cues the second) prompts an internal query as each
corollary is revealed. This is also an example of 'pursuit', where stress-
ing an existing point adds extra emphasis (Den Hartog and Verburg,
1997).

Listing and Puzzle-Solution

Today's Tory party – the party of fox hunting, (A)
Pinochet   (B)
and hereditary peers: (C)
the uneatable,[pause]   (A)
the unspeakable [pause]   (B) (Puzzle-Solution)
and the unelectable.   (C) (Puzzle-Solution)

The extracts above show how CA can be used to understand how political rhetoric is organized. As Table 6.1 shows, these different formats can
also be used to codify the 'ideal type' aphorisms, reinforcing the close
relationship between talk and text for this rhetorical device.

Table 6.1 Twenty aphorisms analysed in terms of five rhetorical formats

Auden	God bless the USA, so large, so friendly and so rich	L, PS
Bacon	Prosperity doth best discover vice, but adversity doth best discover virtue	C, PS
Confucius	He who by reanimating the old can gain knowledge of the new is fit to be a teacher	HP, C
Emerson	Every man I meet is my superior in some way. In that, I learn of him	HP, PT
Gibran	A voice cannot carry the tongue and the lips that gave it wings. Alone must it seek the ether	HP
Goethe	Things which matter most must never be at the mercy of things which matter least	HP, C
Gracián	The least card in the winning hand in front of you is more important than the best card in the losing hand you just put down	C
T. Huxley	The great tragedy of science – the slaying of a beautiful hypothesis by an ugly fact	HP, C
Kenko	...it is vain in all things for a man to set his thoughts on a time he will not live to see	PT
La Rochef'd	If we had no faults we should not find so much enjoyment in seeing the faults of others	PS
Macchiavelli	...if you do not declare your intentions, you will always be a prey of the victor to the delight and satisfaction of the vanquished	PS, C
Mill	If all mankind minus one were of one opinion, mankind would be no more justified in silencing that one person, than he, if he had the power, would be justified in silencing mankind	PS, C
Montaigne	Unless a man feels he has a good enough memory, he should never venture to lie	PS
Nietzsche	He who fights with monsters should look to it that he himself does not become a monster. And when you gaze long into an abyss, the abyss also gazes into you	HP
Santayana	The young man who has not wept is a savage, and the old man who will not laugh is a fool	HP, C
Shakespeare	He that is proud eats up himself; pride is his own glass, his own trumpet, his own chronicle	HP, L
Sun Tzu	All warfare is based on deception. Therefore when capable feign incapacity; when active, inactivity	PT, C
Thoreau	For every thousand hacking at the leaves of evil, there is one striking at the root	HP, C
W. Holmes	What lies behind us and what lies before us are tiny matters compared to what lies within us	C, PS
Wilde	There is only one thing in the world worse than being talked about, and that is not being talked about	PS, C

Note: Position-taking, PT; headline-punchline, HP; puzzle-solution, PS; contrast, C; listing, L.

This suggests that just as in the crafting of effective speeches, part of the skill in crafting aphorisms involves applying common rhetorical techniques (to enhance communication delivery style), and combining formats for message delivery (to increase impact, and keep messages short).

A typology of aphorisms

As an analytical framework, relying solely on rhetorical formats analysis is limited. These ignore the character of the message. Content is not the analytical focus for a conversation-analytic approach, but it is sensible in studying leaders' rhetoric to try to incorporate supplementary indicators of the kind of message that is being delivered, since this will influence the impact of their aphorisms. To explore this, I revisited the authors shown in Table 6.1 to see if there was scope to address the intrinsic character of these aphorisms, as well as describing their formal properties. This indicated two broad dimensions, or continua, on which the character of individual aphorisms could be mapped. This can be illustrated using examples from two authors (Nietzsche and La Rochefoucauld).

First, using the metaphor of two types of lens, a difference could be drawn in terms of the extent to which aphorisms were 'concave' or 'convex', in other words, whether they were designed to draw readers' attention to a particular point (i.e. concave), or to open up possibilities for interpretation (i.e. convex). As an example, La Rochefoucauld's aphorisms typically express a feeling in a pithy, apposite way, directing attention to a specific moment, or mood. In this respect, they are similar to quotations by some of the other writers illustrated in Table 6.1, such as Auden, Gracián, Huxley, Montaigne and Wilde. In contrast, Nietzschean aphorisms, though they are often as memorable and as brief, are more complex since they do not summarize so much as encourage one to think more deeply, and return to the text to discover more:

> ... space is created in which to work *on* something and work *out* something ... one of the virtues of reading Nietzsche's texts is that readers become aware of their own conceptual inventory, and subsequently change this inventory. (Del Caro, 2004: 112, original emphasis)

In this light they share something in common with other writers in Table 6.1: Confucius, Gibran and Santayana; or Zen writing that encourages reflection, rather than immediate recognition (Reps, 1991).

Two examples serve to illustrate this. When La Rochefoucauld states, 'It is easier to be wise for others than for oneself' (1665/1959: 54), this prompts an introspective moment of recognition, encouraging one to reflect on the dangers of hypocrisy. The aphorism is free-standing and there is no need to look for deeper meaning or alternative interpretations. In contrast, when Nietzsche writes, 'There are no moral phenomena at all, only a moral interpretation of phenomena' (Nietzsche, 1886/1973: 78), this is not an easy statement to assimilate, and requires further thought, since it attacks the ontology of ethical systems which lay claim to knowledge of the good.

As well as a distinction between 'concave' and 'convex' aphorisms, a contrast can be drawn between those aphorisms that are 'creative' and those that are 'destructive'. This distinction seems to hold within the body of work of a single writer, so for example some of La Rochefoucauld's maxims are pieces of constructive advice, 'To try to be wise all on one's own is sheer folly' (La Rochefoucauld, 1665/1959: 67), whereas others are cynical indictments, 'The evil that we do brings less persecution and hatred on us than our good qualities' (ibid.: 40). Similarly, Nietzsche's aphorisms are on occasion joyous expressions of creative thought, 'He who attains his ideal by that very fact transcends it' (Nietzsche, 1886/1973: 73), and on other occasions vituperative outbursts, 'The vanity of others offends our taste only when it offends our vanity' (ibid.: 88). Considering these two continua together suggests a preliminary four-fold typology for aphorism based on both the convex–concave axis, and the creative–destructive axis. Combining this with the earlier mentioned formats provides a basic technique for analysing or crafting aphorisms; one that addresses delivery style, as well as the character of a message. This is illustrated in Figure 6.1:

Aphorisms can be used to warn of an unspecified challenge ahead (destructive, convex); they can signal the need for change and innovation and creativity (creative, convex); they can mark out and undermine an unfavourable alternative position or strategy (destructive, concave); they can illustrate a favourable alternative that is clearly understood and known (creative, concave). Using the example extracts from Tony Blair's speech (above) illustrates the work aphorisms can do in political rhetoric: 'These forces of change driving the future: don't stop at national boundaries... they are universal' (Q1); 'Today at the frontier of the new Millennium I set out for you how, as a nation, we renew British strength and confidence for the 21st century' (Q2); 'Today's Tory party – the party of fox hunting, Pinochet and hereditary peers' (Q3); '10 years ago, a fifteen-year-old probably couldn't work a computer. Now he's in danger of living on it' (Q4).

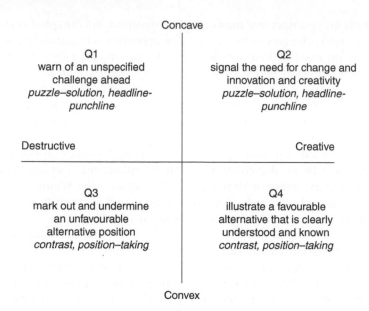

Concave

Q1	Q2
warn of an unspecified challenge ahead *puzzle–solution, headline-punchline*	signal the need for change and innovation and creativity *puzzle–solution, headline-punchline*

Destructive | Creative

Q3	Q4
mark out and undermine an unfavourable alternative position *contrast, position–taking*	illustrate a favourable alternative that is clearly understood and known *contrast, position–taking*

Convex

Figure 6.1   Two dimensions on which to locate aphorisms

Different rhetorical formats can be employed to craft aphorisms in any of these four quadrants, but if leaders set up clear relations of opposition (contrast), or outline a particular concrete stance (position-taking) this is more likely to be indicative of a 'concave' type. If leaders pose challenges (puzzle-solution), or use notably dramatic delivery modes (headline-punchline), this is more likely to be indicative of a 'convex' type. Listing, or 'pursuit', to provide emphasis is likely to be prevalent across the different types. Creative aphorisms can direct attention to past successes, thereby emphasizing a shared history or continuity (Shamir, Arthur and House, 1994) or to future prospects, which may be a characteristic of charismatic rhetoric (Bligh, Kohles and Meindl, 2004). Destructive aphorisms can emphasize points of departure between leaders which may prove decisive in a campaign or leadership struggle (Clayman, 1995). They may also create a climate of uncertainty and fear that can be exploited, or that alerts people to potential threat.

Aphorisms in context

So far, the chapter has centred on the delivery format, treating the aphorism as an isolated fragment. There has been little emphasis on the context for an aphorism. The framework above (as other typologies are) is static and therefore limited. It is more informative about specific utterances than the total substance or impact of what is said. One advantage of this is that in contrast with more interpretive methods, it makes analysis more transparent; there is unlikely to be debate over whether a saying was an example of 'listing', say. It also offers advantages over programmatic content analysis, where focus on thematic elements may be less revealing about the way in which messages are received. A disadvantage is that the impact of messages is more finely nuanced than simple dichotomies such as 'concave' versus 'convex' allow. Impact also depends on the context. Below, I develop the argument to incorporate two dimensions of context that are key to understanding the impact of an aphorism. These can be summarily referred to as *sequence* and *setting*. Sequence describes the timing of the aphorism: not just in the narrow sense of the delivery (though that is important), but timing relative to other events, and relative to other parts of a speech. Setting describes the place, in its widest sense, in which the aphorism is uttered: not just the arena or forum, but the wider political, social and historical context.

In the following two sections, to illustrate context-sensitive applications of the above framework, two different examples of powerful rhetoric are studied: Marcus Antonius' funereal speech in *Julius Caesar* and Winston Churchill's first speech as Prime Minister. These are from different genres, respectively: literature (fiction) and historical record (non-fiction). They are also from different eras: the sixteenth century and the twentieth century. What they have in common is they are inspirational, momentous examples of oratory.

Antonius offers an ideal example in the sense that great dramatic works can offer insight into the mundane. Though fictitious, there is much in it that resonates with contemporary leaders' rhetoric. In Shakespearean drama his is arguably the most pivotal speech and it is chosen here because it is an excellent example of the importance of sequence. This is not just sequence in the sense of timing within his speech, but in relation to prior events, since he addresses a crowd shortly after Brutus. Churchill's speech is also an exemplary work. He was a renowned orator and this speech, as well as being one of his briefest, is among the finest (Cannadine, 1990). It marked a turning point in his parliamentary career, but also influenced the history of the last century. Here this speech is used to illustrate the importance of setting. In the following sections each speech is studied to develop the earlier framework and establish the dynamic, situated nature of leaders' aphorisms.

Marcus Antonius – the importance of sequence

At Caesar's funeral *(Julius Caesar,* Act III scene ii), Brutus convinces the angry mourners that Caesar had to die to save Rome from dictatorship:

> Not that I loved Caesar less, but that I loved Rome more...as he was ambitious, I slew him. There are tears, for his love, joy, for his fortune; honour, for his valour; and death for his ambition. (Shakespeare, 1599/1962: 834)

Brutus is an impressive orator. He uses common devices, such as contrasts, lists and pairs to good effect (above), and opens with, 'Romans, countrymen, and lovers', a phrase echoed in the more famous beginning to Antonius' speech. Brutus is sufficiently compelling that the mourners unanimously forgive him, even calling on him to be their next leader. However, he then leaves and Antonius delivers a brilliant and impassioned speech that begins as a funeral address and ends with a call for revolution. There is much in this remarkable speech, and one feature of it is it contains some memorable aphorisms: 'The evil that men do lives after them; the good is oft interred with their bones'; 'If you have tears, prepare to shed them now'; 'This was the most unkindest cut of all'; 'I have neither wit, nor words, nor worth'. As well as the familiar lists, pairs and contrasts, Antonius deploys other popular, if occasionally disreputable, tactics: the backhanded compliment, 'I am no orator, as Brutus is'; his use of false modesty, 'you know me all, a plain, blunt man'; and his shameless duplicity running from, 'I come to bury Caesar not to praise him' through to, 'Good friends...let me not stir you up to such a sudden flood of mutiny'.

It is beyond the scope of this chapter to analyse the whole speech here, however one aspect helps develop the earlier framework. A common rhetorical device, repetition, is used to brilliant effect by Antonius and in a way that illustrates the situated, dynamic potential of aphoristic rhetoric. Analysis of this also illustrates the limitations of content-based approaches by shedding light on the importance of sequence. Antonius adopts and usurps Brutus' rhetoric by repeating and gradually subverting the charge against Caesar of ambition. This is a powerful move since 'death for his ambition' is the point of greatest emphasis by Brutus (as in the extract from his speech above). The first time he does this, Antonius seems to be merely describing what has happened: 'The noble Brutus hath told you Caesar was ambitious...Brutus is an honourable man; So are they all, all honourable men.' Shortly afterwards he describes Caesar as a 'friend, faithful and just', and follows this with, 'But Brutus says he was ambitious; and Brutus is an honourable man.' Here, Brutus is no longer 'noble', or part of a group and by contrasting 'friend, faithful and just' with 'Brutus says he was ambitious', Antonius creates a sense of ambiguity and unease. Through repetition, subtle variation and contrast, the juxtaposition of 'ambition' and 'honour' becomes a source of unendurable tension.

Whereas Brutus' listing serves as emphasis, by repeating Brutus' words, Antonius is able to undermine the idea that Brutus is honourable, first raising questions in his audience's mind, then provoking them to fury. Successive challenges to the charge of ambition are juxtaposed with Brutus' 'honourable' label: 'When that the poor have cried, Caesar hath wept; ambition should be made of sterner stuff'; 'He [Caesar] both brought many captives home to Rome, whose ransoms did the general coffers fill; did this in Caesar seem ambitious?'; 'on the Lupercal I thrice presented him a kingly crown, which he did thrice refuse: was this ambition?' Each of these is followed by, 'But/yet Brutus says he was ambitious: And Brutus is an honourable man.'

The sense of the fragment, 'Brutus is an honourable man' changes dramatically over the course of Antonius' address. Using the earlier framework, these changes could be described as shifts from creative/neutral and concave (where it is simple description), to neutral/destructive and convex (where it prompts questions), to destructive and concave (where it becomes obviously bitter and sarcastic), to destructive and convex (as he moves the crowd to mutiny). The ways in which this fragment is deployed are qualitatively different even though the content remains the same and this illustrates the importance of sequence in determining impact. Antonius speaks to such effect that he is able to whip the crowd into murderous rage. They become so incensed they kill an innocent poet (Cinna) simply for having the same name as one of the conspirators. The ultimate impact is that Brutus and his allies are driven from the city and Antonius raises an army to hunt them down.

Churchill's first speech as Prime Minister – the importance of setting

Churchill's first Prime Ministerial address to parliament (13 May 1940) remains a hallmark of oratory. Jenkins (2002: 591) describes it as 'more a call to battle stations than a speech', but with 'several phrases which have reverberated down the decades'. Churchill's wartime accession to Prime Minister followed a period of unease and instability. Chamberlain, whom he succeeded, was widely perceived as weak and during a debate on the British debacle in Norway faced openly hostile and savage criticism, which prompted Chamberlain to ask for a vote of confidence. The resulting majority was an inadequate mandate, and rebelling Conservatives refused to cooperate with the government unless it included Labour and Liberal members. Labour members refused to serve under Chamberlain, and Churchill became leader of a coalition government (Mercer, 1989). He first entered the House of Commons as leader on 13 May 1940, and 'encountered a less than enthusiastic reception', as a few – overwhelmingly labour and liberal members – raised some 'thin cheers' (Jenkins, 2002: 590). In contrast, earlier in the day Chamberlain had been uproariously greeted by the Conservative politicians.

Churchill spoke as one sensitive to the immediate political context. He had an intimate knowledge of parliament having first been elected in 1900. He had also served in both the Liberal and Conservative parties. Leading a coalition government would prove challenging to any leader, but these difficulties were heightened by the recent deposition of Chamberlain and the climate in the chamber. In light of this, and of the challenges lying ahead, offering clarity and a sense of purpose were key. Churchill chose to make a very short statement. Remarkably, it was only 627 words long, and of these, half are given over to a formal request to pass a resolution recognizing the new government. Churchill then prefaced the remainder of his speech with an apology for the 'lack of ceremony'. He continued:

> I would say to the House, as I said to those who have joined this government: 'I have nothing to offer but blood, toil, tears and sweat'. We have before us an ordeal of the most grievous kind. We have before us many, many long months of struggle and of suffering. (The Churchill Centre, online at winstonchurchill.org)

This opening is remarkable given the turbulent political context. In the face of indifference and quiet hostility from many in his own party, he begins with a stark admission of his limitations, but also with compelling determination. In terms of the earlier mentioned rhetorical formats, the passage above and his speech as a whole stand as one of the most dramatic examples of 'position-taking' in the history of political rhetoric. Churchill does this in a way that establishes his integrity, 'I say...as I said', and acknowledges his weakness 'nothing to offer' while committing to personal sacrifice 'blood, toil, tears and sweat'. The theme of sacrifice, at first personal and specific, or in terms of the earlier framework 'concave', dramatically shifts to being inclusive and 'convex' with the repetition of the phrase 'we have before us' and the unbounded notions 'ordeal of a most grievous kind' and 'struggle and suffering'. Churchill strives to frame the situation, first in terms of his abilities and limitations, but then in wider terms as he orients his audience to future hardship.

Given the events preceding his accession, it could have been tempting for him to establish his credibility by signalling a change in direction from Chamberlain, or by setting out a contrastive vision of the future using more concave types of aphoristic phrasing. Instead, he offers a personal pledge then uses simple language to signal a common threat that makes his concise call to arms inclusive and hence more powerful. The climax to his speech comes in the following passage framed by two rhetorical questions.

> You ask, what is our policy? I can say: It is to wage war, by sea, land and air, with all our might and with all the strength that God can give us; to wage war against a monstrous tyranny, never surpassed in the dark, lamentable catalogue of human crime. That is our policy. You ask, what is our aim? I can answer in one word: It is victory, victory at all costs, victory in spite of all terror, victory, however long and hard the road may be; for without victory, there is no survival. (ibid.)

What is striking about these passages and questions is that they set out little other than sheer determination. The use of repetition and listing emphasizes this determination, as well as the sense of scale: 'by land, sea and air', 'wage war…with all our might…wage war against a monstrous tyranny'; 'victory at all costs…victory in spite of all terrors…victory however long and hard the road may be'. Churchill does not offer any specific initiative, any reform, or even the promise that he can do things better. Instead he signals future threats and challenges in a dramatic and compelling way. He creates a sense of clarity of purpose through his use of rhetorical questions and repetition, but simultaneously describes an expansive, far-reaching account of the threat ahead by using lists and convex phrasing, 'a monstrous tyranny never surpassed'.

It is worth noting that achieving such seemingly simple language and phrasing is a skill Churchill had developed over many years as both a writer and speaker. Shakespeare is synonymous with superb writing, but there are points of comparison with Churchill's speeches when considering the degree of craftsmanship, and with his prolific output. Churchill wrote his own speeches and Weidhorn memorably describes him as a 'phrase forger' (Weidhorn, 1972). Weidhorn identifies his earliest use of the phrase, 'blood sweat and tears' as being in reference to the Boer war, some 40 years before the speech above. Churchill described war as, 'toil, waste, sorrow and torment' in an article to the *Evening Standard* in 1936 (Churchill, 1939), but his speech to parliament is the first place where he chose to use 'blood' and 'toil' together (Langworth, 2006), and with such personal reference. The bold and striking way in which he gave his first Prime Ministerial speech is emblematic of his oratory throughout the war and the setting for this speech also needs to be understood in terms of future events. Jenkins writes that 'his purpose and his method were to promote a mood of defiance', something that produced, 'a euphoria of irrational belief in ultimate victory', and suggests that the national mood was partly 'a product of the mesmerizing quality of Churchill's oratory' (2001: 589–90).

Discussion

The speeches chosen and discussed in some detail illustrate two features germane to assessing the impact of aphorism: sequence and setting. The importance of incorporating these alongside the typology is that this offers additional scope to explore the aphorism not as an isolated fragment, but as part of a wider constellation of ideas and events. This includes consideration of the way in which aphorisms are deployed within the context of a speech, but it also extends to the wider context. The categories concave & convex, and destructive & creative are shown as opposite poles on a continuum (see Figure 6.1). These continua are also represented as orthogonal since there is no intrinsic relationship between whether an aphorism is creative, say, and whether it is convex or concave. In contrast, the contextual features of sequence and setting illustrated in discussion of the two speeches from Shakespeare and Churchill are not mutually exclusive. They are interrelated and also not commensurable.

This treatment of context constitutes an important development of the earlier framework since it suggests a way in which a static account can be supplemented with an acknowledgement of process. Sequence and setting influence one another in a recursive manner, and part of the power in leaders' use of rhetoric lies in being able to reframe and change perceptions as to the context. In this sense, even during the brief course of a speech, the effects of the sequence and setting are relationally constituted and not simply a given (Grint, 2000; Morrell and Hartley, 2006); 'leadership involves the social construction of the context that both legitimates a particular form of action and constitutes the world in the process' (Grint, 2005: 1470–1). It is one way that a classical approach to rhetoric (focus on formal, intrinsic properties of arguments) might be informed by more contemporary work on talk and discourse (consideration of context).

Here I suggest the circumstances immediately preceding an aphorism form part of both the setting as well as the sequence. They also contribute to the impact. Churchill faced a hostile audience at a time of crisis, and this setting would have thrown into greater relief the stark, simple language and phrasing he employed, thereby influencing the sequential impact of his speech, a 'lack of ceremony' followed by the promise of 'nothing to offer but blood, toil, tears, and sweat'. Antonius is also sensitive to the setting for his speech as he faces a crowd whom Brutus has just won over. He carefully orders and organizes what he says so as to incite mutiny. His climactic call to riot would have been suicidal if he had opened with it shortly after the crowd chose Brutus as their leader. Shakespeare's chilling illustration of the fickleness of crowd mentality has contemporary relevance as it illustrates the malleability of 'leader' and 'follower' interrelations (cf. Collinson, 2005).

The above analysis suggests a preliminary technology for analysing aphorisms. They can be coded using the five rhetorical techniques used in conversation analysis, as well as being described in terms of two continua: convex or concave, creative or destructive. In addition to being a tool for analysis, this preliminary typology could be used to sculpt aphoristic writing to suit a particular context, perhaps to consolidate a position or to bring about or manage change. Crafting and deploying aphorisms also requires sensitivity to the context, here summarily described in terms of setting and sequence.

In common with metaphors, aphorisms can offer a way of framing a situation or phenomenon since they are memorable (Morgan, 1997). To this extent they may be useful in communicating a shared worldview, however, this is also a limitation since it may engender group-think or entrench division. Aphorisms may also be cynically appraised where participants feel the realities of life are more complex than a short saying allows. This suggests that the element of closure needs to be carefully considered in crafting an aphorism because it may constrain thought or oversimplify. Aphorisms may be useful starting points for conceptualization, rather than representing a definite end point. A second limitation is that any analytical tool has advantages and drawbacks; a 'technology of aphorism' could be criticized as an attempt to codify the tacit, and hence a form of commodification. If this aids rhetoric, that could be for good or ill (Clayton, 2004). In defence, this approach offers an alternative approach from which to evaluate rhetoric. This can be a benefit to speech writers, but it can also be a basis for critique.

Rhetoric in texts

Rhetoric in political speeches has been comparatively well researched but the insight of turn-taking does illustrate one way in which contemporary insights from applied (discursive) psychology have informed the use of ancient techniques. Briefly (for more detail see Morrell, 2006b), a second avenue is to describe an approach to doing this with texts rather than talk. As well as in speeches, using and combining rhetorical formats in texts can make messages particularly memorable or salient. There are points of commonality with the rhetorical analysis of talk and the analysis of texts and this can be developed by drawing on a particular approach to literary criticism: Formalism (Morrell, 2006b, 2008).

Formalism was 'a school in literary scholarship which originated in 1915–16, had its heyday in the early twenties and was suppressed about 1930' (Erlich, 1980: 11). Its proponents (Schklovski, Jakobson, Tynjanov, Eikhenbaum and others) advanced an extremely influential and innovative approach to studying literature (Onega and Landa, 1996), but their analyses also incorporated political speeches and texts that were 'non-fiction': Formalist critique was a sociological as well as aesthetic endeavour (Greenfeld, 1987). This is one reason it was silenced by the emergent Stalinist regime – some Formalist work was effectively lost for decades, only to emerge later and have a significant impact on the development of structuralism. For two leading lights of Formalism: Jakobson and Tynjanov, the proper goal of criticism was to examine how various devices (like the examples above of contrast and lists, but also many more) could be deployed to achieve effective narrative (Any, 1990; Steiner, 1984). Formalism can be thought of as an approach to literary criticism that focuses on how narratives are made compelling, and hence powerful. Perhaps the central contribution of Formalism was to move away from a focus on the content of works towards techniques for analysing how that content was organized – hence the parallels with the study of rhetoric.

To give an example from recent political history, I have analysed a text dealing with political reform by Tony Blair's New Labour government, of arguably the most cherished public institution in the United Kingdom, the National Health Service (NHS). The policy document quoted below was published prior to legislation, to set out the case for reforming the governance of the NHS (in simple terms, this was a move to a more market like system). Here is the opening to that case for change:

> At the start of the twenty-first century England needs a new approach to the health of the public, reflecting the rapid and radical transformation of English society in the latter half of the twentieth century, responding to the needs and wishes of its citizens as individuals harnessing the new opportunities open to it. (DH, 2004: 2)

This passage is underwritten by an influential New Labour theme, the 'teleological discourse' (Allen, 2001: 288), an implicit trajectory of improvement in the policy narrative. NHS reform is represented as necessary to 'sustain and build upon an historic track record of progress' (DH, 2004: 2). Claims to the inevitability of social progress can be contested from different analytical stances, for instance a rejection of enlightenment fantasies (Lewis and Kelemen, 2001: 256ff). Another basis to do this would be to accept Aristotle's position that we do not make advances in practical sciences such as politics in the same way that we make advances in other sciences (such as medicine). To assume otherwise in the context of healthcare limits scope for critical assessment. If, however, progress is seen as one theme within a narrative, it is simpler to acknowledge that alternative accounts could be created. It also becomes easier to identify rhetorical devices that support the case for this particular narrative.

The introductory passage above glosses over complexities in healthcare governance by establishing relations of 'entailment' (Fairclough, 2000), which imply that widespread societal change necessitates certain specific reforms in healthcare. The extract is also a rich example of enthymeme (Dyck, 2002; Hamilton and Redman, 2003), what Aristotle describes as 'the substance of rhetorical persuasion' (*Rhetoric*, 1345a15). Enthymemes take the form of an argument that comprises two propositions: an antecedent (A), and the consequent that is deduced from it (C); but where an implicit premise (P) is suppressed. The extract above suggests that:

> a new age (A) '21st Century England'
> necessitates radical reform (C) 'a new approach'
> because current structures are inadequate (P)

societal change (A) 'transformation of ... society'
necessitates response to citizens as individuals (C) 'responding to
needs'
because that is the best way to provide healthcare (P)

technological change (A) 'new opportunities'
necessitates changes to modes of organization (C) 'harnessing'
because current working patterns are obsolete (P).

Each of the tacit premises could be challenged, but the case for change
is rhetorically strengthened by finessing discussions about the appro-
priateness of reform, whether this relates to abilities to respond to societal change, to engage with consumers or to use new technology.

Bevir (2003: 456) argues that the stories told about policy by New
Labour seek 'to tame the contingency of social life ... to make social
life governable'. However, 'the process of simplification distorts their
understandings of social life in ways that contribute to the failures that
plague their attempts to govern it'. Analysis of policy documents can
offer suggestions as to why there are differences between policy rhetoric and its outcomes. Since these outcomes are experienced, as well as
influenced, by an audience 'who do not generally make up the policy
elites' (Schofield and Sausman, 2004: 245), identifying themes used by
the authors of NHS reform offers an alternative basis for analysis.

Academics have a role to play in critically examining policy reform,
and in refining and developing frameworks which can offer conceptual
clarity. Where there is a lack of precision in use of key concepts and
complexities in understanding accountability requirements, there is
value in trying to identify the structures underpinning reform. Political
administration is not a science and does not allow for certainty or precision. If we are awake to rhetorical devices used by leaders and governments, this can make us more informed citizens and support Aristotle's
position that we are then in a position to deliberate on the basis of arguments, rather than on how they are presented.

7
The *Nicomachean Ethics*

This chapter introduces Aristotle's work on ethics, focusing on the *Nicomachean Ethics*, though it makes some reference to the *Eudemian Ethics* and to *Magna Moralia* – a work traditionally attributed to Aristotle but whose authorship is questioned (Brewer, 2005). My intention is not to draw on the latter two texts to surface differences in nuance or even inconsistencies across these three texts, which might be a fruitful activity for other purposes. Instead, it is to make reference to instances where there may be something additional that can help to consolidate or emphasize important points in the *Nicomachean Ethics*. This reflects the established view that it is in the *Nicomachean Ethics* that we find Aristotle's most complete and considered view of ethics and important themes such as friendship, happiness, the good life and virtue; as well as the grounds for compassion and mercy (Gallagher, 2009; Nussbaum, 2001b). The chapter begins by situating the *Nicomachean Ethics* in relation to other ideas within Aristotle's work, before summarizing and then reviewing some of the main arguments in the text, focusing in particular on his account of intellectual virtues and the notion of *phronēsis* (Reeve, 2006). It concludes with a consideration of the continuing relevance of the *Nicomachean Ethics* from a contemporary perspective on organizations, society and politics.

Aristotle's *Ethics* in the context of his other work

Bobonich (2006: 14) suggests that the *Nicomachean Ethics* 'might well be the most analysed text in the history of Western philosophy'. Like so much of Aristotle's social philosophy, the roots of his account of ethics can be understood as based in a biological analysis of human beings, and in the classificatory scheme he uses. Though a great deal of his work in biology has been superseded or even refuted, there is an appeal in the simplicity of this categorization. He sees a human being as the animal whose unique differentiating property is the ability to reason (attributions of uniqueness and the idea of 'difference' follow the classification scheme outlined in *Categories* and discussed in the chapter on 'Organization, Society and Politics'). In the *Eudemian Ethics* Aristotle identifies what we now take as commonplace, but which he was the first to elaborate with such care, that people can only be blamed for actions which they take voluntarily:

> ...excellence and badness and the acts that spring from them are respectively praised or blamed – for we do not give praise or blame for what is due to necessity, or chance, or nature, but only for what we ourselves are causes of...excellence and badness have to do with matters where the man himself is the cause and source of his acts...acts that are voluntary and done from the choice of each man he is the cause, but of involuntary acts he is not himself the cause; and all that he does from choice he clearly does voluntarily. It is clear then that excellence and badness have to [do] with voluntary acts. (*Eudemian Ethics*, 1223a10–20)

Though they have some passages in common, the *Eudemian Ethics* is usually taken to be written earlier than the *Nicomachean Ethics* and has had less attention from scholars, partly because it is considered comparatively under-developed (Bobonich, 2006). Nonetheless, the extract above makes the point about voluntariness very clearly. What is interesting, in the context of connecting Aristotle's biology with his ethics, is how the idea of voluntariness is developed in the opening sections of book III in the *Nicomachean Ethics*.

In this book, Aristotle suggests it is not enough to have in mind a notion of voluntariness in attributing praise or blame. For instance, animals in general act voluntarily, 'the living creature is moved by intellect, imagination, purpose, wish and appetite...all these are reducible to thought and desire' (*Movement of Animals*, 700b16–19). Also, people can act voluntarily but in ignorance (*Oedipus* killed his father without knowing he was doing so). To blame or praise we must also infer that someone has deliberated, 'choice involves reason and thought' (*Nicomachean Ethics*, 1112a15–17). It is through our ability to exercise reason, the unique property that differentiates us from animals, that we are warranted in assigning praise or blame. This is such a basic and simple idea to us now (in law it underpins our concept of *mens rea* – a state of criminal intent), but in Aristotle it is a powerful concept connecting biology, logic, politics, ethics and rhetoric. Assignation of praise and blame concerns justice, and is tied into how we understand the development of character. Politics is the arena in which such deliberations find their highest expression, and an entire book of the *Nicomachean Ethics* is given over to the discussion of justice, which he sees as 'the whole of virtue [and] the virtue that expresses one's conception of oneself as a member of a community of free and equal human beings: as a citizen' (Young, 2006: 178).

Though Aristotle is responsible for the modern view that ethics is a branch of philosophy, he clearly saw it as something that was practical and enmeshed with political life (Kraut, 2006). Without wishing to lose sight of that, given the scale of the task of introducing and discussing Aristotle's major works in social philosophy, here I have tried to consider these texts in turn. This is partly because trying to draw such a distinction helps to develop a more structured and systematic understanding of his thought. It is not a straightforward thing to do though, not simply because these topics are interrelated, but because of the way that his work is organized (for instance here I have discussed the *Politics* before the *Nicomachean Ethics*, which is to take these two works out of their conventional order).

If we consider the beginning passages of the *Nicomachean Ethics* and then relate them to the beginning of *Politics* we may well question whether Aristotle would even have intended this kind of ordering of his ideas (Deslauriers, 2006). Ross (1991: vi) says of the *Nicomachean Ethics*, 'Aristotle cannot have meant the work to appear in its present form', and Bartlett (2008: 677) suggests that '[t]he first book of the *Nicomachean Ethics* is the proper place to begin one's study of Aristotle's political philosophy'. This is because it is in the opening chapters of the *Nicomachean Ethics* we are offered an account of politics, and political science that starts from first premises:

> ...we must try, in outline at least, to determine what [the Good] is, and of which of the sciences or capacities it is the object. It would seem to belong to the most authoritative art and that which is most truly the master art. And politics appears to be of this nature...though it is worth while to attain the end merely for one man, it is finer and more godlike to retain it for a nation or for city-states. These, then, are the ends at which our enquiry, being concerned with politics, aims. (*Nicomachean Ethics*, 1094a25–b12)

The concluding sections of the *Nicomachean Ethics* pave the way for the *Politics*, but at the same time the summary of the politics offered there is inaccurate (Stalley, 2009), and belies the neat transition implied by the final sentence of the *Nicomachean Ethics* (1181b23–4), '[l]et us make a beginning of our discussion', which is clearly intended to link the two books. It is likely this sequence and some of the text has been imposed retrospectively on Aristotle's original writing, and it does seem his work has suffered at the hands of a later editor (Kraut, 2006), since many passages in the *Nicomachean Ethics* are duplicated in the *Eudemian Ethics*.

The main arguments within the *Nicomachean Ethics*

There are several interrelated concepts in the *Nicomachean Ethics* that make this text the most compelling and enduring work of ethics in ancient philosophy. Before considering these, it is useful to offer a brief summary.

In book I, Aristotle introduces and discusses the notion of the Good for human beings – *eudaimonia* – in the process explaining that we cannot expect too much precision from an inquiry into ethics, but that ethical arguments are still amenable to reasoning. Appreciation of ethical matters is dependent on one's upbringing and on habit (this is an important point of overlap with the *Politics* – the law and civic education are mechanisms the State has for instructing and habituating citizens). *Eudaimonia*, sometimes translated as the good life, but also – often misleadingly – as happiness, is an activity rather than a noun. It is what we do as people when we exercise reason in accordance with what is virtuous or excellent. Aristotle then discusses virtue or excellence – *aretē* in books II–IV. Virtues for Aristotle, unlike the Platonic/ Socratic formulation, are means between vices. For instance, Graafland identifies that (in relation to social interaction) 'sociable, honest, witty, civilized' is the middle ground between 'grumpy, quarrelsome, quasi-modest, rude' (a deficit) and 'coaxing, boastful, scoffing' (an excess). For Plato/Socrates, virtues consisted in the absence, or denial, of vice ('Plato/Socrates' because we cannot be precise about where one ends and the other begins). This is one reason Nietzsche reserves such scorn for Socrates and the notion of the ascetic ideal, '*impoverishment of life ...* the affects grown cool, the tempo of life slowed down, dialectics in place of instinct' (Nietzsche, 1989: 154, original emphasis).

Book V concentrates on a particular virtue, justice, and this is the virtue which receives greatest consideration in the *Nicomachean Ethics*, which is unsurprising perhaps because it is the virtue most associated with the actions of the *polis*. Aristotle calls on two senses of justice – lawfulness and fairness. Book VI outlines, what to modern readers seems like an epistemological contribution, kinds of knowledge: *technē* (art, craft or skill); *epistēmē* (scientific or propositional knowledge); *phronēsis* (practical wisdom); *sophia* (theoretical wisdom); and *nous* (comprehension). These are discussed in more detail below but for Aristotle they belong in discussion of ethics because knowledge is a kind of excellence. The intellectual virtue he concentrates on is *phronēsis*. In book VII he discusses situations where people do not act virtuously, instances of *akrasia*, and also the topic of pleasure (which duplicates passages in the *Eudemian Ethics*). Books VIII and IX are devoted to the topic of friendship – *philia*. The *Nicomachean Ethics* concludes in book X by revisiting some earlier themes and then introducing the *Politics* in a discussion of the contribution of law to ethical development. To review principal arguments more closely, it is helpful to concentrate on the central terms.

Eudaimonia

Eudaimonia has been variously translated as the 'good life', well-being, flourishing or, perhaps least satisfactorily, happiness. Happiness is an unsatisfactory translation for *eudaimonia* because we typically use happiness to describe a disposition, whereas *eudaimonia* is an activity, 'doing well in action (*eupraxia*)' (Reeve, 2006: 204). Aristotle's definition of happiness (*eudaimonia*) as 'activity of the soul in accordance with perfect virtue' (1102a5 in Ross, 1980), prompts us to consider not temporary states, or junctures within our life, but our entire life's course (Bragues, 2006). Hence, his most well-known aphorism (cited in the preface) is as follows: 'one swallow does not make a summer, nor does one day; and so too one day, or a short time, does not make a man blessed and happy' (1098a15). The idea that happiness is an activity is still very powerful and important. It runs counter to the logic of consumerism since happiness is not accomplished through acquisition of objects. The discussion of friendship makes this specific point, 'without friends no-one would choose to live, though he had all other goods' (1155a5–6). Instead of acquisition, happiness consists in pursuing excellence; in other words in carrying out those things that make us most human.

There is another, less obvious implication from Aristotle's view of happiness in the *Nicomachean Ethics*. This comes if we consider the common account of payment for work as 'compensation'. This definition entails that giving time to work is substitution for other more worthwhile activity, namely leisure (see Bartlett, 1994b). Aristotle suggests:

> ...to exert oneself and work for the sake of amusement seems silly and utterly childish. But to amuse oneself in order that one may exert oneself...seems right...relaxation, then, is not an end; for it is taken for the sake of activity. (1176b32–35)

This could be taken as an elitist statement, since not everyone has the autonomy that is necessary to live the good life (Allmark, 2008); for instance Spivak's subaltern (discussed in the chapter 'An Aristotelian Perspective'), or anyone who finds they have to work to support a family. Setting this important qualification aside, and without dismissing it, it is still an interesting relation to draw between happiness and work. It rejects the view of a worker as someone who is compensated for giving up their leisure time (with money that can be used to consume and acquire, and thereby enhance leisure). Instead it suggests work is, or should be, the purpose of living, or, to rephrase this negatively and in Marxist terms, an implication of Aristotle's analysis is that some forms of production negate human potential. On this view Socialism becomes understood as 'the actualization of a potential to be what capitalism prevents most humans from becoming' (Knight, 2007: 105).

That work should be something intrinsically meaningful has always struck me as a more sensible basis on which to plan one's life, rather than working to support a lifestyle, again assuming one has that freedom and privilege. The amount of time spent physically 'at work' is often greater than the amount of waking time spent with friends or family. It seems obvious one should try to enjoy and embrace work and make it meaningful, rather than see it as the means for doing something else. This view of *eudaimonic* happiness has also been used in contemporary psychology, in studies of narrative identity, which explain how:

> ...people fashion and internalize life stories, or narrative identities...to integrate the reconstructed past and imagined future. Narrative identity provides life with unity, purpose, and meaning. To the degree that happiness – especially eudaimonic happiness – depends on a sense of meaningfulness in life, narrative identity should play a key role in personal interpretations of whether one is happy. (Bauer, McAdams and Pals, 2006: 82)

What is interesting about this contemporary account of happiness (in the *Journal of Happiness Studies*) is that it shows how the concept of narrative closely connects *eudaimonia* with the cultivation of virtue. Virtue occurs through habituation and is only cultivated gradually.

Aretē

Arguably the most influential concept in Aristotle's philosophy, *aretē* or virtue (sometimes translated as excellence) needs to be understood in combination with the account of *eudaimonia* (above) and the principle of *phronēsis* (below). I have said above that these concepts are inter-related, but a less generous description of this would be to suggest that Aristotle's system of ethics is circular, since these concepts are interdefined (Charles, 2005: 55). A sceptic might suggest the terms overlap to such an extent that they do not enhance understanding.

A defence against this charge of circularity would be that Aristotle was creating a new language for understanding ethics and by using different terms that overlapped he wanted to describe different aspects of ethical conduct. In a sense he is trying to capture both the content and the process of ethical behaviour. Unlike other foundational projects in ethics, Aristotle does not start with definitive precepts or overriding principles, so one way to break this circularity is to look outside his interdefined terms, to existing opinion about what 'good' means, or to some kind of communal sanction or legislative framework. Unlike most philosophers, Aristotle gives considerable weight to common opinion (*Rhetoric*, 1355a14–16).

There are a number of appealing aspects to Aristotle's discussion of virtue. Whether or not someone is of good character is something we assess over time (Sison, 2003); acting ethically is something we tend to associate with people who can give a good account of their choices, reflecting the role of deliberation, 'practical wisdom is primarily a deliberative capacity' (Reeve, 2006: 205). In contrast to Kantian and Utilitarian ethics, which are the most prevalent alternative systems in applied ethics, virtue allows space for the emotions, and for a narrative construction of the ethical agent (MacIntyre, 1984a). The emphasis on dispassionate obeisance that is involved in following imperatives, or in following some process of commensuration, seems to ignore that emotion is also fundamental to our decision making, our consciousness and construction of self (Greenfield, 2001). Yet many of our decisions are not one-off, isolated choices, but part of the ongoing fabric of our lives. In that sense, we do not make decisions in a dispassionately rational manner, but in light of other choices we have already made, or are yet to make. For Aristotle, the exercise of reason involves considering our emotional response, and cultivating the right kinds of emotional response through habituation. As Reeve puts it:

> Choice depends not simply on what one knows but on the appetites and desires involved in one's choices. For if these are to be as virtue requires, so that we *feel*... we must repeatedly do virtuous actions from childhood on. (Reeve, 2012: 99)

In some contemporary research on decision making, aspects of narrative and emotion are recognized as undermining a purely self-interested 'rational' account of choice (as discussed in more detail in the following chapter). A host of actions within organizations are carried out because of habit, tradition, custom or duty. These are not simply calculated but influenced by social norms, which have themselves evolved in archetypically non-rational ways and frequently involve ritual, culture or superstition (Salancik and Brindle, 1997). Sometimes, organizational decisions are made to preserve consistency because it is more comforting to continue down the wrong path than having to admit an initial error. Relatedly, we may persist in pursuing an irrational course of action because we have already invested time or money in it, a phenomenon known as escalation (Garland, 1990; Staw, 1997).

Technē, epistēmē, phronēsis, sophia and nous

Technē, the root of our modern word technique, refers to the kind of knowing that we associate with both an art and a skill, 'a state concerned with making' (*Nicomachean Ethics*, 1140a20–21). It is a form of knowledge that is perhaps closer to the way in which we use the word craft than it is to technology. *Epistēmē* refers to the type of knowledge (typically: propositional, formalized and codifiable) that we associate with scientific thought, 'that which can be known can be demonstrated' (*Nicomachean Ethics*, 1140b34–1141a1). *Phronēsis* is often translated as 'practical wisdom', or sometimes 'prudence' (Bragues, 2006), and it reflects a learned ability to make judgements in accordance with the development of virtue, and with experience gained over time, 'a reasoned and true state of capacity to act with regard to human goods' (1140b20–21). It is the most popularly discussed intellectual virtue in the social sciences. *Sophia* is perhaps closest to our contemporary understanding of wisdom, an ability to make sense of experience in the light of past experiences, but something more fundamental than that – considered reflection on those experiences, 'truth about the first principles' (*Nicomachean Ethics*, 1141a17). Finally, *nous* is what we might call know-how (rather than the knowing that, which we associate with *epistēmē*), 'comprehension' (1139b17) (see chapter 3 in Reeve, 2012).

For reasons which are not clear, a number of recent authors have simultaneously embraced Aristotle's account of the intellectual virtues, but at the same time seem to have misapplied them. For instance several authors inexplicably state that Aristotle specifies three intellectual virtues: *epistēmē*, *technē* and *phronēsis* (Flyvbjerg, 2001; Gunder, 2010; Halverson, 2004). This leads to some confusion. For instance Halverson states that theoretical wisdom is based on *epistēmē*, omitting that it also requires *nous*. Flyvbjerg (2001: 4) states categorically that Aristotle says *phronēsis* is the 'most important' of the intellectual virtues. Aristotle is unlikely to have thought *phronēsis* the most important. He believes Poetry is superior to History because it deals with universals rather than particulars (which are the stuff of phronēsis), and this reading is not consistent with Aristotle's description of *phronēsis*, 'it would be strange to think that ... practical wisdom is the best knowledge, since man is not the best thing in the world' (*Nicomachean Ethics*, 1141a20–1); while he describes *sophia* as non-instrumental knowing, 'things that are remarkable, admirable, difficult and divine, but useless' (1141b6–7). Reeve (2006: 202) identifies that for Aristotle, 'theology is both the best or most estimable science' (in *Metaphysics*, 1074b34). And both Flyvbjerg (2001) and Gunder (2010) place too much emphasis on intuition as a form of knowledge that is *phronēsis*.

> The source of intuition, just as the Real of the human subject, resides in the unconscious and is unknowable. Further, the Aristolian [*sic*] intellectual virtue of phronesis, is the development of an excellence in effective intuition. (Gunder, 2010: 41–2).
>
> Bicyclists can bicycle because they have the necessary know-how, achieved via practical experiences ... Experience cannot necessarily be verbalized, intellectualized and made into rules. (Flyvbjerg, 2001: 19)

Taking these together, intuition and know-how are closer to the sense of *nous* as comprehension or ability to grasp principles. The value of Aristotle's account (and the benefit of his identifying five different intellectual virtues) lies precisely in his not seeing a separation between rational deliberation and *phronēsis*. Far from *phronēsis* involving something unknowable and unconscious, he says:

> Practical wisdom ... is concerned with things human and things about which it is possible to deliberate; for we say this is above all the work of the man of practical wisdom, to deliberate well. (1141b9–10)

At least one commentator has found themselves frustrated with Flyvbjerg's recruitment of Aristotle, and has been driven to suggest that 'all in all it appears to me that Flyvbjerg's views on Aristotle say more about Bent Flyvbjerg than they do about Aristotle' (Eikeland, 2008: 45). This is perhaps a charge any writer on Aristotle fears, but Eikeland's frustration is understandable because it is unfortunate this term has simultaneously found fresh popularity at the same time as apparently being misunderstood, or applied to promote a view of social scientists as experts by virtue of their possession of *phronēsis* (Flyvbjerg, 2001). Apart from at times conflating *phronēsis* with *nous* and ignoring *sophia* altogether (neither term appears in Flyvbjerg, 2001), it is hard to follow the logic of premising the rebirth of social science on *phronēsis*. *Phronēsis* is developed within a community of practice through the pursuit of particular goods. It is not something an outside expert can 'bring' in to solve problems within that community.

Phronēsis is concerned with matters of reason, precisely because we are human. So it is unlike the kind of *phronēsis* that animals such as fish have (1141a22). That kind of knowledge could be more readily compared with Flyvbjerg's examples of expert procedural knowledge – for example knowing how to ride a bike. Instead though, *phronēsis* requires deliberation and Aristotle explicitly says it is different from states that we might associate with intuition (an unconscious, tacit, procedural or 'unknowable' way of knowing), 'readiness of mind is different from excellence in deliberation' (1142b5–6), nor is it 'skill in conjecture; for this both involves no reasoning and is something that is quick in its operation' (1142b2–3). It is, as Richard Kraut says in the introduction to his (edited) *Guide to Aristotle's Nicomachean Ethics*:

> ... a quality of mind that governs the emotions by making use of clever instrumental reasoning, *excellent non-routinized deliberation* about the proper and ultimate ends of life, and perception of particular facts that play a telling role in decision-making. (Kraut, 2006: 7, emphasis added)

Aristotle allows for us to cultivate excellence and wisdom relating to subjects that are not science and do not allow certainty. He also incorporates the role of emotion and acknowledges that we develop character in ways that can allow us to become more effective and wiser decision makers. But, this is because his model of rationality incorporates emotion and character not because he invites us to abandon rationality, and least of all does he suggest we somehow bypass the active deliberation which is required for life in the *polis*, and for complex decision making.

Philia

A number of commentators have remarked on the fact that Aristotle gives over so much time to the topic of friendship, 'a topic that occupies two of the ten books of Aristotle's *Nicomachean Ethics* and nearly a third of his *Eudemian Ethics*' (Brewer, 2005: 722). Despite the length of consideration he gives to *philia*, and the importance it seems to hold in the text of the *Nicomachean Ethics* 'after what we have said [books I–VII], a discussion of friendship would naturally follow' (1155a3–4), these chapters have provoked far less discussion than the core sections devoted to the good, to the virtues and to the different kinds of knowing. Yet his discussion of friendship has an appeal because (as with other terms) Aristotle uses *philia* very broadly, and at the same time defines it in relation to other concepts (virtue) in a way that seems insightful and elegant (see *Nicomachean Ethics*, 1155b32–35):

> Aristotle uses the term *'philia'* to pick out a broad array of human relationships, ranging from the most intimate relationships between lovers or husbands and wives, through the relationships we commonly call friendships, to the relatively casual and impersonal relationships among fellow citizens. What genuine forms of *philia* have in common, according to Aristotle, is that all of them involve reciprocated goodwill (*eunoia*) between two persons, each of whom is aware of the other's goodwill. (Brewer, 2005: 723)

Friendship is also a virtue, 'it is an excellence or implies excellence' (*Nicomachean Ethics*, 1155a4), and it is the principal means for us to evaluate our own characters since friends can give us insight into our selves that we could never otherwise have (Veltman, 2004):

> ...when we wish to see our own face, we do so by looking into the mirror, in the same way when we wish to know ourselves we can

obtain that knowledge by looking at our friend. (*Magna Moralia*, 1213a20–2)

Sustaining friendship also gives us a way to see connections between virtue, narrative and character. As friendships evolve and develop, they provide a continual source for the replenishment and enriching of one's character.

Applying Aristotle's *Ethics*

In recent work in the social sciences, the most frequently discussed aspects of Aristotle's contribution in the *Nicomachean Ethics* relate to virtue, the good life and to the five ways of knowing (intellectual virtues). What is less frequently discussed are the implications of his account of choice as a basis for making attributions. The following chapter elaborates on this by considering the relationship between decision making and applied ethics, and draws on a paper in the *Journal of Business Ethics* (Morrell, 2004a). There are two exciting things about linking choice and virtues. First, these can be used to understand the ethicality of decisions from the main rival normative systems in applied ethics (Kantianism and Utilitarianism). Aristotle (speaking somewhat anachronistically) gives us a way to see how to relate these different systems together. Second, connections between virtues, character and choice can be applied to understanding ethics and decision making in practice.

8
Decision Making and Ethics

The study of decision making has multiple implications for 'business ethics'. There are some problems with this term, partly expressed in the tired, but largely true joke that business ethics is an oxymoron. Also, a lot of organizations are not businesses. Since it is used broadly within the field (to include public sector organizations for instance), and because the term is familiar, it is used in this chapter. The chapter begins with an outline of some commonly used frameworks for understanding choice in organizations and in society. It characterizes the dominant model for decision making in organizations as rational choice theory (RCT) and contrasts this with the naturalistic theory of decision making, image theory. The implications of using RCT and image theory to model decision making are discussed with reference to three ethical systems. RCT is shown to be consistent with Utilitarian ethics, but not with Kantian or Virtue-based ethics. Image theory is shown to be consistent with each. The chapter identifies a number of implications following from this analysis.

Justification for examining choice in ethics

As discussed in the previous chapter, Aristotle identifies that to assign praise or blame sensibly we infer that someone has exercised choice. To describe an action as chosen involves more than simply considering whether action was voluntary (animals act voluntarily), but in addition implies deliberation, in other words a process (*Nicomachean Ethics*, 1109b30–113a14). Gaining greater insight into this process is relevant to our understanding of ethics. This applies equally whether we evaluate our own actions, or other people's.

It would seem sensible in considering applied ethics, to study some of the most commonly used frameworks for understanding choice in organizational behaviour and in the social sciences. This is because these frameworks are used to explain and describe different stages of decision making, whether in terms of an initial consideration of the problem, an outline of the choice of a course of action, or retrospectively to offer justification for that choice. The most commonly used models of decision making may be conceptual tools for evaluating or generating options, or they can be used to select or reject options. They may also be used to explain a chosen course of action retrospectively, irrespective of whether they were the basis for that choice. More generally, a given framework may form the basis for conceptualizing reasons and motives. Many of these frameworks are restricted to particular domains or decision scenarios though, and they cannot sensibly be applied to understand complex ethical problems. In this light, Morgan's caveat on metaphor also applies here, 'in creating ways of seeing they tend to create ways of *not* seeing' (Morgan, 1997: 348).

Studying decision making processes can enable the identification of assumptions, or partial truths. For example, many decisions taken within organizations are portrayed as driven by considerations of cost and benefit. This is true even in the third sector: just because people in an organization are not pursuing profit that does not mean they have the luxury of being immune to considerations of cost. On closer examination though, across all kinds of organization, decisions presented as commercial may be more tellingly understood in terms of culture (Vecchio, 2000), power (Kanter, 1979), conflict (Camerer and Knez, 1997), politics or tradition (Salancik and Brindle, 1997) or symbolism (Zajac and Westphal, 1997). As individuals, we may have unwarranted assumptions about the way we make choices; for example that we weigh up all the evidence before making a reasoned judgement, and are impassive, or at least aware of our own prejudices and biases. Such assumptions about individual and organizational decision making are prejudicial to ethically aware behaviour.

Beginning with a brief overview of some influential ways to model decision making, the chapter critically evaluates the most popular way of explaining decisions taken in organizations – RCT. It then outlines an alternative account, *image theory* (Beach, 1990, 1998). The implications of using RCT and image theory to model ethical decision making are discussed with reference to three ethical systems: Kantianism, Utilitarianism and Virtue ethics. Considering the more recent literature in this area does not invalidate Aristotle's perspective, nor render it obsolete. Instead the argument here (in keeping with the premise of the book) is that Aristotle's account of choice and of virtue remains comparatively more capable of providing insight into ethical decision making than the other rival normative frameworks of Kantian and Utilitarian ethics.

Decision making

There are a great many ways to model how people make decisions. This section sketches some influential theoretical approaches rather than offering a comprehensive literature review. This necessarily brief overview serves as an introduction to the two models of decision making discussed here.

In the motivation literature, it is conventional to contrast between content and process models, though the two categories overlap somewhat. Content models, which try to answer the question, 'what things motivate a person' (Alderfer, 1972; Herzberg, 1966; Maslow, 1954; McLelland, 1965) are of limited use in understanding ethical choices, since (perhaps like trait accounts of personality) they readily reduce to typologies and struggle to represent an intricate process, such as grappling with an ethical problem. Process models try to answer the question, 'how do you motivate a person' Equity theory (Adams, 1965) and expectancy theory (Vroom, 1964) are among the most influential process models. Implicit in both is a notion of commensuration. In organizational settings this is typically construed as an effort–reward bargain: in equity theory, to balance effort and reward; in expectancy theory, to assess whether increasing effort is worthwhile (goal theory can be understood in these terms too).

In the literature on learning, choice can be construed in terms of behavioural conditioning (Skinner, 1953), or social learning theories (Bandura, 1977). Conditioning approaches emphasize positive (e.g. praise) or negative (e.g. criticism) reinforcement (Vecchio, 2001). Social learning theory stresses the role of imitation and modelling behaviour on others, and forms the basis for many training and development initiatives. Other approaches to choice describe the role of learned schema and shared heuristics, emphasizing automaticity or unconscious following of habit (Schank and Abelson, 1977). Choice is also sometimes explained in terms of the influence of external factors, such as the local environment or community, or the influence of others: peers, family, opinion leaders, and word of mouth. All of these may bias judgement and action by shaping a decision maker's perceptions. More broadly, socially disenfranchised groups may have reduced scope for choice, as captured by Dahrendorf's (1979) theory of life chances, where access to cultural and economic goods varies according to (for example) class, gender or race.

These approaches are summarized in Table 8.1. As well as listing an influential theorist or application associated with each approach, a sample organizational or societal problem for each is offered, together with a 'solution' or answer suggested by that construction of decision making.

Each of the approaches in Table 8.1 can be used with differing levels of success to predict or explain a wide variety of choices, but this brief review illustrates how their utility may be specific to particular domains – for example, it is more appropriate to use motivational theories to encourage or predict choices of particular individuals and connected groups (e.g. in organizational settings), than to understand long-term, complex social processes (e.g. the persistence of structural inequities). However, in Aristotle's terms, as discussed in the preceding chapter summarizing the *Nicomachean Ethics*, each framework is unsuited to providing an analysis for ethical choice. Several 'lessons' from the *Nicomachean Ethics* apply here and serve as a critique of the theories in Table 8.1: that ethics is not a science and does not warrant such precision; that relying on group level categories to explain an individual's actions, or to make attributions of praise and blame, is mistaken (it does not pay attention to particulars); that invoking specific and external determinate causes, such as a role model, life chances, culture, leaves little room for responsibility and personal choice – but voluntariness is necessary to assign praise and blame.

In practice, we are unlikely to employ just one way of understanding a decision scenario, since decisions that involve ethical considerations are also typically complex. Trying to guess at the reasoning or processes behind another's choice will probably involve not one model but recourse to a range of theories, personal and private hunches, and judgement. This judgement is likely to be better informed by an awareness of a range of approaches, together with their limitations.

More fundamentally, our interpretation of the decision making process will be influenced by how we construe people in society. This also does not reduce to one model, but some examples of influential accounts are that people: are political animals (Aristotle); live out a largely predetermined, unconsciously held life plan (Berne, 1961); can be understood in terms of their roles (Goffman, 1969); are engaged in a war of all against all (Hobbes, 1651/1973); or are noble savages corrupted by society (Rousseau, 1775/1984); are rational, self-interested and utility maximizing (RCT); are negotiating complex scenarios relying on

Table 8.1 Approaches to choice and sample organizational or societal problem

Approach	Theorist or application	Sample problem	'Solution' (in theory)
Psychographics	Myers Briggs 16PF	Whom to select from a pool of candidates	Identify personality type suitable for the job
Motivation – content theories	Alderfer's ERG theory	Motivate the electorate to vote	Link voting to one of their needs
Motivation – process theories	Adams' equity theory	What happens if we adopt performance related pay	How will reward be allocated, will it be 'felt-fair'
Learning – conditioning/ reinforcement	Skinner's operant conditioning	Someone is convinced they can't do a task	Positively reinforce (encourage them) when things go well
Learning – social/ observational	Bandura's social learning theory	Train riot police	Use video, role-playing techniques and role models
Learning – schema-based/ heuristic	Video-based market research	How can we get people to buy more chocolates	Identify typical shopper routes, put chocolates in the 'hot spots'
Social – context	Study of Culture	How can we introduce change	Create shared stories, ritual, myths, hero(in)es
Social – demographic	Dahrendorf's life chances	Why is there a gender pay gap	Access to economic goods is unfairly distributed

values, learned goals and schemata (image theory). These final two constructions form the central contrast in this chapter, and are discussed below. Both are more fundamental than the sketch of theories in Table 8.1, since RCT and image theory could underpin any of them.

Rational choice theory

There is no definitive formulation of rational choice theory (RCT) (Zey, 1992), but the term is used here to summarize a common set of assumptions about how and why people choose. The most formal applications of RCT are in modelling aggregated behaviour in markets (Arrow, 1997). This involves adopting several neoclassical assumptions such as equilibrium, competition, complete markets. RCT also involves additional assumptions about the nature of people: they seek to maximize utility (assessed in terms of an internal hedonic calculus); they evaluate alternative options in terms of net gain; they implement options that they expect will result in the greatest utility (Hogarth and Reder, 1986: 2–4; Zey, 1992: 13).

It should be noted that the 'rational' element within RCT does not mean 'has a reason' (someone's reason for doing something could be irrational). Nor is it entirely congruent with the exercise of reason, otherwise any deliberative process could be called rational. Aristotle's account of deliberation (in the *Rhetoric*) involved emotion and took place in a community but was very removed from RCT. Instead, RCT is synonymous with *dispassionate calculation* and with self-interest. It follows that the 'rational' in RCT is very different from the sense of rational in MacIntyre's (1999) *Dependent Rational Animals*, where (as decision makers) humans are understood as interdependent rather than compartmentalized (see also Dobson, 2009; MacIntyre, 1982).

Within many contemporary organizations though, RCT is frequently how decisions of all kinds are characterized, for example through appeals to shareholder value, or to the bottom line or profit. Perhaps most ubiquitous is the imperative to consider the 'business case' for topics where considerations of business should arguably be secondary to, or independent of, those of ethics. Confusion on this point means that questions that relate to ethics (diversity, discrimination, disability, equal opportunities) are often shoehorned into discussion of profitability. Rather than admit unpalatable truths: for instance that covert or indirect discrimination can be profitable, a host of writers promote the premise that 'good ethics is good business'. Whilst it may be true that (say) diversity allows for creativity and for an organization to reflect wider society or that (say) being lawful protects reputation, it is absurd to maintain that the only organizations doing 'good business' are those that are ethical.

Rational choice accounts are parsimonious and theoretically appealing (Hogarth and Reder, 1986), but behavioural analyses of decision making have uncovered multiple problems with them. A wealth of empirical data illustrates how individuals violate basic assumptions of RCT when faced with decision problems (see Mellers, Schwartz and Cooke, 1999 for a review). Adherents to RCT question whether these challenges are truly substantive, and can cite considerable success in modelling a range of decision related phenomena, from traditional market settings to other scenarios, such as incidences of crimes, law suits, marriages (Hogarth and Reder, 1986: 3), as well as studies of gender and religion (Hechter and Kanazawa, 1997). Hechter and Kanazawa (1997) maintain that reservations about rational choice only arise where people misunderstand its application, confusing a macro-level account for an explanation of individual choice. However, one problem with RCT is that the myth of rationality is often invoked to justify choices made on other grounds. Having sketched out how decisions taken by organizations frequently fall short of RCT norms (in broad terms), it is useful to examine more closely the problems with RCT as it applies to individual decision makers.

In RCT the rational individual collects information to generate a range of options. However, this process is costly and uncertain, since the optimal time to stop gathering information is not always clear. Having gathered a range of options, the individual has to evaluate them. This process is usually based on limited information, and hence also uncertain. Since we never face decisions with perfect information, this uncertainty means that many of our decisions involve assessing risk. Risk aversion plays a part in even our most banal decisions (Spies, Hesse and Loesch, 1997). An additional problem is that the environment we each have to negotiate is rich and complex. Faced with an overwhelming number of potential choices, no one has time to weigh up the pros and cons of each and every one. A related point is that many of these options are seemingly identical, so there must be a non-rational basis for some decisions even if it is the psychological equivalent of a coin-toss. Additionally, the emphasis on dispassionate calculation ignores that emotion is fundamental to our consciousness and construction of self (Greenfield, 2001).

Decisions are often not one-off, isolated choices but part of the ongoing narrative of our lives, and we may persist in pursuing an irrational course of action because we have sunk costs, a phenomenon known as *escalation* (Garland, 1990; Staw, 1997). On a grander scale, this is one way to explain projects that go spectacularly over budget, such as the Millennium Dome. On occasions where we have no viable alternative, our only course of action may be appraised more favourably, to reduce cognitive dissonance. This phenomenon – known as the insufficient justification paradigm (Pfeffer and Lawler, 1980) – suggests that utility is better understood as continually constructed rather than calculated. To illustrate, if someone were unhappy about an unethical practice in their organization (perhaps in a university context 'dumbing down' or spoon-feeding students) but felt there was nothing they could do to change the situation, over time they might find their perception of this shifted. They might construe it as a 'necessary evil', or something that 'was happening across the sector', or that they were 'powerless' to influence. A gradual process of accommodation would be easier to tolerate than a continuing dissonance between personal values and organizational practices.

The way a decision is represented – its *frame* – can also influence choice (Rettinger and Hastie, 2001), even where a probabilistic account of two options shows them to be equivalent (Tversky and Kahnemann, 1986). An illustration of this could be where work patterns are reorganized in order to promote flexibility. From an organizational frame of reference, the emphasis would be on flexibility of work, enabling greater responsiveness to customer needs. From an individual frame of reference, however, changes in shift patterns may mean workers actually have far less flexibility (Legge, 1995). Although an organizational decision making tool (such as a cost-benefit analysis) could indicate significant organizational benefits, other costs (to family life, security, stability) would only be articulated if a different reference frame were invoked.

Without necessarily wanting to defend RCT, it is important to qualify this critique. The aim of any theory or model is to balance parsimony with explanatory power and RCT is certainly parsimonious. With a few simple assumptions, powerful explanations can be made about group-level behaviour, perhaps to greatest effect in market situations (Miller, 1986). However, it is this very success that makes RCT dangerous because it is invoked in situations where it is very difficult to hold on to the idea of rational choice, such as when we are faced with ethical dilemmas. Appeals to the business case, shareholder responsibility, or the vagaries of the market can mean denying responsibility for personal choice or corporate responsibility. These appeals are given greater legitimacy if we believe decisions are typically the result of a rational process, which involves dispassionate deliberation and calculation of utility.

Image theory

Several attempts have been made to respond to criticisms of RCT accounts, for example incorporating heuristics, or the importance of learning into second- or third-wave versions of RCT (Simon, 1982). More recently, more radical approaches to understanding decision making, conventionally termed *naturalistic* theories (Connolly and Beach, 1998) reject even the basic tenets of RCT. This section outlines the most well-developed of these alternative accounts (Connolly and Koput, 1997), an image theory of decision making (Beach, 1990, 1998). In contrast to RCT, this holds that the bases for choice are values and personal principles, rather than putatively commensurable variables.

As Aristotle would have appreciated, the need for alternative approaches has arisen because empirical observations suggest decision makers typically do not follow the kinds of processes suggested by RCT (Zey, 1992). For example, Minzberg's observations of managers indicated that many of their decisions were whether to accept or reject a single option, rather than to choose from a range. Other challenges to the normative model of RCT came from Payne (1976) in Beach and Mitchell (1998: 5), who demonstrated that decision makers use different decision strategies in different scenarios, and Tversky and Kahneman's (1986) work on framing (described above). As well as being a response to empirical challenges, image theory addresses a conceptual gap in mainstream models of choice because it places principles at the heart of decision making.

Following image theory, whether a decision is carried out depends on whether the decision maker feels that it fits with their personal values, goals and strategies. These cognitive structures are (perhaps confusingly) collectively called 'images' (Beach, 1990). The first stage of decision making involves 'screening' potential choices (Beach and Strom, 1989), and most decisions are actually decisions not to do something: rejections. This makes sense if we think of the vast demands made on us in coping with the everyday complexity of the social world. Many potential options are never actively considered. The other, less frequent type of decision is the adoption decision. On some occasions one option will survive the screening process. When this happens, decision makers test the option against their personal sets of images: internal values, goals and strategies. If this is compatible and the option 'fits', the decision is adopted (Dunegan, 1998).

On the rare occasions that more than one option survives screening, a test of 'profitability' establishes the best one (Beach, 1990). Whichever option appears most attractive will then be tested against personal sets of images, and if it is compatible, will be adopted. Including a notion of profitability and consideration of alternatives is an explicit acknowledgement that some decisions involve elements of RCT (weighing up competing alternatives, selecting the one perceived most appealing). However, image theory stresses first and foremost that decisions do not typically involve calculation. Most decisions are better understood in terms of intuitive elements, learned rules based on past experience, and

Table 8.2 Contrasting rational choice theory with image theory

	Rational choice	Image theory
The decision maker	Is concerned with maximizing utility, rational, self-interested and dispassionate	Negotiates complex social settings via personal principles and learned schemata
The steps in decision making	1. Gather information about potential options 2. Once a range has been identified, compare them in terms of subjective expected utility (SEU) 3. Select the one that will maximize SEU 4. Implement this option	1. Screen out options 2. If an option survives screening, 'fit' with images is tested. Fit > adoption, non fit > rejection 3. If more than one option survives screening, the most profitable is selected. If it 'fits' it is adopted
The process	*Commensuration* (comparing options in terms of SEU)	Assessing *compatibility* (of options with personal values)

personal principles. This applies even to decisions that are frequently understood in RCT terms (perhaps because they are important and infrequent) such as buying a house or car, or choosing a job (Lee and Mitchell, 1994).

Table 8.2 summarizes the key differences between RCT and image theory across three domains: construction of the person as decision maker; description of the steps in decision making; the underlying nature of the decision process.

Choice and ethics: three ethical frameworks

The implications of choosing between RCT or image theory as a basis for modelling ethical decisions are set out below. This is done in terms of three ethical systems: Utilitarianism, Kantianism and Aristotelian Virtue ethics. These ethical systems are normative, in that they prescribe action and suggest a basis for deciding what ought to be done. Since readers are likely to be familiar with them, each system is only described briefly. As an illustration of how each might be applied, a common ethical business dilemma (how to make someone redundant) is framed in terms of each system. To maintain clarity of argument, revisions or second generation accounts of the basic system (e.g. rule Utilitarianism) are not presented. This allows for an initial exploration of the relationship between construction of the decision making process and ethical system.

Utilitarianism

Summary: Principle-centred philosophy, based on the goal of maximizing utility and a 'hedonic calculus'; consequentialist.

Approach to problem of how to make someone redundant: Consider certain principles (costs involved, how to minimize unhappiness) and weigh up the likely consequences of the action. Which approach on this occasion will cause the least pain to the employee, yourself and other stakeholders?

Kantianism

Summary: Principle-centred philosophy, based on two versions of a categorical imperative that enshrine principles of universalizability and reflexivity; deontological.

Approach to problem of how to make someone redundant: Consider certain principles (fairness, existing ideas of best practice) and reflect on how you would feel if the roles were reversed. What would be the implications if every redundancy were handled in this way?

Virtue ethics

Summary: Dispositional or narrative tradition of ethics that emphasizes the cultivation of virtues and pursuit of the good life; teleological.

Approach to problem of how to make someone redundant: Consider how the action will reflect on your character, and serve to shape both yourself and the person you are making redundant. How will you be able to reconcile the way you make someone redundant with your existing ideas about what it means to behave ethically?

The two accounts of decision making can be related to these ethical frameworks as follows.

Rational choice theory

This is most readily associated with Utilitarianism because of the close link between a hedonic calculus and principle of maximizing utility. Although the point of reference in Utilitarianism is external (utility for the greatest number), it is a matter of translation to make a rational choice account of decision making fit a Utilitarian analysis of an ethical problem. Using the example above, RCT would represent the decision on how to make someone redundant as a choice between a range of options. These would be compared with one another in terms of their subjective expected utility. This would involve a manager weighing up some relatively tangible sources of utility (productivity, cost of making someone redundant), and other less tangible ones (reputation, one's own discomfort at having to do make someone redundant). RCT suggests that as a decision maker, one's final choice would be the option that maximizes utility on this occasion.

Proposition 1a: RCT is consistent with Utilitarian ethics.

It could be argued that RCT is compatible with Kantian ethics, if we accept that imperatives circumscribe a domain of action within which rational choice operates. This is analogous to the idea that businesses or individuals need merely operate within the 'rules of the game' (Friedman, 1970 in Chryssides and Kaler, 1993), whether these are laws, or for individuals, or Kantian maxims. However, accepting that Kantian principles influence business decisions is inconsistent with a RCT construction of choice insofar as the initial evaluation of what constitutes a legitimate option depends on principles, rather than any calculation. Again, using the example above, we could see that certain options that would potentially maximize utility (to make a group of workers redundant by using a text message because it is cheaper) could be ruled out because they violate principles of common decency and fairness.

Proposition 1b: RCT is inconsistent with Kantian ethics.

RCT is least compatible with an ethics of Virtue, since these ethical systems typically emphasize the importance of context and narrative in any understanding of the good life (MacIntyre, 1984a). Virtues are not commensurable, and different people will have different sets of virtues. The end goal of Virtue ethics is to achieve the good life, rather than to maximize utility. In terms of making someone redundant, it is not possible to translate the imperative to develop moral character, or pursue one's own sense of what is right into a calculus.

Proposition 1c: RCT is inconsistent with Virtue ethics.

Image theory

Image theory can be compatible with Utilitarian accounts of decisions, insofar as one's personal principles could be based on Utilitarian ideals. More generally, the notion of profitability suggests a way of comparing two or more options in a probabilistic way. However, most decisions are seen as non-rational and so there are few areas where Utilitarian principles apply exclusively. Finally, the ultimate test for adoption is whether an option fits with one's values. The choice on how to make someone redundant could legitimately involve considering the cost of several options, but it is likely other considerations will weigh more heavily. Some choices may not even enter into one's conscious thought, but be screened out automatically – some managers would not dream of making someone redundant unless it were face to face for example. They may also recognize that the option likely to result in maximum utility is not operable because it conflicts with their personal sense of what is right, or their organizational culture.

Proposition 2a: Image theory is consistent with Utilitarian ethics.

Image theory can be consistent with Kantian ethics, since a categorical imperative can be understood as part of the decision maker's set of principles. Any option that does not fit with these would be rejected. On one level, this kind of reasoning influences redundancy decisions because there are legal considerations which set the boundaries of reasonable behaviour. More importantly though, because making someone redundant is likely to invoke concern and empathy, the decision process will often involve reflection and consideration of how it would feel to be on the receiving end, in other words, consideration of the categorical imperative.

Proposition 2b: Image theory is consistent with Kantian ethics.

Image theory is compatible with Virtue ethics. Principles are learned and values dependent on a particular context, which is consistent with the development of narrative (MacIntyre, 1984a). Pursuit of the good life as an end involves the development of personal habits and rules. Again, returning to the example, some managers may develop a personal style for handling redundancy that is consistent with their self-image and the organizational environment. These considerations may take precedence over either Utilitarian or Kantian principles because they reflect the way a process is handled in a particular context. For example, in industries where industrial espionage is a concern, once the decision to make someone redundant has been taken, they may be escorted from their desk by a security guard and be barred from working for a competitor for a set period. Though this could be seen to violate some ethical principles (respect, consideration for others), it may be accepted as an industry norm.

Proposition 2c: Image theory is consistent with Virtue ethics.

Evaluating decisions

Rationality and rationalization

Linking the literature on RCT and image theory to mainstream ethical theory has implications for how we approach Aristotle's problem of how to assign praise or blame sensibly. One problem with the Utilitarian principle is that it is abstract and cold, and difficult to apply in situations where there are competing ideas about what constitutes the greatest happiness, or whether other principles should take precedence (Velasquez, 2002). This can mean that decisions are taken on other grounds, and then retrospectively rationalized to fit the language of greatest utility. Similarly, many decisions within business are framed in the language of balancing costs and benefits, even though other factors that are seldom articulated – such as politics, power and ritual may be more significant (Kanter, 1979; Salancik and Brindle, 1997; Zajac and Westphal, 1997). It is in such cases that the dangers of RCT as myth (Bradley et al., 2000) become apparent.

For instance, someone could justify casualization of a workforce by appealing to a business case, where implications were translated into a common metric using a cost-benefit analysis (e.g. predicted reduction in cost of labour – benefit; predicted increase in labour turnover – cost). This decision may actually be motivated by short-term, personal interests, or a desire to appear tough to the stock market, or to undermine a rival business function. Casualization could simply be a ritual following of what other companies in the sector are doing. None of these factors can be articulated if we accept the rational cost-benefit justification at face value. Additionally, if we accept the empirical evidence that suggests that very few decisions are enacted following the normative model of RCT, this signals greater scepticism when it comes to evaluating the stated reasons for practices. Rejecting RCT allows us to consider alternative bases for choice, such as the part that principles and personal values play in our decision processes.

> Proposition 3: Rejecting RCT enhances ability to evaluate decisions in organizations from an ethical standpoint.

Commensuration

On one level, a common metric (of utility, or profit) is useful because competing alternatives can be assessed using a process of commensuration (Espeland and Stevens, 1998). However, there is a substantial body of literature to suggest people do not simply rely on commensuration when making decisions (Minzberg, 1975; Payne, 1976; Pfeffer and Lawler, 1980; Salancik and Brindle, 1997; Tversky and Kahneman, 1986; Zajac and Westphal, 1997). This implies the need to redirect attention towards other ways to model decisions. Whereas discussions of utility and general principles are often impersonal, emphasizing the role that individual values play in shaping action makes discussion of ethics more immediate. Linking this discussion with the literature on decision making is also a way of reaffirming the status of ethics as an applied discipline. In this light, one avenue for developing image theory is in studying the nature of decision makers' personal principles (Beach, 1998).

Ethical theorists are perhaps uniquely placed to shed light on the value image, given their rich experience in devising and discussing ethical dilemmas and problems. For example, many challenges to Utilitarianism undermine the utility principle, which was originally constructed to allow commensuration in otherwise 'messy' problems (Nussbaum, 2001a: 112–13). The 'messiness' remains difficult to resolve if we cling to alternative principles, or a notion of rights, rather than a utility principle. Consideration of images (learned, personal principles) is likely to be prompted wherever decision makers understand, or represent, potential options as incommensurable because they will not have a basis for comparison on a common metric (Espeland and Stevens, 1998). This suggests that one way in which the merits of RCT and image theory can be tested is to evaluate decision makers' responses to different problems. These problems could be devised to represent alternative scenarios, from pure cost-benefit decisions (with minor ethical implications) to major ethical dilemmas. Decisions that involve consideration of options in terms of a common metric (here, for the sake of brevity, 'commensurate decisions') can be modelled using either RCT or image theory. Decisions that involve consideration of principles (here, for the sake of brevity, 'incommensurate decisions') cannot be modelled using RCT, but they can be modelled using image theory.

> Proposition 4a: Commensurate decisions can be modelled with RCT.
>
> Proposition 4b: Commensurate decisions can be modelled with image theory.
>
> Proposition 4c: Incommensurate decisions cannot be modelled with RCT.
>
> Proposition 4d: Incommensurate decisions can be modelled with image theory.

One way to develop this idea is to devise scenarios designed to provoke consideration of the different images. For example some decisions might relate strongly to the value image (beliefs about tolerable behaviour in organizations), or to goals (what was acceptable to have as a long-term organizational aim), or strategies (what was acceptable behaviour in pursuit of such an aim). This is illustrated in Figure 8.1.

I suggest the value image only meaningfully applies in situations where there is an ethical dimension. This image also necessarily involves a degree of incommensurability since it represents the decision maker's personal principles or moral rules. Although ethical implications are impossible to avoid ('investing in machinery' may make workers feel threatened, or lead to redundancies), the scenarios on the left of the figure are meant to represent occasions when evaluating an option does not involve consideration of whether people can get hurt, so 'negotiation of a contract' does not involve redundancies, extortion, or threats for example. Correspondingly, the ethical dilemmas on the right are also idealized, in the sense they refer to situations with no risk. This is to avoid ways in which a utility calculation could creep in, for example where the risk of getting caught and subsequent penalty could be weighed up against the anticipated benefit from infraction. Scenarios designed to tap the strategic image need to be formulated so as to represent choice on a particular occasion in pursuit of a goal, else they will take the form of enduring principles, that is value images.

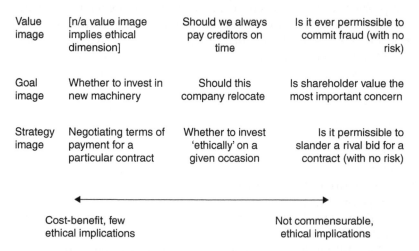

Value image	[n/a value image implies ethical dimension]	Should we always pay creditors on time	Is it ever permissible to commit fraud (with no risk)
Goal image	Whether to invest in new machinery	Should this company relocate	Is shareholder value the most important concern
Strategy image	Negotiating terms of payment for a particular contract	Whether to invest 'ethically' on a given occasion	Is it permissible to slander a rival bid for a contract (with no risk)

Cost-benefit, few ethical implications ←——————————————————→ Not commensurable, ethical implications

Figure 8.1   Values, decision scenarios and commensurability

Accounts and behaviours

Using Figure 8.1, scenarios could be devised to study three different stages of decision making: consideration and framing of the problem, the process of choice, and justification for that choice. This would provide an empirical test of the position advocated here, namely that image theory provides a better way to understand ethical decision making than RCT. Identifying a number of different scenarios is important to provide a means for assessing the comparative merits of RCT and image theory. The above analysis suggests that decision makers' observed behaviour (during consideration and framing of the problem, and the process of choice) and their accounts of the decision (justification for that choice) could be modelled using both RCT and image theory for some scenarios. For other scenarios, decision makers' accounts and their observed behaviours cannot be modelled using RCT.

Recalling that ethics is not a science and does not allow for the same standards of precision, the key difference between these scenarios will be the extent to which they allow a process of commensuration. One potential research strategy would be to explore this in an organizational setting, identifying discrete decision scenarios that could be studied in more depth using a mix of methods. For example, one could study a particular kind of decision process (e.g. a selection procedure) using ethnographic methods to observe decision behaviours, then analyse the key decision maker's justification for the final decision. If studying this process reveals that personal principles play an important part, or that the decision maker acts unwittingly in a biased way, the decision is unlikely to be successfully modelled using RCT because this depends on commensuration.

For commensurate decisions (assessing options in terms of a common metric):

> Proposition 5a: Accounts and behaviours can be modelled with RCT.
> Proposition 5b: Accounts and behaviours can be modelled with image theory.

For incommensurate decisions (assessing options in terms of principles):

> Proposition 6a: Accounts and behaviours cannot be modelled with RCT.

Proposition 6b: Accounts and behaviours can be modelled with image theory.

A second research strategy could be to use a more artificial laboratory setting, where participants respond to different scenarios by selecting from a set of predetermined options. For incommensurate decisions, one would expect that decision times are significantly different from commensurate decisions. Note, decision times need not always be longer, since under image theory, options could be screened out almost automatically, where they did not fit with one of the decision maker's principles.

Proposition 7: Decision times will vary between incommensurate and commensurate decisions.

Conclusion

This chapter began with an overview of several ways to understand the decision making process: theories of motivation and trait approaches; theories of learning; accounts that emphasize the context or frame for a decision; accounts implying sociological determinism (see Table 8.1). This exploration is warranted because in considering ethics in organizations, it is important to be aware of some of the most commonly used frameworks for understanding choice. Following Aristotle's account in book III of the *Nicomachean Ethics*, greater insight into decision processes provides a sounder basis for assessing the ethical merit of a particular course of action. It is also useful to identify assumptions that are prejudicial to ethically aware behaviour, as well as to show how some accounts of decision making are limited to certain domains. This selective review provided the context for comparing and contrasting two more wide-ranging accounts of choice: rational choice theory, the dominant account of decision making in the social sciences (Zey, 1992); and image theory, a newer, naturalistic theory of decision making (Beach, 1990).

Initially, the implications of using RCT and image theory to model decision making were discussed with reference to three ethical systems. RCT was shown to be consistent with Utilitarian ethics, but not with Kantian or Virtue-based ethics (propositions 1a–c). Image theory was shown to be consistent with each (propositions 2a–c). Recognizing the limitations of RCT can alert us to the dangers of rationality as a myth (Bradley et al., 2000) and enhances our ability to evaluate business decisions from an ethical standpoint (proposition 3). The chapter then identified a number of research propositions, illustrating how the relative merits of RCT and image theory could be tested, to test the position advocated here, namely that image theory offers a superior basis for studying choice in business ethics. These propositions stress the importance of commensuration in analysing different decision scenarios. For decisions that involve consideration of options in terms of a common metric ('commensurate decisions'), RCT and image theory can both be used to model the decision process (propositions 4a–b), as well as to study decision behaviours, and accounts of those behaviours by decision makers (propositions 5a–b). For decisions that involve consideration of values and principles ('incommensurate decisions'), RCT cannot be used, but image theory can (propositions 4c–d and 5c–d). In image theory, the role of screening and use of principles in the decision process suggests that decision times will differ between scenarios that involve commensurate decisions and those that involve incommensurate decisions. This analysis has multiple implications for understanding ethics in organizations as well as demonstrating the continuing value of an Aristotelian perspective.

9
The *Poetics*

This chapter introduces Aristotle's work on aesthetics, more specifically the text *Poetics*. There are aspects of Aristotle's aesthetic covered in other works, for instance the *Rhetoric* and the *Nicomachean Ethics*. The *Poetics* is comparatively short and fairly simple to summarize, even though its significance and consequences are quite momentous for aesthetics as well as other disciplines. Accordingly after a general introduction to the significance of the *Poetics* in the context of ancient Greek life, this chapter briefly outlines its principal arguments and situates it in relation to other ideas within Aristotle's work, before consideration of the continuing relevance of the *Poetics* from a contemporary perspective on organizations, society and politics.

The context for the *Poetics*

It is hard to imagine exactly how central the role of drama and poetry was in Greek life but these art forms were not seen simply as diversions or entertainment, they played a part in religious festivals, civic instruction and shaping of history and culture, even at times taking on the form of competitive sport. It is clear the Greek citizen took drama very seriously. For instance, the poet Phrynicus staged a tragedy in circa 493 BC titled *The Capture of Miletus*. Miletus was a city the Persian King Darius had captured after a six year campaign and which he consequently annihilated. Phrynicus' play was successful to the extent that he was, 'fined a huge sum in thoroughly democratic fashion for reminding the Athenians of their sorrows' (Cartledge, 2009: 59).

Though it addresses different art forms including poetry and music, in essence the *Poetics* can be thought of as an analysis of drama that moves beyond simple description or categorization, to a search for underlying structure and aetiology (Russell and Winterbottom, 1989). In doing this, Aristotle deploys the same methods he relies on in his writings on biology to discuss the nature of art and of how it is able to imitate life, to educate and entertain, and to impassion. The *Poetics* is, in this sense, a dissection of the aesthetic.

It is the first example we have of literary criticism, but also more widely it is a scientific treatise on aesthetics. Although it focuses principally on tragedies and how to construct them, Aristotle's account of aesthetics applies not simply to drama but to all forms of art, and draws centrally on the concept of *mimēsis* (representation or imitation). The *Poetics* includes discussion of two of the most famous Greek playwrights: Euripides and Sophocles; but some of the core concepts and frameworks Aristotle uses – relating to: characters, plot, sympathy, action can be applied to study contemporary work in theatre or film. It is not going too far to suggest that it could still be used as a toolkit for devising drama. Indeed later writers have taken the *Poetics* to be a kind of manual on how to construct drama – for instance on how to make the central characters more sympathetic, or to make the action more compelling and realistic. We can see this in the following passage:

> A good man must not be seen passing from good fortune to bad, or a bad man from bad fortune to good. The first situation is not fear-inspiring or piteous, but simply odious to us. The second is the most untragic that can be ... it does not appeal either to the human feeling in us, or to our pity, or to our fears. Nor, on the other hand, should an extremely bad man be seen from falling from good fortune into bad. Such a story may arouse the human feeling in us, but it will not move us to either pity or fear; pity is occasioned by undeserved misfortune, and fear by that of one like ourselves ... There remains, then, the intermediate kind of personage, a man not pre-eminently virtuous and just, whose misfortune, however, is brought upon him not by vice and depravity but by some fault, of the number of those in the enjoyment of great reputation and prosperity. (*Poetics*, 1452b33–1453a17)

Often the hero or heroine in a film is a character who is noble in some ways but also flawed because otherwise the audience could not sympathize with them, 'a man not pre-eminently virtuous and just'; for instance: Han Solo (*Star Wars*); Rick Blaine (*Casablanca*); Ellen Ripley (*Alien*); and a host of characters played by the likes of Bruce Willis, Arnold Schwarzenegger, Sylvester Stallone, Julia Roberts and Angelina

Jolie. Though Hollywood has settled on the conventional happy ending to its films, there are other parallels in terms of plot construction, which Aristotle describes as the 'soul of tragedy' (*Poetics*, 1450a39, Butcher translation). For instance the following passages set out the basics of plotting:

> ... a whole is that which has beginning, middle and end. Beginning is that which is not itself necessarily after anything else, and which has naturally something else after it; and end is that which is naturally after something itself, either as it is necessary or usual consequence, and with nothing else after it; and a middle, that which is by nature after one thing and also has another after it. (*Poetics*, 1450b26–31)

These ideas (beginning, middle and end) seem simple and self-evident, but this is only because they have been absorbed into our culture at such a deep level that we no longer notice them as analysis, but take them to be description, or recounting of truth. We can even read into Aristotle a warning for contemporary directors about a reliance on special effects:

> ... fear and pity may be aroused by the spectacle; but they may also be aroused by the very structure and incidents of the play – which is the better way and shows the better poet. The plot in fact should be so framed that, even without seeing the things take place, he who simply hears the account of them should be filled with horror and pity at the incidents. (1453b1–5)

Unlike Plato's dialogues, which were literary works designed for a contemporary audience, the most famous and influential of Aristotle's writings are private drafts or notes for lectures. Although he did write works similar to those of Plato, it seems clear that he would not have wanted the principal texts associated with his views of ethics, politics, rhetoric and aesthetics to be seen in the form in which they are handed down to us today. Works like the *Poetics* only resurfaced 200 years after his death and we can certainly not interpret that this represents his entire thinking on aesthetics. For instance, though the *Poetics* does not discuss comedy, it is implied that this is something that will be examined later.

Plato's position in relation to poetry is quite a complex one. Although in the Republic Plato seems to suggest poetry would be abandoned in the ideal state (other than in praise of Gods or noble men), he quotes liberally from contemporary poets in all his dialogues, as indeed does Socrates (whom we principally know through Plato – hence elsewhere my use of 'Plato/Socrates'). Whereas Plato seems to distrust *mimēsis*, it is this aspect of aesthetic forms that Aristotle embraces, '*mimēsis* as representation is elevated in the *Poetics* to the status of philosophical learning and inference' (Haskins, 2000: 22). From Plato we can take an essential source of suspicion or doubt in relation to poetry. It can bypass rationality because it can inflame passion, and by imitating action it opens space to imagine radically different lives or represent potentially harmful alternatives. Consequently poetry can corrupt the character or soul. Aristotle acknowledges that art has the ability to move one's emotions but sees this as having potential for a restorative or ameliorative effect: *katharsis*.

Katharsis is sometimes interpreted as referring to a purging of emotions, or a kind of bleaching or cleansing of emotion. But it is very unlikely this is the sense that Aristotle would give to *katharsis*. For Aristotle, emotion is part of what makes us human and indeed it is central to an account of the virtues. Virtuous choices are not those that are made purely rationally or that are dispassionately calculated, but they involve an emotional response. The key to determining virtue is that this is learned, and that we have the right kind of emotional response in the right degree and in a manner that is appropriate to the situation. So *katharsis* will not simply be getting rid of emotion, rather it will be a kind of calibration, or learning about emotion: a journey (through *mimēsis*) which leads to greater self-awareness and the cultivation of character. In discussing Halliwell (1998), Dadlez (2005: 355) suggests:

> ...the satisfaction Aristotle believes we find in tragedy involves its providing an avenue for the rehearsal of our moral and emotional dispositions, affecting our future capacities for response through habituation.

Similarly, Aristotle delights in the fact that poetry does not represent reality, 'the poet's function is to describe, not the thing that has happened, but a kind of thing that might happen' (*Poetics*, 1451b1–2). It is because of this ability of poetry to represent other futures or alternative states of affairs that he sees it as superior to history:

> Aristotle aligns poetry with philosophy because the poets' political teaching serves the city at the same time that it anticipates political philosophy. In the *Poetics*, Aristotle states that poetry is more philosophical and serious than history since poetry speaks of things with respect to a whole... and history speaks of particular things. (Bartky, 2002: 445)

So in a number of ways the *Poetics* is a deliberate challenge and radical alternative to the view Plato put forward of poetry's role in society, and yet one curious aspect of the *Poetics* is that Plato is never mentioned.

The main arguments within the *Poetics*

The *Poetics* is comparatively short and begins with a general theoretical account of literature before focusing on tragedy as a paradigmatic form. It concludes with a brief discussion about epic poetry that makes multiple references to the Iliad. The reason Aristotle seems to prefer drama to narrative (epic poetry), despite its drawbacks, is that it protects the plot from authorial intrusion. Because there is a narrator, there is the possibility of multiple lines of action and 'it is possible to put in many parts which are accomplished at the same time.' This gives 'splendor' and 'diverts the listener' (*Poetics*, 1459b23, Butcher translation). Drama accomplishes *mimēsis* more readily because the audience is an eyewitness to the events: in watching a drama unfold we do not have to trust a narrator who tells us what motivates characters, or moves events around; and drama introduces elements that distract, entertain and more immediately induce pity or fear. In drama we attend to the logic of the sequence, judge it based on our intuitions about action, and, if it is compelling, we can make appropriate inferences about how people behave. Two central ideas in the *Poetics* are *katharsis* and *mimēsis*. The force of *mimēsis* is that it is not simply copying, which might be the ordinary sense we have of imitation. Worth (2000: 335) nicely helps us to overcome this difficulty that confronts us as contemporary readers (because, as with other terms from Aristotle, there is no direct translation). '*Mimēsis* is not an imitation of reality but a direct reference to it, in which we can come to understand reality more clearly.'

The differences in Aristotle and Plato's/Socrates' perspective on poetry can be understood in terms of the role of *katharsis*. *Katharsis* is sometimes translated as purification or purging, yet in Aristotle's aesthetic the idea of *katharsis* is more subtle than any notion that emotions should be banished or evacuated. For Aristotle, emotion is central to identity and character and so ridding oneself of emotion would not be desirable. As Reeve (1998: 61) argues:

> By provoking powerful emotional responses in the citizens, tragedy allowed them not only to explore these fears in an imaginative and illuminating way, but to experience their community and shared values in a sustaining and reassuring one. Each member of the audience

felt pity and fear at what he witnessed on the stage, but aided by the very shape of the amphitheater each also saw his fellow citizens, rich and poor, feel them too. The politically educative role of tragedy, again operating both cognitively and affectively, consisted to a large extent in its ability to facilitate this communal achievement on the part of the audience.

Bartlett describes *katharsis* as 'a kind of palliative for the shortcomings of political life' (1994a: 395). For *katharsis* to play a role in the development or maintenance of good character, it can be seen as a more delicate process than purging, perhaps closer to recalibration, where 'poetry has a place in calming the passions' (Bartky, 1992: 608). In terms of the art form most closely associated with ancient Greece, tragedy, *katharsis*, plays a part in civic instruction:

> ...tragic catharsis is able to tame the greed of human desire [and] serves to prepare the soul of the citizenry in the best democracy by teaching what is worthy of being feared and pitied. In teaching what is worthy of fear and pity, tragedy makes political deliberation possible, and in so doing encourages men to see that happiness (*eudaimonia*) depends on the right order of the city. Aristotle's defense of tragedy is, in this view, based on his belief that the *demos* is educable. (ibid.)

Alongside *katharsis*, *mimesis* or imitation is fundamental in Aristotle's aesthetics, and also I would argue in his social or practical philosophy since it is the basis of learning (Nussbaum, 2001a). Artistic forms for Aristotle are aesthetically pleasing as acts of representation, which he describes at the opening of the *Poetics* as 'modes of imitation' (*Poetics*, 1447a17, Barker translation). For instance, Aristotle writes that the wellspring of poetry is an instinct of imitation, 'lying deep in our nature' (*Poetics*, 1448b6, ibid.). Similarly, in a discussion on music in the *Politics* (1340a19–1340b18), he says: 'Rhythm and melody supply imitations of anger and gentleness, and also of courage and temperance...even in mere melodies there is an imitation of character.' Both extracts show his view that it is by imitation and by developing an aesthetic appetite that we can learn. *Mimēsis* gives a way to see how we can acquire knowledge even without direct experience. The comments in the *Politics* are interesting because they connect aesthetics with virtue, and to the *polis* (they are taken from a discussion on the role of music in civic education).

Aristotle's *Poetics* in the context of his other work

Though the *Poetics* deals with more than poetry and drama, Aristotle's discussion of the role of these art forms in political life has attracted considerable attention (Bartky, 2002; Curran, 2001; Ferrari, 1999; Reeve, 1998). In contemporary democracies it is certainly the case that poetry is often political, but it is perhaps rare (in democracies) that poetry is an activity carried out in service of the state, or aligned with the state's interests. It is not common for poets to integrate with political life and, perhaps as a consequence of Romanticism, the figure of a poet is of one who stands outside convention. Poetry is an alternative mode of expression, often one that is invoked or deployed when political discourse is insufficient, or that can constitute an effective challenge to particular policies that may be simultaneously, but separately, under attack from political opposition. In the *polis* however, poetry can be seen much more readily as something acting in support of the state. It 'preserves and transmits the myths of the city and as such is a conservative force' (Bartky, 2002: 449).

Alongside other forms of art, such as drama, poetry could be seen as providing moral guidance (Nussbaum, 2001a). As I've suggested elsewhere:

> ...the famous tragedies contemporaneous with Aristotle are not so much diversions as they are instructional stories for navigating life in the first *Polis*. *Antigone* describes the struggle between personal and civic duty – the moral imperative to follow the higher laws of the Gods and act dutifully towards one family, on the one hand, and having to obey the tyrant's diktat on the other. *Oedipus Rex* demonstrates that, despite leaders' intentions, confidence or power, they are ultimately subject to forces beyond their control – even the most powerful are constrained and subject to the will of the Gods. (Morrell, 2007: 498)

Reeve (1998: 61) suggests, 'the Athenian theater was itself a political institution'; and Bartky (2002: 449) suggests a close connection between poetry and governance:

> ...the catharsis of fear and pity requires a serious threat to the well-being of the nomoi, the laws or conventions of the hero's city (1453b18). By effecting this catharsis poetry is able to perform its

central educational role because it evinces in citizens the recognition that their happiness depends on the proper ordering of the city. Since poetry is essential for the proper education of the citizens and the well-being of the city it is both the preeminent mimetic art, and among the chief concerns of the statesman.

There are two main ways in which I think of the *Poetics* in the context of Aristotle's other work. The first of these is in terms of a distinctive approach informed by Aristotle's biology, so the *Poetics* can be considered as a dissection of the aesthetic. The second is in terms of the sections in the *Nicomachean Ethics* which describe the five different intellectual virtues, or what we can call ways of knowing. These have various translations but (writing in the context of management) Arjoon lists them as:

> ... sophia (theoretical wisdom), epistēmē (science), nous (intuitive understanding), phronēsis (practical wisdom or judgement), and craft expertise. (Arjoon, 2008: 226)

The Barnes edition translates these terms: *sophia* as 'philosophic wisdom', *epistēmē* as 'knowledge', *nous* as 'comprehension', *phronēsis* as 'practical wisdom' and *technē* (the final one in the list above) as 'art'. As discussed in Chapter 7 on the *Nicomachean Ethics*, it might seem curious to a contemporary audience that these comments on epistemology appear in a treatise on ethics, but for Aristotle the five intellectual virtues are only to be understood in relation to moral virtues. Arjoon continues:

> The moral virtues (justice, fortitude and temperance) represent the fundamental modes by which an individual approaches a human good as discerned by practical wisdom. Together, the four virtues (practical wisdom, justice, fortitude and temperance) comprise the cornerstone or cardinal virtues; all other human virtues can be understood as components associated with the cardinal virtues which lay the foundation for a unified character. Practical wisdom appropriates a particular human good directly by the action of the intellect which determines how best to actualize that good; justice directs external actions in such a way as to conform to reason; fortitude and temperance moderate the passions in such a way that the individual spontaneously desires what is truly in accordance with the specific good of the human person.

This distinction between different ways of knowing has been extraordinarily influential, if occasionally misapplied, and even the simplified or erroneous accounts of these intellectual virtues still seem to provide us with something far more useful than our catch-all term 'know' which can refer equally to certainty based on experience, propositional knowledge, declarative and procedural knowledge. Flyvbjerg (2001: 2) argues that 'attempts to reduce social science and theory either to *epistēmē* or *technē*, or to comprehend them in those terms are misguided'. This is because it leads to impossible comparisons with other (natural) sciences where these forms of knowledge are the essence of disciplines. A consequent problem is that the social sciences become divorced from, rather than enmeshed with, the social world. This means that processes of political inquiry and the prospects for informed action are compromised. The relevance of this for reading the *Poetics* is that Aristotle's aesthetic can be interpreted as supporting a kind of engagement with the world that allows scope to develop wisdom, *but* without immediate empirical experience. It is because we learn through imitation that art allows us to develop intellectual virtue.

This is relevant in the context of higher education and in terms of considering learning about organizations because the vast majority of students undertaking degrees in business or management have little immediate experience of business and no experience of management. In the absence of management experience, there is potential for there to be a disconnect between theoretical and practical knowledge. A full-blooded scepticism about this would seem to suggest that placing academic education (*epistēmē*) prior to activities that require practical experience (management) is wrong headed. To date my teaching experience is in business schools and I will restrict discussion to this context to develop the argument in detail, but I think the broad points about pedagogy could be applied to other social sciences in higher education. This is perhaps more justifiable given the current context for higher education. Universities have historically been understood as places that enabled teaching and research; activities seen as intrinsically worthwhile (and in that way compatible with an account of virtue where the goal lies in the activity itself rather than some product). Now, across the social sciences, and the humanities, we are judged as though we exist to create individuated products that can be ranked and classified, such as journal articles, research contracts, and a certain kind of student whose worth is predicated on market value, and whose assessment of the student experience can be expressed as a number.

As Grey (2005) points out, even from an extremely sceptical position, a business degree can be useful in the sense that it can have a symbolic significance or imbue students with cultural capital. This applies even if the academic content of such a degree is not directly useful in the way that, say, knowledge of physics is to an engineer or an architect. In this sense one could say that degrees in business and management are not in themselves relevant, but at the same time that this irrelevance does not mean they are of no value. This is because a number of things come along with such a degree: membership to a loose club of a sort, things that identify one as a member – such as jargon and cultural resources that can be later cashed in for privilege and insider status.

There are problems with this sceptical position on the value of academic knowledge in business and management, and a dogmatic or extreme position is indefensible in some areas (employment law, logistics or operations management). At the same time, the main counterargument to this scepticism has always seemed rather specious to me in the area of organizational behaviour, or loosely 'management'. This is usually expressed in terms of equipping students with tools that can later come in useful as they pursue a managerial career. The reason I struggle with this is that it relies on the idea that by pursuing a business and management degree, students acquire resources that somehow lay in wait until they are triggered later on by the appropriate (managerial) experience. This seems to suggest that management *epistēmē* is like killifish spawn, which can survive years of drought, lying dormant and then hatch when rain appears:

> The annual killifish *Austrofundulus limnaeus* lives life on the edge. The Venezuelan ponds where it lives rapidly evaporate in the dry season, killing off the adults and exposing their mud-buried embryos to extended periods of drought...The key to the embryos' survival is that they go into periods of dormancy, or diapause. (Podrabsky et al., 2007: 2266)

The idea that having these eggs (*epistēmē* in relation to management) leads to more effective management is quite easy to call into question. We could simply ask how much sense it then makes to infer that business schools are the best managed faculties in a university, or that departments of management are the best managed departments in a business school. Both these things may be true in particular institutions but, *a priori*, they are not universally true.

Even if we do not sign up to this almost fatalistic account of management education, a problem remains which I have elsewhere described as the problem of learning. This relates to the conundrum of how it is possible to acquire *phronēsis* (or *sophia*) in the absence of experience. In the context of learning about leadership Grint describes this in the following way:

> The problem for our perplexed leader is that Aristotle suggests that *phronesis* cannot be directly learned because there is no formulaic element to moral discernment or prudence [it is] something only achieved through experience and reflection. (Grint, 2007: 238–41)

The *Poetics* offers a way to try to resolve this conundrum of a route *phronēsis* (or *sophia*) in the absence of experience. In the context of higher education it suggests a more coherent approach to teaching about organizations which does not rely on a dormancy fantasy.

Applying the *Poetics*

The application in the following chapter is close to the orthodox view of the *Poetics* (see also Belfiore, 1992; Halliwell, 1986). This sees the *Poetics* as a guide showing how art can play a role in supporting civic life through education:

> ...the value of tragic action is a practical value: it shows us certain things about human life. And these will be things worth learning only on a certain conception of *eudaimonia*... the great tragic plots explore the gap between our goodness and our good living, what we are (our character, intentions, aspirations, values) and how humanly well we manage to live. (Nussbaum, 2001a: 380–2)

Ferrari, interestingly, takes the view that the *Poetics* is a way of evaluating what makes a work of literature effective in its own terms (it would be overstating his argument to say that this is 'all' the *Poetics* is). He does concede that the tide is against him and in favour of the view that 'the *Poetics* is part and parcel of his larger interest in the moral education of the citizen' (1999: 181). There are two problems with this narrow view of the *Poetics*, the first is that it runs counter to the clear evidence of connections across the rest of Aristotle's work – not simply in practical philosophy, but in biology and logic as well. The second is that Aristotle does suggest very clearly that poetry has a role in, 'setting out universal truths' (Kemal, 2001: 410). In a famous passage that is usually read as defending poetry from the attack on poetry by Plato (Bartky, 1999 being a notable exception); Aristotle states:

> ... poetry is something more philosophic and of graver import than history, since its statements are of the nature rather of universals, whereas those of history are singulars. (1451b5–7)

He goes on to say that what makes someone a poet is that:

> ... he is a poet by virtue of the imitative element in his work, and it is actions that he imitates. (1451b28–9)

Since quite early on in the *Poetics* Aristotle says we take delight in imitation, and that human beings first learn through imitating (1448b6–9), it is difficult to imagine anything other than that Aristotle sees imitation as core to learning, that art forms offer us a way of contributing to civic education and that aesthetic engagement can be linked to the intellectual virtues. The following chapter outlines an attempt to apply what I take as the foundational element within the *Poetics* to encourage learning in students of organization theory. This foundational element is the notion of *mimēsis*.

10
Bolshevism to Ballet in Three Steps

This chapter applies Aristotle's work on aesthetics to contribute to understanding a personal and professional topic of interest, namely how to support learning about organizations in the classroom. Narrative, which is a central theme in this chapter, is an interdisciplinary topic area and has links to our understanding of ethical life, as well as to how power is understood and represented. So as well as clear links to considerations in the *Poetics*, narrative has links with *Politics* and *Ethics*.

Teaching about organization

The chapter outlines an approach to teaching business school undergraduates about some fundamental concepts in organization studies. This is based on a comparative analysis of three film extracts from: Eisenstein's *Battleship Potemkin* (1925) and *Strike* (1925), and *Billy Elliot* (2000). Similarities and contrasts across these extracts portray different theoretical perspectives on power and resistance. It draws on Aristotle's aesthetic and the intellectual virtues of *epistēmē*, *sophia*, *technē*, *nous* and *phronēsis* to advocate this approach as one that can help introduce undergraduates to the distinction between a classical Marxist account of revolution (class consciousness among the workers is sufficient), and a Marxist–Leninist account (revolution must be led by a vanguard of socialist intellectuals). To illustrate why this is important, we can begin with a pessimistic account of learning in business schools:

> The notion that management actions trigger reactions on the part of groups of employees is difficult to transmit. The majority of undergraduate students have not yet been bosses. Most have been employees, particularly in low-wage jobs in the service sector, and many

can recall specific instances in which they were mistreated. What they have almost no first-hand knowledge of is any form of collective action or collective retaliation. (Taras and Steel, 2007: 179)

Taras and Steel's intriguing study makes a case for deceiving students in order to teach them about collective action. They pretend to change the basis for allocating marks midway through a course; this encouraged students to complain as a group. They describe deception as a last resort once more traditional methods such as 'cases, films, open discussion, role-playing' had 'failed'; 'deception was intended to elicit behaviours in them that would have them band together collectively for fear of reprisal. We wanted them to retaliate against us, and hence know what it feels like to feel outrage' (ibid.: 185–7).

The approach here suggests it remains possible to teach students about this topic and related topics without resorting to deception. This may be desirable since Taras and Steel's approach depends on reproducing inequalities in the employment relationship, 'students would learn a deeper and more valuable lesson by having their boss – their professor – betray them in a deception ploy' (ibid.: 194). I feel very uncomfortable understanding teaching in these terms and so have tried to look for other possibilities, though this is not to displace or devalue Taras and Steel's study and the approach advocated here should not simply be seen in that context.

Taras and Steel relate impressions of students in North America and until quite recently it is possible that presumptions of students' ignorance about collective action also applied in the UK. However, proposals by the coalition government to introduce increases to tuition fees changed that for many prospective and current students. Tens of thousands of students and lecturers protested against these cuts in central London and across the UK. In the wake of redundancies attributed to reductions in higher education funding, some undergraduates occupied University buildings to protest against potential redundancies to academic staff. This collective resistance was quite selfless and came at personal risk, both physical and in relation to their careers as students. These kinds of actions fit Fleming and Sewell's (2002: 862) definition of 'traditional' views of resistance in terms of, 'formalized, organized acts, dependent upon some transcendental principle'. They also suggest that understanding the principles of collective action is not so far beyond the reach of contemporary undergraduates, at least in the UK.

In organization studies, interest in theories of 'traditional' resistance has waned somewhat; at the same time there has been a surge of interest in alternative modes of resistance in the workplace (Edwards, Collinson and Della Rocca, 1995; Fleming and Spicer, 2003; Gabriel, 1999; Sturdy and Fineman, 2001). It remains to be seen whether the experience of protest will fundamentally change how undergraduate students studying in the UK approach subjects such as organized labour and organized resistance. Nonetheless, recent events show 'traditional' forms of resistance are of considerable contemporary interest for students in the streets. As such, they may also benefit from attention within the lecture theatre.

This chapter presents a pedagogical case study that offers a way to encourage students to interpret and analyse collective action without resorting to deception or exploiting imbalances in power. In doing so it restates the importance of considering 'traditional' resistance and contributes to theoretical understanding of an important issue in industrial relations: attitudes to collective action amongst the young (Lowe and Rastin, 2000). It begins with an account of why there may be barriers to understanding this topic for contemporary undergraduates, and illustrates an approach to teaching it based on comparative analysis of film extracts that relies on aesthetic engagement and a differentiation between the intellectual virtues.

Business schools and pedagogy

One of the concerns of contemporary pedagogy in business schools is that undergraduates are at risk of retaining or absorbing an uncritical perspective on management and organizations (Prichard, 2009). Unless otherwise prompted or encouraged to become 'critical beings' (Dehler, 2009, passim), students may not question a number of tacit managerialist norms and assumptions. Examples of such assumptions could include the taken-for-granted legitimacy and unchallenged authority of management; the assumed fairness of relations between labour and capital; ignorance about issues relating to unionization and forms of collective action; acceptance of the corporation as the dominant and also most legitimate and desirable organizational form; and a general, uncritical acceptance of current formations of society and social institutions (including the role of business schools and business education). It is partly in this context that the topic of collective action can be understood as a difficult one to teach (Taras and Steel, 2007). At the same time, encouraging students to question such assumptions, and broaching ideas that relate to leadership and collective action are important undertakings, because these concern the dynamic between power and resistance, arguably the central theme in the social sciences (Haugaard and Clegg, 2009).

There are a number of potential explanations for why contemporary undergraduate business students may succumb to managerialist assumptions (or why they may find it hard to identify these as assumptions). It may be because these are taken for granted in the mainstream of wider society, an expression of Lukes' ideological face of power, where people accept a state of affairs, 'either because they can see or imagine no alternative to it, or because they see it as natural and unchangeable, or because they value it as divinely ordained and beneficial' (Lukes, 2005: 28). As either MBA or undergraduate students, it may be because they experience an institutional logic within business schools that rests on such assumptions: that there is a right to lead or manage, that leadership consists in directing work organizations, that management and the ability to control the labour process are desirable things, that these can be taught, and so on (Gabriel, 2005; Sinclair, 2007). Perhaps then there is less chance of these ideas being subjected to sustained, spirited criticism in a business school (Grey, 2005).

Part of this wider context in terms of organized labour is that the proportion of workers who have never been members of a trade union is increasing in both the UK and US (Booth, Budd and Munday, 2010). There may also be generational differences in attitudes to collective action. For instance Bergman, Westerman and Daly (2010: 122–3) state that students in US business schools, as members of 'generation me', are increasingly narcissistic, which could imply a reduction in consideration of common goals; although it should be acknowledged that in terms of attitudes to collective action, relations between individual, social and union identity are causally complex (Frege, 1996: 406–7).

Perhaps those who start off fundamentally questioning such assumptions do not select a business degree in the first place. Or, having chosen such a degree, it may be there is a tacit acceptance, or 'contract of cynicism' between students and their lecturers (Watson, 1996: 458–62). Under the terms of such a contract, business schools are not expected to address issues of fundamental substance, but to provide discursive resources that can be traded in later for advancement in educational or managerial careers, 'mantras have their purpose [and] reiteration of patent nonsense has its functions. It does not scare the customers' (Clegg, 2003: 376). Management education then plays more of a symbolic role in a process that is largely about rites of passage, socialization and accreditation rather than learning. Processes of professionalization may mean that 'business school students simply ape what is required of them rather than creatively engage with the problems of practice' (Chia and Holt, 2009: 472). It may even be some students are exercised by these kinds of concerns in other spheres, for instance in engaging in protests about tuition fees, or green politics but that they see this as separate from their business degree. Critical approaches to pedagogy attempt to restore the status of the classroom as a space for possibility and critique, as opposed to the potential alternative, 'the domestication of students for the purposes of reproducing authoritarian systems' (Dehler, 2009: 38).

Power and resistance

As well as these broader contextual explanations, at the level of particular disciplines, it is fair to say that many of these managerialist assumptions go unquestioned in the mainstream (and predominantly North American) literature on behavioural analysis (Austin, 2002). The field of corporate governance, which ostensibly explains and limits abuses by management, is 'overwhelmingly' (Daily, Dalton and Cannella, 2003: 371) and 'without doubt' (Benz and Frey, 2007: 100) 'dominated' by agency theory. This can be seen as a symptom of a broader issue: that there are limitations in terms of how power is construed and represented in this mainstream literature (Linstead, Fulop and Lilley, 2009: 278–315). The conventional and most popular treatments of power in business and management are agent-centric and concentrate on 'episodic power': 'discrete, strategic political acts initiated by self-interested actors' (Lawrence et al., 2005: 182) (e.g. Robbins and Judge, 2007: 468–501). For instance, the most influential account of power is French and Raven's (1959) five bases of power: coercive, reward, expert, legitimate, referent (six if you include information power separately).

Though the secondary literature on French and Raven captures the essence of this account, it has often been represented rather simplistically. For instance, French and Raven (ibid.: 150) begin by acknowledging the diffuse aspect to power, 'processes of power are pervasive, complex, and disguised in our society', and they refer to the roles of tradition and culture, and the acceptance of social structure in determinations of legitimacy. In contrast to the way their framework is often interpreted (as identifying several things that make an individual more or less powerful), they emphasize relations, 'phenomena of power and influence involve a dyadic relation between two agents' (150). Accordingly they place equal conceptual importance on the role of resistance in determining influence (151). These subtleties have been lost in some of the secondary literature and unfortunately in terms of its intellectual legacy, it is the bare bones of the framework that survive and which contribute to a simplistic account of power across several disciplines.

Many people, not simply students, clearly find merit enough in these bare bones. For students facing the pressures of assessment, it may be comforting because there are five (six) things to remember which is manageable but at the same time can feel like an accomplishment in the context of giving an exam answer. For lecturers there may be parallel benefits – it is simple to recall and transmit. Yet French and Raven's framework (at least in the way it is typically presented or recalled) is not suited to challenging assumptions about the nature of society, the fairness of the labour process under capitalism, the right to manage, or the mechanisms underpinning collective action. In themselves, these bases overlook the extent to which power may be diffuse and embedded; a legacy of tradition and routine (Foucault, 1991). They also say little directly about underlying structural causes, such as what constitutes expertise, or who determines legitimacy, or what criteria make people accept a form of control as legitimate (Clegg, 2010; Lukes, 2005). In these important respects, the way that French and Raven's framework is recalled supports many of the above managerialist assumptions.

There is a clear epistemological justification for teaching students alternative perspectives on power. Accounts emphasizing agency alone are not sufficient to explain the different forms power can take in organizations (Clegg, 1989a); nor do they explain the phenomena of organized resistance to power (Foucault, 1991; Foucault and Gordon, 1980). This applies whether we restrict the sense of organization to refer to the firm, or to include wider society and other forms of association, thereby 'placing IR into a larger political-economic framework' (Heery and Frege, 2006: 603). As well as the clear epistemological justification, there are also two kinds of ethical justification. First, in terms of their education and development at the academy, it is appropriate to make available to students as many tools as possible to think critically about the world. Reducing education to legitimation or professionalization is highly problematic, 'it would be to our peril, in my view, if we accepted [the] thesis that business schools were created primarily to legitimate business and to professionalise business people' (Francis, 2010: 213). Second, and relatedly, the way in which we represent social phenomena has important consequences, since these phenomena are influenced by how we describe them (Ferraro, Pfeffer and Sutton, 2005, 2009). Teaching about alternative accounts of power, and the role of collective action, can offer a counterpoint to what Ghoshal calls the 'gloomy vision' of management as a world populated by self-interested agents (Ghoshal, 2005: 82–4). Rather than understanding power as an attribute or property of individual agents, accounts that emphasize power relations can offer a wider perspective on control and resistance (Clegg, 1989b).

In teaching business and management, a course on organization studies is one logical place for students to be made aware that these assumptions (about how society is structured, and the right to manage and so on) are open to question and criticism. These objectives are not unique or original; nor do I mean to imply others have not identified and addressed these or similar objectives in other courses. What I am proposing for consideration however is a novel route to realizing them, one that can be readily applied and improved upon and that is based on encouraging empathy via a theory of aesthetic engagement.

Epistēmē, technē, nous, sophia and phronēsis

A few textbooks include or prioritize structural and systemic perspectives on power (see for instance Bratton et al., 2007: 92–3; Linstead, Fulop and Lilley, 2009: 278–315; Wilson, 2010: 301–3). The main two candidate theorists for these perspectives on power, respectively, Marx and Foucault, feature prominently on many courses on organizational behaviour. Even though a good number of undergraduates have not had paid employment, given their experiences of school, and of university, and in particular the punishment/discipline of exams, there is a readily available route to help them relate to some of Foucault's central ideas about power and the disciplinary functions of classification and ranking (Foucault, 1991).

The students who are the focus of this case have come across Marx, in an introductory course in their first year. But, as the Taras and Steel quote which opened this chapter suggests, collective action was, until very recently in the UK, an unfamiliar experience to many business school undergraduates (and for undergraduates in other social sciences). Even for those with experience of collective action, such as participation in protests against increased tuition fees or staff redundancies, there may be difficulties connecting such experience with what is taught in a lecture theatre. This is perhaps a particular problem within business schools, as opposed to other faculties such as politics or sociology. There is a danger that the logic of a business school and its association with managerialist assumptions leads to a contract of cynicism and a disconnect between the world of theory, which becomes understood in relation to success in exams and professionalization; and the world of practical experience. One of the compelling aspects to Taras and Steel's study is that it unites these worlds.

The potential for a disconnect between theoretical and practical knowledge is clear. Capable students may be able to reproduce propositional knowledge, or what Aristotle called *epistēmē* (a facility to recall such propositions could also be understood as an art or skill – *technē*; ability to appraise arguments based on such propositions could include *nous*). For instance, as mentioned when it comes to assessment, they can recount that a person called Marx said something like 'capitalism means workers are never paid the full value for their labour'. But this is very different from the *sophia*, which Aristotle used to describe a form of knowing that was able to make sense of experience (Grint, 2007), and it is even further removed from *phronēsis* or practical wisdom (see chapter 3 in Reeve, 2012). Flyvbjerg (2001: 2) argues that 'attempts to reduce social science and theory either to *epistēmē* or *technē*, or to comprehend them in those terms are misguided'. This is because it leads to impossible comparisons with other (natural) sciences where these forms of knowledge are the essence of disciplines. A consequent problem is that the social sciences become divorced from, rather than enmeshed with, the social world. This means that processes of political inquiry and the prospects for informed action are compromised.

As Lowe and Rastin's work on young people's attitudes to union suggests, enabling students to experience these different kinds of knowing may be important in terms of the long-term prospects for organized labour. 'Views about unions are emergent during youth, solidifying with age and experience' (2000: 217). The age range Lowe and Rastin identify for this kind of crystallization of attitudes towards unions is between 15 and 24. As a greater proportion of young people enter higher education, and a greater proportion take business degrees, business schools will become increasingly important spaces within which students either learn to engage with, or disengage from, organized labour. In the face of a number of contextual factors discussed above (the nature of wider society, the institutional logic of business schools, students' life stages and their preconceptions about management education), there are barriers that militate against collective action being understood in any terms other than as *epistēmē*. What the remainder of this chapter sets out is a way to make students more able to relate to a structural account of power to make sense of experience. This is done through comparative analysis of three films: *Battleship Potemkin* (1925) and *Strike* (1925), and *Billy Elliot* (2000). The approach is one that can be adapted and applied and this is a straightforward and clear route to identifying and challenging some managerialist assumptions about the labour process, the nature of society and the right to manage.

Bolshevism to ballet in three steps

After some intentionally brief background information, I show students selected extracts (approximately two minutes each) from three films: Eisenstein's *Battleship Potemkin* (1925) and *Strike* (1925), and *Billy Elliot* (2000) – these are described in more detail below. The reason for providing minimal background is so that, as far as possible, the experience of watching these extracts is immediate and not coloured by the kind of preconceptions associated with *epistēmē* (for instance the topic or theories these clips relate to). Before a plenary discussion, the students are shown each of these extracts in turn and asked to analyse them by making notes, being encouraged to draw comparisons and contrasts. As far as possible, the subsequent plenary is led by students' own descriptive analysis and their interpretations of comparisons and differences, but if the discussion stalls, it can be illustrated with revisiting appropriate sections of the extracts, with reference to key frames shown on a slideshow, and guided with supplementary questions. The aim is to avoid an instructive *epistēmē* mode and instead encourage reflection.

At the end of the session, a 'wrap up' summarizes the discussion and is an opportunity to communicate any important ideas not identified by the students themselves. In the years of the course so far (2009, 2010, 2011), the students' discussion has identified some readily apparent differences in context and in the development of film and cinematography, as well as underlying theoretical differences which are influential in terms of the representation of power. These contrasts are referred to at later parts of the course, in particular during a session which discusses the contribution of Marx to organization theory. At the end of the course, in addition to an exam, part of the assessment asks students to work in groups and present an application of organization theory to evaluate a film or a film extract. So this session helps to frame the overall course.

Using film is not new (see Bell, 2008). The claim for why this example is worthy of discussion is based on: the assumed challenges faced in teaching this particular topic; the merits of a compare and contrast technique; the suitability of these clips, in particular Eisenstein's work; and a principle of aesthetic engagement that allows scope to shift from *epistēmē* to *sophia*. The following three sections or 'steps' relate how to use these films. Based on experience of working with a variety of films, these extracts in particular make it comparatively easy to help students relate to alternative representations of power, evaluate mechanisms precipitating organized resistance, and thereby reveal limitations in simplistic accounts such as the demotic version of French and Raven (1959), or the agency view of power with which they are familiar.

Step 1 – *Strike*

A production of the First State Film Factory in 1925, *Strike (Stachka)* was intended as the first part of a series of propagandist films about the workers' movement in Russia. *Strike* recreates an uprising at a factory in Tsarist Russia that was brutally suppressed. Alongside *Battleship Potemkin* (step 2 below) it is an account of one of several ultimately unsuccessful mutinies and uprisings in Russia in 1905, which prefigured the 1917 revolution (Lynch, 1992).

Strike portrays how the lumpenproletariat – workers in a Tsarist factory – are exploited and spied upon by the owners of the factory. In the opening scenes where we see the factory in operation, images of chimney stacks and machinery are intercut with a close-up of the face of an obese, top-hatted figure who is laughing and stroking his chin, 'The Director' is a caricature of the bourgeoisie, he puffs on a large cigar and sits down smugly to work behind a large desk. The inciting incident in *Strike* comes when one worker is falsely accused of theft and hangs himself – there are grotesque contemporary parallels with this incident and events at Foxconn:

> Since March, five workers have tried to take their own life in the Taiwanese company's [Foxconn] Shenzhen factory; no less than 12 workers have died of unnatural causes in the past two years. In early April, one migrant worker committed suicide and another one failed his bid to end his life. Foxconn, a leading supplier for Apple, Nokia and Sony, has been under the spotlight since July 2009 when Sun Danyong, a 25-year-old employee, leapt to his death after management accused him of stealing an iPhone prototype. The problem has become so severe that the company has been dubbed the 'suicide express'. (Asia News, 2010)

The suicide prompts a strike which is initially successful and at first the workers develop their demands communally. Over time, and in the face of provocation by state-sponsored collaborators, the unity of the workers disintegrates and organized protest descends into riot. A liquor store is looted which is the pretext the governor uses to call in the military. The strike is crushed and ultimately the workers are shot and left dead lying in a field.

The extract from this film that the students are shown is towards the end of *Strike*: the brutal quelling of the rebellion. As unarmed crowds flee, tumbling down steep hills, the military advances on them and they are shot; a short time later we see them lying strewn across a field. During these scenes of rout and carnage, Eisenstein intercuts with another sequence: of a bull in a harness that is led out to be slaughtered by having its throat cut. The modern disclaimer 'no animals were harmed during the making of this film' would not apply here. The struggles of the bull are intercalated with the killing of the peasants and the violent ends to both scenes juxtaposed. This technique, known as intellectual montage, has the form of an equation: slaughtered bull + shot workers = workers are cattle.

This is now such a familiar cinematic device that to modern eyes it can even seem laboured or overly literal. Even so, Eisenstein's choice of imagery is stark and this still shocking example is brutal enough that it remains arresting and encourages students to start thinking about one portrayal of power and resistance. Based on experience of having used other film, this sequence is certainly more gripping than the scenes of *Modern Times* or *Metropolis* for instance, however well these communicate the drudgery and alienation of mass production.

Step 2 – *Battleship Potemkin*

In his account of the most famous military uprising in 1905, Eisenstein depicts the mutiny aboard the *Battleship Potemkin* as sparked by a disagreement over the sailors being made to eat rancid meat. Gathered round a carcass, a number of sailors complain the meat is 'not fit for a dog' and could 'walk overboard' by itself. But it is inspected and passed fit by the ship's surgeon who says the maggots on the carcass are dead (the point of view of the camera shows writhing maggots through his glasses). The ship's cook smells the meat and because it is so rotten decides to serve it in the form of a borsch (soup). This is discovered, and some men refuse to eat it instead buying their food from the ship's canteen. When the men are next on deck, the captain gives an order that anyone who did not eat the soup should be hanged; several men try to escape but are bundled together and covered in a tarpaulin so they can be shot.

Just as the order to fire is given by a senior officer, an ordinary sailor Vakulinchuk shouts (subtitled) 'Shipmates! Who are you firing at?' This sparks the mutiny which leads to the officers being killed and during this Vakulinchuk also dies. The ship is lying off the port of Odessa where there is simultaneously a workers' uprising. Vakulinchuk's body becomes a focal point and the interests of workers and sailors align as there is cooperation among the two groups. A brief utopian period is ended when the uprising is brutally suppressed by the military. This is the extract the students are shown next: the quelling of the rebellion in the Odessa Steps sequence, one of the most famous of all film sequences (Corrigan, 2007: 28–33).

The Odessa Steps sequence begins with an idyllic scene of celebration and carnival as the people of Odessa gather on the steps to celebrate the uprising on the Potemkin. This scene is brutally and rapidly transformed from celebration to massacre, as soldiers march down the steps in file, opening fire on the unarmed crowds below as they attempt to flee. Some people are shot as they lie injured on the steps. Others hurl themselves downward and among many scenes of carnage we see a young boy being shot in his mother's arms as she holds him up to the troops and pleads for his life. Another mother who is shot falls down dead, nudging a pram with her infant in it. This begins tumbling down from the top of the steps; a symbol for the failing, nascent revolution it careers out of control down the steps before the closing scenes of this sequence show soldiers battering innocents by bringing the butts of their rifle barrels down on their faces. The point of view shows these blows raining down towards the camera.

Step 3 – *Billy Eliot*

Set during the turmoil of the 1984 miners' strike, *Billy Elliot* (2000, directed by Stephen Daldry) tells the story of an 11-year-old boy whose father and brother are striking miners (his mother has recently died). Billy discovers he has a gift for dance when the boxing club he attends has to share the same building as a ballet class (the ballet class has been moved to make space for a soup kitchen). Against this background of conflict and poverty, and in the process challenging stereotypes about sexuality and class, Billy discovers himself to be a dancer and his teacher secures him an audition with the Royal Ballet.

Thinking Billy was still attending boxing lessons, his father and brother are at first hostile and disbelieving when they learn of his dancing, but eventually support his talent in the face of the severe financial hardship thrown at them by the strike. At one stage Billy's father even goes to cross a picket line, but his brother persuades him they can find another way to support Billy. They do so and at the close of the film we see Billy as a young man, dancing in *Swan Lake*: as Lancioni (2006) points out, he takes on a role that is traditionally a female one. This is one of a series of transformations in the film: the realization for Billy that dancing sets him free; the change in Billy's father and brother as they oversee his escape from their world and later take pride in his achievements; the defeat of the miners' union and caving in of the strike; the fracturing of friendships as there are divisions between strikers and 'scabs'; and the changes from childhood to adolescence in Billy's friends.

The extract the students are shown is a chase sequence where Billy's older brother Tony is pursued by the police across the streets and through the houses of his town. The sequence begins with a shot of a mass of strikers running down a steep hill but the focus for the rest of the chase sequence is on Tony, and the closing scenes show the chase from Billy's perspective. Though set to music, there is barely any dialogue (at one point, a police officer shouts 'he's a union leader' which is the motive for the chase). Billy's brother is defiant throughout and at one point spits on the ground in front of ranks of riot police, at another he throws down a mug of tea before trying to escape. He is caught in a memorable scene as he runs along a street criss-crossed with clotheslines that are draped with white linen. One of the sheets falls across him, covering his face and torso, and mounted policemen beat him to the ground with batons. The sheet which falls on him makes it impossible for him to see or for us to see his face; pure white at first it becomes stained with his blood as he falls to the ground before being bundled into a police car.

Discussion

As acknowledged, showing film extracts is not new. However the rationale for these three 'steps' depends on the choice of the extracts, the principle of comparative analysis, and the intention of encouraging a form of learning suited to this topic that takes into account some of the potential barriers to learning. The process is simultaneously simple and arresting. It is simple in that it brings a familiar and relatively recent account of industrial conflict in *Billy Elliot* alongside two of the earliest and most influential film accounts of revolution: *Battleship Potemkin* and *Strike*. Almost all students are familiar with *Billy Elliot* and it needs little introduction in terms of the plot, or the cultural context (a twenty-first century character-based dramatic film), and yet (unsurprisingly) none to date have come across Eisenstein. These earlier extracts are arresting because of their shocking violence and also their sheer scale which is still remarkable 80 years after these scenes were filmed.

Because of this unfamiliarity, comparison and contrast is a good way of introducing students to influential cinematic portrayals of ideology, to techniques of representation and the importance of perspective in both a theoretical and literal sense as best shown in Eisenstein's early works. The juxtaposition is intended to develop students' skills in reflecting on vicarious experience – something which both Daldry's and Eisenstein's work is powerful enough to provoke. The possibility of vicarious experience is how one can connect Aristotle's theory of different forms of knowledge with his concept of aesthetic engagement. Provided an aesthetic experience is sufficiently compelling and can evoke sympathy and recognition amongst an audience, the use of drama can support a move beyond *epistēmē* to *sophia* (cf. Levy, 2005: 23–4). Paradoxically perhaps, because two of the extracts are silent, they require greater attention and involvement since the experiences are not mediated through language. To develop a sense of how this can work, the sections below outline some learning points in terms of comparisons and contrast.

Comparisons

There are a number of close parallels between Eisenstein's films and *Billy Elliot*. There are obvious parallels in the crowd scenes where both directors show a mob running down a steep hill and both use the motif of descent to underline the powerlessness of the pursued and the failure of collective action. Steps feature in several places in the mise-en-scène during the chase sequence in *Billy Elliot*, though in a far more understated way than in *Battleship Potemkin*. Billy's older brother Tony is shown running down the steps at the backs of the houses, at one point leaping an entire flight, a smaller scale parallel with the crowds hurling themselves down the Odessa Steps. During one of the shots where Tony runs out of the back door of a house, we see a space hopper lying on the flight of steps. This marks the time period but, in another echo of Eisenstein, Daldry shows a jarring, incongruous image of childhood innocence amidst oppression and conflict. At one point, we see a close-up of policemen's boots tramping down a flight of steps in pursuit of Tony. This echoes one of the most famous images in Eisenstein: in *Battleship Potemkin*, he shows the revolt about to be put down with images of disembodied, regimented boots marching down the Odessa Steps (Corrigan, 2007: 29).

The boots illustrate uniformity, and the deliberate concentration on the lower half of the soldiers reinforces that this is impersonal, brutal class conflict. There are analogues in *Billy Elliot* when we see a mass formation of riot police beating their batons on their shields.

Whilst running through the houses of his town to try to escape the police, at one point Billy's brother has a door held open for him by the pensioner who lives there. She helps keep him one move ahead of the police. In another house which he is running through, he grabs a mug of tea from a kitchen surface. Daldry's subtle indicators of a sense of community are easy to draw attention to, and the solidarity between townspeople and striking miners offers points of comparison with the alliance between the sailors and citizens of Odessa. It is straightforward to connect these scenes to the more theoretical idea of class interest.

In both *Strike* and the *Battleship Potemkin* Eisenstein develops techniques which have been incorporated into a visual lexicon with which modern filmgoers are subconsciously familiar. The use of intellectual montage is the most obvious example of this, and the device (from *Strike*) of intercutting between a bull being slaughtered and the quelling of the revolt can seem overly literal to modern filmgoers. Though not montage in Eisenstein's sense – since it is not 'colliding' independent shots (Kiernan, 1990) – Daldry's use of the white linen sheets at the end of the chase sequence conveys some similar images: of innocence, powerlessness and anonymity. This is a subtle blending of images rather than a juxtaposition but the role of symbolism in representation is as apparent as in *Strike*.

There is another more general point of familiarity for the students with the Odessa Steps sequence. Eisenstein juxtaposes the order of the ruling class with the fragility and chaos of the revolution by showing an infant in a pram tumbling down the steps – the most famous sequence in Eisenstein's work. There are a number of homages to this in other film and it has been parodied in the *Naked Gun* film, which some students have seen and remember. A similar theme features more recently in the UK in an advert for Kellogg's *Crunchy Nut Cornflakes*, which shows a supermarket trolley with a baby in it careering down concrete steps. The man chasing the trolley stops it and we see he is interested only in the cereal. This soulless paean to consumption is unintentionally as bleak in its own way as the Odessa Steps sequence.

Contrasts

In terms of historical context, there are comparisons and contrasts to be drawn between the alignment of class interests portrayed in the

Battleship Potemkin and its violent suppression, the subversion of the workers' uprising in *Strike* by agents of the state, and the miners' strike. There is a fracturing of the working class in the miners' strike as shown in *Billy Elliot* but it is more complex and subtle, and took place over a longer time period. In *Battleship Potemkin*, there is a short-lived alliance between the citizens of Odessa and the revolutionary sailors, whereas one feature of the miners' strike was the split into those who stayed on strike and those who did not.

Another point of comparison and contrast was in the bussing in of police officers from other parts of the country; nicely illustrated in the chase scene from *Billy Elliot*, which is set to the soundtrack of the Clash's *London Calling*. Asking students what song was playing in that extract and why can help guide that discussion. The troops brought in by the ruling class in *Strike* and *Battleship Potemkin* are drawn from that ruling class, and illustrate the alliance between the military, the Tsarist regime and industry. In the miners' strike, though they were often brought in from other parts of the country, the police were mainly working class and their role ordinarily is central to the regular administration of the state. In this more complex context an interesting question to ask students to speculate on is whether there can be the moment of realization of 'class consciousness' that Vakulinchuk prompts by asking his shipmates who they are firing at. This can lead to discussion of the strength of socialization processes in organizations such as the police force and also the complexity of assigning a class status to such a distinctive organization.

The three films are obviously made in very different circumstances and with different ends. In the wrap up, one idea to explain to the students is that the propagandist films of the early Eisenstein supported a post-revolutionary regime (Kiernan, 1990). A consequence of this is that they reflected the political ideology of the period, and showed conflict as the product of class struggle (a Marxist view) rather than a result of heroic actors (a Hegelian view). Eisenstein's portrayal of powerful characters (like 'The Director') as caricatures, and workers as mass heroes, is faithful to the account of revolution as class struggle. This is not the case in all his later work notably *Ivan the Terrible* Again, state-sponsored, this time under Stalinism, that film represents Ivan as a hero: production was personally ordered by Stalin (Moynahan, 1997). The absence of individually heroic figures in *Strike* and the unconventional hero of the *Battleship Potemkin* (Vakulinchuk, who dies early in the film) contrasts with the character-driven drama of *Billy Elliot*.

The political content of both of Eisenstein's films is apparent from their opening sequences and these are also useful to consider towards the end of the classroom discussion. Both films open with quotations from Lenin which can be shown as text on a slide. These can work well towards the end of the session to reinforce that the themes of power and organization can be thought of in far wider terms than the boundaries of the firm, or powerful agents. *Strike* begins with the following quote attributed to Lenin:

The strength of the working class is organization. Without organization of the masses, the proletariat is nothing. Organized it is everything. Being organized means unity of action, the unity of practical activity.

A central theme in *Strike* is how the unity of the strikers was undermined and fractured. In the context of Eisenstein's later work, *October*, this quote can be seen as his explanation for why the uprisings in 1905 were unsuccessful and the later 1917 revolution was successful; the 1917 revolution was organized by Bolshevik revolutionaries including Lenin. Lynch (1992: 48) lends some support to this representation, '[i]t is a remarkable feature of the 1905 revolution how minor a role was played by the revolutionaries'. This raises a dividing line between Marx and Lenin and some perennial questions for Marxist accounts of revolution: are class interests, mass heroes and class consciousness enough, or do revolutions need leaders? if leaders are necessary, what is to stop their new regime becoming another form of domination? (see Hosking, 1992: 22–8).

Setting that context aside, the quote as it stands is arresting, and can be used to encourage students to think more widely about a different core sense of 'organization' – as an activity and as a vehicle for power, rather than a formal, bounded institution. The quote broadens the terms of reference of 'organization' to move beyond the firm to wider society and other social forms: unions, protest groups, social movements. It opens space for collective action to be seen as organization. It is also helpful in encouraging students to think about the limitations of agency views of power, with which they are familiar from other modules in their degree, since it is organization of a class united by common interest rather than under a single leader (though there remains the problematic question of who organizes). Lenin's quote recuperates 'organization' from the managerialist sense it can have in the mainstream literature on organizational behaviour.

Battleship Potemkin also begins with a quote from Lenin:

Russia is going through a great historical moment. The revolution has flared up, its flames are spreading wider and wider enveloping new areas, new strata of society. The proletariat stands in the van of the militant forces of the revolution.

References here to the 'strata of society' and 'the proletariat' make it clear again to the students that this is a representation of class struggle. Although one of the sailors on the *Battleship Potemkin*, Vakulinchuk, is central to the revolt beginning, he is by no means a typical hero figure. He dies early in the film and is clearly representative of his class.

Some rather theoretical points about agentic power and structural power can be brought out by asking students to identify differences in the portrayal of the 'main characters'. In *Billy Elliot*, it is obvious who the main characters are; in the sequences from *Strike* and *Battleship Potemkin*, it is not – because there aren't any in the contemporary sense in which we understand characters in film. The intellectual montage (workers as cattle) shows Eisenstein's resistance to individual hero figures. There is also a contrast in terms of how conflict is represented. In *Billy Elliot* we see the miners strike through Billy Elliot's or his brother's or father's eyes (and occasionally via context-setting sounds and images from the media) but Eisenstein relies much more heavily on third-party camera placement, particularly in showing the violent suppression of the strike scenes. This creates a sense of distance and observation that is at once more separate – since we do not see the action from any one person's point of view – and also more immediate – since we are directly confronted with these images, rather than imagining how a character is reacting to them.

For instance, the scene from *Battleship Potemkin* where Vakulinchuk incites the mutiny is a very brief sequence that illustrates the effects of perspective and different kinds of camera shot. When the order to fire is given, the camera moves to a close-up of Valinchuk shouting 'Shipmates! Who are you firing at?' It then shows a close-up of the conflicted and hesitant face of one rifleman, before moving to a wider shot that shows the rank of rifles wavering. Eisenstein then uses a mid-shot of the senior officer (S.O.) shouting 'Shoot!' before showing another close-up of the riflemen, this time we see two of them who look at one another and then begin to lower their rifles. The camera moves back to another mid-shot of the S.O., then an overhead (crane) shot of the deck of the Potemkin, showing the S.O. striding towards the riflemen, the effect is to show how he is a small (now powerless) figure. This is followed by an extreme close-up of his face showing his futile screams demanding they fire.

So, to underline the crucial moment in the mutiny – a moment where there has been (in Marx's terms) a realization of class consciousness – Eisenstein uses this series of cuts that emphasize crisis and awakening of the working class (the riflemen) and show panic and the disappearance of power among the ruling class. In doing so, he lays bare the mechanisms for revolution.

Such examples make it easier and more immediate to understand these things through the medium of film even though this comparison introduces some complex and influential ideas relating to (i) contrasting portrayal of crisis in Hegel and Marx; (ii) the difference between contemporary accounts of power as the province of individuals (the received 'agency' view of power in organizational behaviour), versus power as the product of systemic constraints and ideology (critical theory perspectives); (iii) class conflict and the changing nature of class; and (iv) ideology, propaganda and film. It does this by relying on vicarious experience as a route to *sophia* rather than *epistēmē*.

Conclusions

This course is designed to offer a critical perspective on organizations and organization theory. Accordingly some of the themes introduced are unfamiliar to the students and some of the approaches and interpretations advocated draw more on political science and critical social theory perspectives than on the typical literature on 'organizational behaviour'. There are some quite complex ideas to communicate relating to power and ideology. Film is an excellent medium to introduce these ideas even though early twentieth-century Russian silent films are not particularly easy viewing for most filmgoers, and it is a challenge to make them accessible for modern students. Selecting brief extracts that are still visually arresting, even shocking, to twenty-first century eyes and comparing these with more familiar material help encourage students to engage with these works. *Billy Elliot* helps by virtue of its familiarity, and then as the innovator of such stark, shocking imagery, Eisenstein proves an excellent starting point for thinking about film and representation. Eisenstein's work is so clearly driven by a particular ideology so it is a useful departure point for thinking about whether ideology features in less obvious and more subtle ways and in more complex contexts.

Hughes (2005: 616) suggests that 'it would be problematic to limit understandings of resistance solely to conscious acts of opposition to capitalist authority. Equally, it is problematic to view resistance as residing solely in the sphere of work.' Nonetheless, it may be that there will remain a distinction in students' minds between the kind of organized resistance which led to tens of thousands of them protesting in central London, and the kind of collective resistance associated with strikes and industrial conflict, or – arguably – with the UK riots of 2011. It may also be that the mass protests remain a kind of dramatic spectacle for some (this description is not to undermine or call into question its authenticity) and that this means they are likely to remain separate from other forms of subtler resistance. Fleming and Sewell (2002: 863), suggest – at least as a research strategy – that this kind of separation and variegation of forms of resistance is possible:

Rather than looking for patently grandiose and global strategies of insurrection we may instead find it in the commonplace cracks and crevices of intersubjective relations and other quiet subterranean realms of organizational life.

It is open to question as to whether any direct experience of politics in relation to a specific issue will lead to more fundamental reappraisal of the way society is structured, or scrutiny of the relations between labour and management (capital); or as to the role of business schools and the ultimate value of education in such schools. Any such changes would represent an opportunity to develop and enrich the method described here, rather than invalidate it.

There are some fundamentally challenging questions about this approach and it has limitations. For instance, is the use of film a kind of concession to a desire to be entertained in our age of spectacle? Does this example encourage any deeper engagement outside the classroom? It is unlikely for instance that students would then go on to read Marx. Could this approach even be inspiring future managers to understand the mechanics of organized resistance and thereby make them able to pre-empt or frustrate it? Addressing such questions is partly a matter of critical reflection.

Perhaps it remains a partial and impressionistic assessment, but, informed by an Aristotelian aesthetic, this does suggest a way of encouraging students to move from a propositional knowledge, *epistēmē* (understanding of collective resistance) to one that is closer to *sophia* (the ability to apply learning to experience). It engages them and gives them the opportunity to show that they are able to apply theory in interpreting the different cases. It also suggests ways of overcoming a contract of cynicism (Watson, 1996). This approach is useful because although they have some kinds of organization in common (school, university) not all have work experience. However, they are all able to draw on examples from film. It tries to address the challenge that some of the concepts to which students are introduced could otherwise only live in the abstract, or that there could be a continuing separation between struggle and resistance on the streets, and the representation of leadership and power in the classroom.

Often the students make (what seem to me) novel and perceptive comments on the film extracts. This happens much more frequently than in a standard lecture format, and is a very different dynamic from when they are asked to comment on a written case study, or identify problems with a theory, or apply a theory. One of several highlights in the course so far came in 2009 during the group assessment, where a group completely unprompted chose to analyse the film *Das Leben der Anderen* (The Lives of Others) (2006). This film gives an account of life in cold-war East Germany focusing in particular on the surveillance mechanisms of the secret police. In their interpretation of this, the students demonstrated that it showed how surveillance could be internalized to the extent that writers would self-censor (one of the central characters is a dramatist). They explained this well in terms of Foucault's disciplinary power, drawing parallels with practices in the workplace.

For the sake of balance, a low point was having two groups who, independently, had each chosen to analyse the horror film *Saw*, where a psychopathic killer torments his victims by setting them grotesque tasks (such as crawling through a barbed wire tunnel, or sawing their own foot off). What was doubly disconcerting, though revealing, was that whereas neither group found anything in Marx and Foucault to say about a psychopathic killer, they both found it straightforward to apply (a simplistic account of) French and Raven – the most influential account of power in mainstream organizational behaviour

There is a potential incoherence in this approach. It is purportedly one that makes students aware of structures supporting power, and yet it takes place in a lecture theatre – a context that can entrench power relations. The political events of 2010, continuing protests over tuition fees, and the 2011 riots could make such an approach appear overly theoretical or Laputan, and it may be insufficiently 'real' in comparison with Taras and Steel's method of encouraging immediate, personal feelings of betrayal and injustice. In the absence of seeing the session, one could challenge the extent to which students are 'guided' rather than lectured. Another limitation is that a session with such emphasis on Eisenstein, though intended to discuss a propagandist account, could become itself propaganda.

One way these issues are addressed is by raising them as questions for the students to reflect on. These subjects are raised at different times throughout the course, and in particular in the context of a separate session on disciplinary power which calls attention to things like the organization of space in the theatre, the structure of the timetable, time given over to questions, nature of assessment, presumed expertise of the lecturer and so on. These are all noteworthy and important to challenge, because they can support the power imbalance in the relationship between lecturer and students. More particularly in the design of this session, a way this potential imbalance is addressed, is that most of the space is given over to the students and the attempt is to make the discussion led by them as far as possible. The 'wrap up' includes some discussion of the limitations of Marxist accounts of history and crisis, indeed the students typically raise some of these limitations themselves.

Though it is done here for the sake of concision, it is misleading to write about students as though they are a homogenous group. In another potential incoherence, this closes down space to criticize aspects of capitalism in higher education (massification, consumption), and also to challenge the 'contract of cynicism'. There are differences across these students, but there are also sufficient similarities to enable a shared learning experience, and common points of familiarity and unfamiliarity. Inspired by Aristotle's aesthetic and the notion of *mimēsis*, this is a route to teaching about important themes in the study of organizations, society and politics, and one that can easily be adapted and improved upon.

11
What Is 'Public Interest'?:
A Case Study

As the chapter on the public good argues (and using the terms synonymously), 'public interest' is a central concept in public administration. In an important and basic sense, we understand effective governance as that which contributes to the public interest. Key features of civil society that protect the public interest can be taken for granted in established democracies. However, in many contexts we cannot assume a tradition of citizenship, or stable government, or rule of law, or basic infrastructure. Examining what is in the public interest in developing countries can be useful to identify these taken-for-granted assumptions, and to re-examine this ubiquitous and enduring concept. This chapter does this through a case study of land rights reform in post-conflict Nicaragua which draws together themes from organization, society and politics.

Public interest is an ancient idea that remains at the heart of writing on religious, social and applied ethics (Carcello, 2009; Dorrien, 2008; Hollenbach, 2002; Morrell and Clark, 2010; O'Brien, 2009). It is also core in the contemporary literature on public administration (Barabashev and Straussman, 2007; Bozeman, 2007; Dillman, 2008; Lewis, 2006; Morrell, 2009; Rhodes, 2009). It is used here to capture the core senses that public good, public interest and common good have as consideration of shared benefit. As Lewis (2006) has identified, these terms can have different nuances but at their core they each chime with Rawls' (1999) definition of common good, 'certain general conditions that are in an appropriate sense equally to everyone's advantage' (also cited in Carcello, 2009: 11).

Recent papers in the literature on public administration use public interest and public good in ways that overlap or are congruent and at different levels of analysis. Grandy (2009: 1119) aligns public interest with collaboration and citizenship, 'the values of collaboration, the public interest, and citizenship'. This mirrors Simo and Bies' (2007: 125) operationalization of cross-sector collaboration, as 'orientation toward the public good'. Vigoda-Gadot and Meisler (2010: 73) use public interest to discuss outcomes associated with public work, in the same sense in which Moynihan and Pandey (2007: 40) use public good. Barabashev and Straussman (2007: 380–1) identify corrosion of the public good in an absence of neutrality among public workers, where, 'personal interests dominate the public interest'. This echoes earlier work by Frederickson (1990) and Frederickson and Hart (1985) which emphasizes virtue in public officials.

The academic literature on public interest and public good runs parallel with practical attempts to implement good governance. For example, for the United Nations (UN), questions of good governance are intimately linked to the public outcomes that governance systems deliver. The UN Economic and Social Commission for Asia and the Pacific (UNESCAP, no page) identifies '8 major characteristics' of good governance: 'participatory, consensus oriented, accountable, transparent, responsive, effective and efficient, equitable and inclusive, and follows the rule of law'. This operational definition ties in with the accounts in the papers cited immediately above and also Lewis' (2006: 694) summary of the four aspects of public interest: democracy, mutuality, sustainability and legacy. At the same time as an apparent consensus about the scope and reference of these terms, there are well-acknowledged problems with using public interest (Schubert, 1962), and it is in addressing these that this chapter seeks to contribute. It begins by identifying two central conceptual problems. This provides the theoretical context for an illustrative case study – analysis of the property forum in post-conflict Nicaragua. This context prompts reappraisal of some basic assumptions in our understanding of public interest.

The problem of attainment and the problem of operationalization

There are two main problems with using public interest which are touched on in the earlier chapter on public good, but which, in application to a particular setting, require more discussion. The first is that public interest is unattainable. Societies are pluralist and governing is a never ending process, where aspirations are limitless, resources finite and ultimate goals and values conflict. Two recent theorists draw helpful distinctions which can serve as resolution to (what I call) the problem of attainment.

From a societal perspective, Bozeman (2007: 17–8) defines public values (shared normative criteria about governing, and the rights and duties of citizens) in terms of public value (a criterion for judging the extent public values seem to be achieved). Public interest is a way of judging progress, without commitment to a utopian destination. From an individual perspective, Lewis (2006) suggests public interest is an ongoing obligation, which is consistent with the idea that administration involves pursuing equity and discharging an obligation to future generations (Frederickson, 1994). This also resolves the problem of attainment by showing public interest as a process rather than an end state. For Bozeman and Lewis good governance is understood in terms of the extent to which it contributes to public interest.

As well as the problem of attainment, the second problem with using public interest is that of definition, summed up by Schubert's (1962) suggestion that public interest, 'makes no operational sense' (in Denhardt and Denhardt, 2007: 67). To resolve this, one could suggest it need not necessarily be seen as a problem as much as it may be part of understanding good governance. Governing is in part an attempt to articulate and address such questions: to ask what public interest is, and for whom, and whether given policies will contribute to it. This difficulty (of operationalizing public interest) is well understood. However, there is an aspect to it which is important and which has not been given sufficient attention in the literature. This is that our understanding of public interest is based on Western models of an institutionalized public that can assume basic infrastructures and democratic capacity.

Postmodernity, publics and societies

Part of the value of broad terms such as public interest is that they prompt scrutiny, making us ask what they mean in any given context. For instance, the terms 'public' or 'society' can be misleading since there are multiple publics or perhaps even societies, depending on the frame of reference for a given problem. Berkman and Plutzer (2005) capture the essence of this in the title of their study of governance in US public school districts, *Ten Thousand Democracies*.

In developed countries, public interest is associated with various institutions and infrastructures. This can be expressed in terms of relations between the state and its citizenry, or the government and its electorate, or a distinction between civil society and the market, or the – sometimes blurry – distinction between private and public goods (Morrell, 2009). These kinds of distinctions can still apply in developing countries, but in practice the difference in context may be so stark that we must revisit some basic assumptions underpinning our understanding.

For instance, no matter what form a developing country's government may take, it is likely that, in comparison with developed countries, private multinational corporations (MNCs) will have a disproportionate impact as part of the mix of institutions which make up market and civil society. MNCs are political actors, but neither 'public' nor 'common'. They may produce public goods, like health and education, and take on tasks traditionally carried out by national governments (Walsh, Weber and Margolis, 2003); they can also offer a basis for regulation, stability and peace in civil society, and influence the rules of global trade (Scherer and Palazzo, 2008). In each of these senses MNCs influence not just their immediate contracting environment, they influence a wider system. This dynamic is potentially obscured if we use terms such as public or common that we have grown familiar with in developed contexts.

Terms such as public, society or common can also imply a coherence and stability which may be illusory in extreme cases where there is ethnic hatred, or recent conflict, or disease or famine. Public and common can wrongly imply a collective capacity within civil society or a sense of shared identity. Comparative governance studies suggest such assumptions may be misplaced. In the developing world, there are some very obvious and very pertinent 'bads', such as war, famine and disease, which do not feature in developed countries.

A typical 'first world' model of good governance includes democratic participation, a professional civil service, the rule of law and so on. 'Bad' governance would be signalled by non-democratic governments, rent seeking among public officials, a corrupt judiciary and the like. These accounts are not transferable to all contexts. In extreme crises, they are insufficient. They may be unrealistic, incompatible with entrenched traditions, or neglect 'bads'. We can still pursue the public interest in developing countries, even if that is by minimizing 'bads', but we may not be best placed to do so if we start with a first world governance shopping list, or assume fundamentals. As Klingner (2006: 776) suggests, in some contexts, rather than a GPS navigational device (global positioning system), we need a GDPS: a global development positioning system. 'Public interest' can remain part of such a system.

Comparative public administration

Interest in governance in the developing world is both a cause and consequence of the critical literature in postcoloniality (Spivak, 1999). This makes reliance on such an established concept as public interest problematic, since this is a pre-modern, even ancient term. Richards identifies that some feminist scholars reject the notion of a difference between public and private; the private sphere can be the repository where women's concerns are relegated, 'the insistence that there is such a thing as a generalised common interest has typically served the advantage of male elites who define the content of "public" and "private" (2004: 11–12)'. O'Brien's (2009: 25) analysis of common good echoes this as he suggests contemporary readers are sensitized by 'postmodern sensibilities' that make us, 'suspicious of the idea that a good can be anything more than a perspective on reality that reflects the best interests of a certain elite group, often hiding behind the veil of the common good'. Mindful of such considerations, comparative public administration reflects an interest in questions that lie at origins of the discipline (and the *Politics*). Studying embryonic democracies and emerging nation states allows us to chart the development of government, and to speculate on the effects of various forms of government, and reforms on their respective citizenries (Grindle, 2007).

Recent comparative studies examine forms of government and their effects on industrialization in Brazil, India, Nigeria and Central Korea (Kohli, 2004); reforms in Bolivia, Argentina and Venezuela (Grindle, 2000); and Peru (Ryan, 2004). Intra-state analyses include study of the manipulation of collective history in Iraq (Davis, 2005a); the consequences of state development goals on marginalized groups in Chile (Richards, 2004); the history of public administration (Maheshwari, 2005) and governance (Purnima, 2005) in India; and examination of traditions and variants of bureaucracy in Ethiopia (e.g. Mengistu and Vogel, 2006).

Collectively these studies show that comparative analysis is difficult not only because of the variety of types of government and administration, but also because of differences in levels of socio-economic development, demography, ethnic conflict, the nature of civil and market society, capacity (technology and other infrastructures), the values of existing political institutions, and diverse traditions. All these are contemporary contexts, yet many of the questions they prompt go to the roots of the discipline and the origins of our ideas about public interest (Kraut, 2002).

Examining this is still valuable today. In developing countries, the relationship between governance, democratization and the public interest is a complex one that can challenge assumptions we might make in the developed world. Conventional theories of democratization can assume a pre-existing readiness for democracy in civil society. This may not be the case, even though democracy is seen as a precondition for good governance (Kim et al., 2005). For instance, it can be a mistake to assume decentralization fosters democracy (Grindle, 2007; Ryan, 2004) or that ostensibly liberalizing reforms result in liberation for all publics (Richards, 2004). Klingner (2006: 777) suggests that perhaps the key governance question in comparative public administration is how to develop capacity in 'fragile countries'.

The following sections examine land rights reform in Nicaragua and use 'public interest' to increase our understanding of governance issues in such contexts. The empirical research for this section was conducted by Nicola Harrington-Buhay, a Deputy Director at the United Nations Development Programme (UNDP) (Morrell and Harrington-Buhay, forthcoming).

The case of the 1995 Property Forum in post-conflict Nicaragua

In 1995, the time of the property forum, Nicaragua was consolidating its nascent democracy. A revolutionary movement had deposed the dictator Anastacio Somoza in 1979 and brought the Sandinista Front of National Liberation (FSLN) to power. The FSLN government was debilitated throughout the 1980s by a civil war that had its origins in ideological differences but was multi-class in character (Everingham, 2001). The war caused 30,000 deaths and severe economic and social disruption (Arnson, 1999). A Central American peace plan in 1987 helped pave the way for the end of the war two years later. Democratic elections in February 1990, with international observation led by ex-President Jimmy Carter, resulted in peaceful transfer of power to an opposition party for the first time in Nicaraguan history. In April 1990, Violeta Barrios de Chamorro was sworn in to lead a government of the National Union of Opposition, known also as the Government of National Reconciliation.

Resolution of property problems was central to the 'triple transition' overseen by the Chamorro government: from war to peace; from a centralized to a market economy; and from isolation to international integration. Land rights reform is not just about equity or wealth redistribution. A tradition of private ownership of property is at the core of contemporary models of democracy. In Russia for instance, one marker of transition has been a move to a protective attitude to private property (Barabashev and Straussman, 2007). In Nicaragua, the property problems had their origins in the system of large estates, a legacy of Spanish colonial rule, and the FSLN's decision to use land repartition as its principal tool of political and economic change. During the 1980s, properties were confiscated from the Somoza family and associates, but also from any citizen who left the country for more than six months. Those who lost property became known as the *confiscados*. Though this term is accurate in terms of recent history, it disguises a far more entrenched pattern of inequity of land ownership. Given the historical legacy of Spanish rule, and earlier injustice dating back at least as far as the 1800s, a far greater proportion of the public had already been disenfranchised over time.

Property reforms were guaranteed under the 1987 constitution and supported by numerous acts of legislation. Expropriated properties were not titled to the state, nor did the government transfer title to the beneficiaries: rather, beneficiaries of land reforms were 'assigned' property for use. Land redistribution covered almost half Nicaragua's land, benefiting 43 per cent of peasant families (Cardoso and Helwege, 1992). When the FSLN unexpectedly lost the national elections in February 1990, it made frantic efforts to legalize individuals' property rights before handing over power. Laws were urgently passed that gave legal titles to beneficiaries of land reform and to individual Sandinista officials who held titles to urban properties on behalf of their party. The laws generated huge administrative complexity, resulting in mass transfer of confiscated property by the Sandinista government and multiple claims to the same property. They provoked controversy, becoming known by those opposing them as the *piñata* (a papier-mâché figure filled with sweets hung at parties: blindfolded children break it with sticks so sweets rain down).

At the heart of the property dispute lay a fundamental debate over whether the gains of the revolution or sanctity of private property rights should take precedence. While this remained unresolved, the often violent disputes to which it gave rise were a major source of instability. Legal uncertainty over ownership blocked investment and economic recovery. A complicating factor came in the form of claims by US citizens, some 70 per cent of whom had been Nicaraguan at the time of expropriation of their property. US citizens' claims represented only a quarter of the total, but came to dominate US foreign policy towards Nicaragua. In 1994–5, Congress threatened to cut bilateral aid and block multilateral assistance to Nicaragua from the World Bank due to insufficient progress on resolving outstanding property claims of US citizens.

The importance President Chamorro attached to peaceful resolution of the property issue was illustrated in her transition protocol with the Sandinistas in 1990, which affirmed 'the need to bring peace and legal security to the Nicaraguan families who have been assigned urban and rural properties by the State, harmonising their needs with the legal rights of Nicaraguans who have lost their property' (Lacayo Oyanguren, 2005: 299 [Nicola's translation]). Chamorro's government came to the view that the only viable solution was the return of appropriated properties where possible, and compensation to owners of properties that could not be returned. Since the government was effectively bankrupt, compensation would be made using government bonds. Issues to resolve included how the government could finance the bonds, whether and how much existing occupants of land and houses should pay for their property, and how to resolve multiple claims on individual properties and provide legal security to occupants in the interim. Progress was difficult: by 1994, legal disputes over property continued to affect 40 per cent of dwellings (Hendrix, 1996/7) and a quarter of cultivable land (Carter Center, 1995).

The property forum

What makes Nicaragua an unusual and compelling case is that the basis of land rights reform can be traced to a specific event, the UN property forum in 1995. The forum was of critical importance owing to its contribution to specific outcomes and also in its symbolic role as a watershed moment in Nicaraguan history on this vital issue. It offered an excellent opportunity to focus on public interest: there was a clear and specific problem, with divisions across different parties, that was addressed via a salient, time-bound process. It also allowed identification of respond ents who had played a central role in this process. That the event was so momentous and that different respondents' accounts converged on key points gave confidence that they were still able to recall it and its effects over a decade later. Importantly too, the event was far enough in the past to allow them to see it in its historical context.

In 1994, the UN General Assembly (GA) requested the UN Secretary-General to provide Nicaragua 'with all possible assistance to support the consolidation of peace, in areas such as...land ownership and land tenure in rural areas' (UNGA, 1994). At the request of the Chamorro government, the UNDP, and University of Wisconsin Land Tenure Center, had been providing advice on the property question. UNDP and the Carter Center had also been sounding out the willingness of different constituencies to find a solution. The Property Forum, co-sponsored by the UNDP and the Carter Center, provided a venue for this public exchange. This took place on 4–5 July 1995 and involved 58 high-level representatives from Chamorro's cabinet, the National Assembly, political parties, the Supreme Court, and organizations representing former property owners, bondholders and beneficiaries.

Ex-US President Carter's involvement with Nicaragua over time gave the Carter Center credibility as an event co-sponsor. He had been instrumental in Somoza's downfall in the 1970s and in persuading the Sandinistas to accept electoral defeat in 1990. For many, the neutrality of the UN made it a logical institutional 'home' for an event of this kind, the political risks of which were recognized. The principal agreements reached at the Property Forum were (in sum): security for small property holders; compensation for expropriation of former owners; occupants of larger properties to purchase or return them; agreements to be translated into specific decisions and laws within three months (Carter Center, 1995). In November 1995, a comprehensive Property Law was passed by the National Assembly. This legalized ownership of small properties for 200,000 beneficiaries of land reform, confirmed the transfer of properties to demobilized contra-revolutionary and army soldiers after 1990, and guaranteed compensation to previous owners except the Somoza family.

Data collection

Adopting a case study design, the empirical research involved analysis of documents contemporaneous to and subsequent to the reform, and interviews of forum participants asking them to recall the event and reflect as to whether it achieved the goal of contributing to the public interest. Case studies allow deep probing into a specific set of issues, and are particularly suitable where it is not easy to separate events from their context (Yin, 2004). Our focal questions were (i) who benefited from the forum and its legacy, and (ii) what constituted benefit – thereby addressing the problems of attainment and operationalization. Preliminary telephone interviews were used for orientation, to identify key figures in the forum, gain access, and inform design of the interview schedule.

The bulk of the empirical research was carried out during a visit to the capital, Managua, in April 2006 by Nicola.

We chose interviewees who had occupied senior decision making roles in their respective arenas at the time of the Forum, with the aim of ensuring a cross-section of relevant groups. Given the seniority of these figures and the limited number of forum participants, it was not possible to guarantee anonymity. However, respondents were guaranteed that quotes would not be attributed and that descriptions would not compromise confidentiality (while allowing adequate contextualization). Nicola also made it clear that interviewees could speak off the record or withdraw at any time (neither of these happened). The interview schedule and design satisfied institutional research ethics committee criteria, and was consistent with relevant professional associations' ethics guidelines (the American Political Science Association, the American Society for Public Administration). Interviews were held with 14 key informants: a minister-equivalent from the administration in office at the time of the site visit, four ministers from the government of Violeta Chamorro, four representatives of the political opposition and unions, two high-level technicians deployed in the Forum by its sponsoring institutions, and two influential commentators from civil society. Nearly all were male, with the only female being a commentator from civil society – the Forum itself included three women amongst 58 people (Carter Center, 1995). All but two interviewees were Nicaraguan.

The research combined a semi-structured interview schedule, with critical incident technique. This involves asking interviewees to focus retrospectively on the character and consequences of a particular, salient event (Chell, 2004; Gremler, 2004). Retrospective reporting is open to a number of biases (recall error, retrospective rationalization, social desirability) (see Miller, Cardinal and Glick, 1997). Nonetheless, even a decade later, the salience and specificity of this event was likely to mitigate many biases. This is partly corroborated by research suggesting episodic memory and autonoetic (self-referencing) consciousness are the most stable forms of memory (Symons and Johnson, 1997; Wheeler, Stuss and Tulving, 1997). There was good evidence of inter-rater reliability in that recollections by different respondents tallied. As noted above, it would have been impossible to tell shortly after the reform the extent to which it had been successful. Evaluation after some time is not only defensible but desirable.

Interviews were conducted in Spanish in all but one case, and all recorded. Interviews lasted between one and two hours. Each was transcribed in full by a Nicaraguan national before being checked for accuracy and sense in Spanish (Nicola is fluent in Spanish) and, once translated, in English by me. In addition to these main interviews, a number of more informal interviews were carried out with representatives of international organizations, national statistical institutes and local think tanks; principally to explore issues of measurement of public interest in the Nicaraguan context. These interviews facilitated access to additional documents not otherwise available through official repositories in the Carter Center or via the UN.

Findings

The forum

Interviewees noted the Forum was one in a chain of efforts to find consensus on property rights. A recognized contribution of the Forum was the bringing together of issues on which the government and society had been working for a matter of years but which were losing momentum or were blocked politically. The Forum itself was thus not necessarily about finding solutions, but rather about advancing what existed. Nevertheless, virtually all interviewees attributed the passage in November 1995 of Law No. 209 (designed to bring legal closure to the property issue) to the political agreements reached in the Forum.

When asked about the benefits created by the Forum, interviewees cited: (i) security for both sides (for the beneficiaries of land, that the property they had received would not be taken away, and for the *confiscados*, confirmation of compensation); (ii) official recognition that a party had been wronged, counterbalanced by an upholding of the rule of law; (iii) a boost to the system of compensation by bonds, thereby diluting the possibility of parties to opt for violence; (iv) removal of political obstacles, with agreements reached in the Forum re-opening the possibility of foreign aid. Interviewees cited a number of outcomes resulting from the process itself. These included a sense of confidence in an emerging democracy which is owned by Nicaraguans.

In the view of a Chamorro minister, the broader impact was felt by the fact that 'the government confronts a problem, a seemingly very serious one, it finds a solution'. Property reform was seen by respondents as a metonym, as noted by a technician, 'property was the most acute symptom of a larger inability to get on'; and as having a symbolic significance, for a representative of the *confiscados*, 'if the problem of property could be weakened, diluted, without needing to resort to violence, it must be [possible to do] the same with other things.' The process itself came to be seen as an exemplar for reaching other agreements.

Interviewees were also asked how the benefits they identified from the Forum had come about. The presence of the UNDP and the Carter Center were crucial. The neutrality of the UN and its continued presence in Nicaragua throughout the war made it a privileged interlocutor between government and wider society. UNDP had an established record in mediating sensitive issues of transition. As a Chamorro minister put it, 'The United Nations...was fundamental in assembling, designing and the drive to ensure a critical mass.' This enabled 'a solution that was Nicaraguan, not imported.' Different constituents referred to the Forum as providing 'oxygen' (a government minister), and 'breathing space' (a union representative), serving to *amortiguar* – cushion sensitivities (a representative of the *confiscados*; from *amortiguador*, meaning shock absorber). Third party involvement was deemed by all but one interviewee to be crucial. As a Chamorro minister commented, 'it isn't because we don't have the intellectual capacity or the legal preparation...our big problem is interests, we put personal interests above those of the country'. This was echoed by a technician: 'Nicaragua being so polarised, it [would have been] very difficult to find people in-country acceptable to both sides'.

With hindsight, the presence of external parties to *amortiguar* is perhaps an obvious ingredient in successful reform in some contexts, though such external influence can have other less positive consequences (as noted below). This was not an anticipated finding, partly perhaps owing to a reliance on Western models of public interest and good governance. These do not incorporate the *amortiguar* role since Western democracies are generally developed, stable states and reforms come from within. This kind of role is also absent in ancient models of comparative governance, where much time is spent discussing the nature of the ruler and constitution, but little on the role of actors beyond the *polis*. It may be that since these ancient models come from a time of warring and often self-sufficient city-states (Kraut, 2002), the role of an *amortiguar* is harder to envisage.

Costs and benefits of the forum

Interviewees were also asked about aspects of the Forum that resulted in a diminishing of public interest. At the time of the event, these were considered by interviewees to include: (i) non-agreement by one central partner, which weakened the outcome and was to affect its sustainability; and (ii) the perception some groups benefited more than others, 'the hardest criticisms came from the *confiscados*...where there is greatest grief' (technician). There was also the fundamental question of actual or potential diminishing in public interest for those who were not present or represented in the Forum. A Chamorro minister noted, 'the negotiation was much more influenced by [the need] to respond to the interests and demands of one sector of the population that...was in conflict'. Access of the poor to land was not given the same profile as other issues. In the medium to long term, a burgeoning national debt resulted from compensation of *confiscados* with government bonds. This was exacerbated by the government's failure to set limits on compensation levels up front. This was a major loss to any who did not benefit directly from land reforms or compensation agreements. In the view of a technician, 'The ones who lost were the citizens, renters, VAT payers who neither gained nor lost but had to pay for it' (through taxation).

Another diminishing of public interest lay in perceived opportunity costs. One ex-minister felt there was an unhelpful prioritization of political over economic objectives. They felt land rights reform was used to tackle a social problem of demobilization and unemployment, and satisfy a political need to compensate certain groups. This resulted in a lost opportunity to regenerate the productive sectors of the economy.

One challenge in evaluating the extent to which good had been created through the Forum was the impossibility of knowing what other outcomes might have been possible, and whether the alternatives to what was achieved were themselves more pressing and threatening 'bads'. One civil society commentator made the point that 'without reconciliation, who knows what would have happened?' It may well be that the benefits created by avoiding a return to conflict are not commensurable with economic growth or even stable government or a rule of law. Such stark trade-offs between public 'bads' exist only in extreme environments. A number of interviewees echoed the view expressed by a *confiscado*:

> At the end of the day, how many people died in the process of recovering their properties? Very few, compared with the significance of the problem, because the life of property has no direct relation with the satisfaction of peoples' lives...How much blood was shed for this very complicated problem of property? Little – little blood was shed...Nicaragua came out of it with lower costs than it could have.

Though it is overly simplistic to state definitively that this is what has happened here, the extract is enough to suggest that sometimes public interest (public good) may be better understood as a choice to avoid horrific 'bads'. This is not the case with developed country models of public interest. Whilst these acknowledge the fundamental importance of domestic peace and stability, for the citizens of developed countries, this is an abstract rather than material reality. In keeping with Lewis (2006), interviewees were asked about the sustainability of any benefits. Most felt some of the benefits generated were lost as a result of partial or discriminatory implementation of agreements. A technician said it proved difficult to keep agreements 'nailed down'. When President Chamorro's successor slowed the implementation of agreed solutions, this generated renewed expectations among *confiscados*, also provoking reactions among beneficiaries of the reforms. Pressure from US Congress meant the Nicaraguan government had to make swifter progress on resolution of US nationals' claims. A minister from the Chamorro government felt this resulted in 'practically discriminating' in their favour, and strengthening the position of groups of *confiscados* in relation to other constituencies.

An influential civil society commentator noted that public interest was harmed by the fact that agreements reached on property were only partial solutions for 'the underlying problem'. This chimed with the assessment of a high level union representative that 'there was no plan to consolidate social peace in the countryside.' Land titles were not accompanied by the means of production such as credit or technical assistance. As a result, many of the poor (and ex-combatants) opted to sell their land, leading to overall re-concentration. A minister-equivalent from the government in office at the time of the visit noted that even more than ten years on, 'as long as we don't offer a real alternative for … rural people, it will be difficult to move towards a resolution.' Most interviewees considered the property problem to be reduced not resolved.

A lowest common denominator of values

During the interviews, questions of what constituted or contributed to public interest elicited most of the elements in the operational and academic definitions which opened the chapter. It seemed clear in this research that the question of public interest had featured in interviewees' thinking long before the interviews. Responses were well considered and varied, and included shared objectives and established 'rules of the game'; methods to bring about consensus and institutionalized consensus; mechanisms for dialogue and goal setting across sectors; wide recognition of inequity and the need to reduce it; the capacity to reconcile differences without resorting to violence; the ability to over-come vested interests in the status quo (Snyder and Mahoney, 1999); governmental legitimacy and coherence between its espoused and real intent (Brinkerhoff and Brinkerhoff, 2002); capacities for governing, and capacities for public service delivery; a sense of nationhood, and national ownership of solutions.

Interviewees also specifically identified: peace, security, political and economic stability and basic infrastructure. Each had personally experienced the alternatives to every one of these. One ex-government ministerial respondent suggested that what was lacking in Nicaragua was 'a lowest common denominator of values'. For us this comment illustrated the benefit that can come from deliberation and discussion of public interest. It provides a basis to express divergent goals and rec-oncile priorities in relation to each other. Indeed perhaps 'a lowest com-mon denominator of values' is the most essential or basic social good (cf. Rawls notion of primary social goods discussed in Crocker, 1992).

Finally, interviewees were consulted on how to measure the creation and diminution of public interest in this context. These questions reflect our interest in the problem of operationalization. To provide additional data and a form of triangulation on this, representatives from interna-tional institutions and local think tanks based in Nicaragua were also interviewed. A final stage of analysis drew on supplementary discus-sions with officials at the World Bank and the Instituto de Estudios Nicaraguenses. What follows reflects inputs from each.

Discussion

Operationalization of public interest

To operationalize public interest in this context involved trying to iden-tify measures of progress in the resolution of property problems. This included the functioning of land and credit markets, as well as public perceptions of the continued importance or otherwise of the property problem, and also ways to capture improvements in state–society rela-tions (on the premise that difficulties finding solutions to the property issue reflected broader weaknesses in governance). Elements selected included the existence or otherwise of political processes that permitted peaceful resolution of social conflicts, inclusiveness of those processes, confidence in the efficiency and effectiveness of the judiciary/rule of law, and the State's capacity to respond to societal demands. In terms of an analytical model, our thinking was informed by Bozeman's (2002) criteria of public value failure. The problem of operationalization is addressed in Table 12.1.

Table 11.1 A case study of public interest in Nicaragua's reform of property rights

Public interest	Good governance	Measures
Rights to land and property	Increasing the numbers of titles benefiting the poor; granting indigenous land rights	Structure of land ownership, degree of concentration by class; government commitments met; land with legal title
Land in use as a factor of production	Supporting land being used for production; investing in farm technology; transparency of land market; poor can access credit	Land market value; agricultural productivity; loans made to the poor; prosecutions for corruption relating to land
State support of industry (agriculture)	Coherent strategy supporting farmers: technical, marketing assistance, access to credit etc.	Number of people employed profitably in agriculture; crops grown; fair working conditions
Public perceptions	Confidence in government and in systems and infrastructures of administration and property reform	Attitudinal (opinion surveys), participation levels, priority given to property issues in surveys, voting
Democracy	Engaging with various publics in goal setting, planning and decision making, and feedback on property disputes	Number and types of *concertación* (consultations) that are ongoing; agreements reached; commitments met
Deliberative capacity	Increasing participation across all classes in consultative processes relating to property	Conflicts of interest manifested publicly; solutions negotiated; engagement by class, race, gender
Rule of law	Institutional capacity to enforce property reform; knowledge of and faith in judicial process by citizenry; access to justice	Public trust in judiciary (participation in judicial processes, attitudinal surveys); number of cases not represented by lawyers

Continued

Table 11.1   Continued

Public interest	Good governance	Measures
Institutional competence	Financial, technological and human capacity to plan and spend, to learn and innovate;	Public trust in government; service quality satisfaction; number of cases of government corruption tried and resolved
Peace and security	Reduce use of arms or force in property disputes; improved security relative to other countries in the region	Ranking of property as a cause of crime; levels of crime related to property
Pluralism	Inclusive political process; fair distribution of land; groups previously in conflict live in peace	Participation of disenfranchised in politics, society and economy
External perceptions	Seen as stable and well governed	Improved country credit rating; increased levels of FDI and trade

The first two columns in the table offer an account of public inter-est and good governance in this context. The problem of attainment is addressed in column three, where quantifiable measures are suggested as ways of tracking enhancement of the public interest. This shows the need to consider assumptions about civil society that may be taken for granted in developed contexts.

Who are the public?

One challenge of the case study lay in understanding what and who constituted the public. The question 'who was the public?' was put to each interviewee and each interviewee was also asked whether the pub-lic was adequately represented in the Forum. Government respondents saw the public ultimately as the nation, in whose interests an agreement on property was sought. While acknowledging this 'public' comprised many groups, two ex-ministers considered the public to be appropriately represented. They had quite a limited account of public, namely those directly implicated in property disputes and their representatives.

Other commentators thought there were gaps in representation. One union representative indicated participants were 'those most visible' in relation to the laws in question. The union members and one technician each noted the 'real powers' of the time were present, but not the poor and the landless. As one civil society commentator put it, 'Poor peasants in general don't have the structure, the mechanisms, the information to make their concerns and demands heard, and therefore at the end of the day [merely] receive the results of those macro negotiations.'

The divergence of views about who constituted 'the public' with regard to the Property Forum reflects differing perspectives on what the Forum was designed to achieve. For a union representative, 'Carter did not come to resolve inter-class conflicts, he came to see how to make the *hacienda* [the main house on a large estate] work.' Frederickson (1991) notes that responses to the question of 'who is the public?' depend directly on the purpose for which the question is asked, suggesting the need to explore and explicitly define the public when operationalizing public interest. This is important for nascent democracies, where public policy can be driven by the interests of the dominant coalition rather than of the nation (Auchter, 1996). This applies more generally in Latin America where serious deficiencies have been noted in terms of the lack of control citizens can exercise over the State's actions (PNUD, 2006).

In addition to these groups comprising the public, a range of external partners (the UN, World bank, donor countries, MNCs) were cited as directly influencing Nicaraguan policy. A Chamorro minister stated:

We had to negotiate with these organizations continually as if they were part of our public... that is the problem of a poor country, especially one coming out of a war. It has to incorporate...as part of its public which it has to please, not only internal groups with a political, economic or union voice, but also the international community, United States, the financial institutions.

The influence of external partners is not surprising given Nicaragua's history of external intervention and its dependence on foreign aid. Even so, the influence of these bodies who are not the 'public' is a function of the specific circumstances of a developing democracy. These kinds of influence are not as keenly felt, or articulated, in the established constitutions of developed nation states (nor are these articulated by Aristotle). Some of the pressures emanating from external actors stemmed from Nicaraguans now nationalized as US citizens. This adds a further layer of complexity to the question of 'the public' in the specific case of Nicaragua.

One obstacle highlighted in the interviews, and supported by opinion polls (Instituto de Estudios Nicaraguenses, 1999), was the absence of a sense of 'nation' and thus a national vision that would unite different parties to tackle key problems in the country. Interviewees suggested the memory of civil war required a reassertion of even the most basic values. Part of the problem with reaching wider agreement is the use and interpretation of polarizing terms such as 'conflict,' 'triumph,' 'defeat' and the 'dispossessed' which interviewees used and are typical in Nicaraguan discourse. These convey and create continuing division, making dialogue more difficult, reinforcing group identities and entrenching difference (Crossley and Roberts, 2004).

Public interest needs to be understood in light of social and institutional arrangements (of actors, institutions, the role of the state, government and governance) and also in relation to language use (Kohn, 2000). Public interest is contested and local: what one group sees as an act of requisition (*confiscar*) another might see as robbery (*despojar*). An agreement (*pactar*) resulting in or a consequence of *solidaridad* (solidarity) may be *triunfo* (victory), *derrota* (defeat) or *choque* (shock – in the sense of earthquake) – each of which referred to the overthrow of the Somoza government. Given the crucial role of dialogue in the democratic process, including its potential to unify or polarize partners (Crossley and Roberts, 2004; Davies, 2007), this context suggests the issue of language use should be given more formal consideration in public interest frameworks. In established democracies, though they are pluralistic, 'public' is a more coherent and stable entity than in post-conflict developing countries such as Nicaragua.

Conclusion

Currently, property seems no longer to be as pressing a problem. Interviewees commented anecdotally that in the early to mid-1990s, property appeared in first, second or third place in surveys of public opinion. Whilst Nicola was unable to trace opinion polls as far back as that, in 2005, the population did not identify property as a major problem confronting the country (CID/Gallup, 2005). Nonetheless, Nicaraguans are still poor, indeed many are relatively poorer than in 1995. The number living on less than one US dollar a day (i.e. extreme poor) doubled from the mid-1980s to 2001, totalling 43 per cent of the population (Instituto Nacional de Estadisticas y Censos, 2001; Flores Silva, 2005). Many groups remain excluded from the economy, with income differentials between men and women, for example, at 2.2 to 1 (UNDP, 2005).

While it is difficult to establish causality between property ownership and economic well-being in the case of Nicaragua, research suggests a link between the two in other Latin American economies (de Soto, 2003). A core goal of UNDP's support was to help Nicaragua consolidate democracy and strengthen capacity for good governance (UNDP, 2006). In this regard, World Bank governance indicators suggest Nicaragua lags behind other parts of Latin America in a number of critical areas, including attitudes towards democracy, trust in politicians and views on those in power being driven by their own as opposed to national interests (drawing on Latinobarometro survey data 1996–2005, in Kaufmann, Kraay, and Mastruzzi, 2006).

What constitutes good governance is always contested, yet some of the key features of civil society that are pivotal in developed models of good governance, and that contribute to public interest are taken for granted. However, in many contexts we cannot assume a tradition of stable government, or of civil society, or a rule of law, or basic infrastructure. Examining public interest in developing countries such as Nicaragua is useful to identify such taken-for-granted assumptions, and to prompt re-examination of this fundamental and enduring concept.

12
Where Do We Go from Here?

There is an old joke that tells the story of a stranger asking for directions. I have heard it several times set in different contexts that correspond to the nations and regions of the UK. One version of it is this:

> An English tourist is driving in the Irish countryside, lost and looking for the route to Galway. He stops in the middle of a small village as he sees a local at the side of the road and asks him for directions, 'excuse me, could you tell me the best way to get to Galway please?' The villager pauses, and replies, 'ah, well, you don't really want to be starting from here'.

Like many jokes about 'outsiders' and 'insiders' this has a dark side, if it relies for humour on stereotyping: an assumed eccentricity based on place or ideolect ('ah, well'), or a set of traits assigned to a given nationality that has historically been oppressed by a colonial power. It could also be an emancipatory story if it challenges presumed power relations – perhaps these might be reinforced if the driver is in an expensive car say, or arrogant, or has a pronounced upper class accent. This story has always appealed to me because of the simple truth that wherever we want to get to, we have to start from somewhere. There is always a context for our choices and motivations, and for our ways of understanding organization, society and politics. We start any journey of ideas from a particular set of historical and social contingencies. Contemporary scholars in the social sciences are no different.

We start from a position where the most influential thinker in the history of our planet saw his species as one kind of animal, rather than as divine; and where his taxonomic zeal as a biologist shaped, or created, a variety of disciplines and practices. We start from a position

where generations of subsequent editors ignored this thinker's presumed wish that the books he actually published in his lifetime were
the ones he wanted a wider public to see. We start from a position where
this thinker's works in ethics and politics survived the collapse and rise
of empires: preserved by Arab scholars who over time reconciled them
with monotheism in a way that made them palatable to later Christians
(Rubenstein, 2003). We start from a position where this thinker's seminal work on aesthetics – the *Poetics* – was rediscovered in the first century BC having been left lying in a hole in the ground. And, we start
from a position where greater understanding of these original texts
helps us to see the continuing value of an Aristotelian perspective on
Organization, Society and Politics.

In a single text, it is very hard to give an account of Aristotle that
does justice to the breadth of his work, even if this text is to restrict
itself principally to his practical philosophy. It would be harder still, if
not impossible, to engage adequately with over two thousand years of
subsequent writing inspired by his work. What I hope to have done here
is more modest. It is to try to inspire and interest readers to see Aristotle
in something of a new light – from the introduction and application of
his work offered here, and by explicitly linking his original texts to contemporary problems in organization, society and politics. To do this, I
returned to the source of his practical philosophy and in particular the
following works: *Politics, Rhetoric, Ethics,* and *Poetics.* This return to the
root, ancient wellspring of so many of our ideas in practical philosophy
is also an attempt to radicalize and re-imagine the contemporary discipline of organization studies, connecting it to broader and older questions about society and politics.

A number of questions are addressed in this book: how do we evaluate the legacy of an administration? what is the basis for ethical decision making? how can we criticize the arguments made by power?
how do we try to teach 'wisdom'? and what is in the public interest?
To examine these, we are always starting from somewhere. In many
situations, and unthinkingly, we have no choice other than to start
with Aristotle's approach to classifying, to logic and empiricism, and
the very disciplines in which thought is structured. Perhaps, as insights
from postcolonial studies may suggest, we do not want to be starting
with such grand reifications as 'public' or 'society', but this is on some
level inescapable.

Aristotle's work has clearly lasted. One contemporary aesthetician
begins their study into a perennial problem in aesthetics, '[c]an the fictional or make-believe prompt emotions just like the ones that the real

world prompts?' and concludes that, 'Aristotle had the answer all along' (Worth, 2000: 338). Less positively, in some ways the development of post-Aristotelian thought has required a very slow process of unlearning. In *A History of Western Philosophy*, first published in 1946, Bertrand Russell suggested:

> ...since the beginning of the 17th century, almost every serious intellectual advance has had to begin with an attack on some Aristotelian doctrine; in logic, this is still true at the present day. (Russell, 1984: 173)

Russell sees Aristotle's posthumous fame and his subsequent condemnation as equally excessive but in a sense if we are still disagreeing with Aristotle's ideas centuries later, they still provide an opportunity for us to learn: a dialectic. The extended case study in this chapter, and which has brought this book to a close, revisits the notion of public interest/common good: *koinon sumpheron*, but it also identifies limitations with Aristotle, as expressed in the challenges posed by postcolonial studies.

Cicero described Aristotle's writing as being a 'flumini aurum' a river of gold (Botley, 2004: 59). The Foucauldian concept of Episteme suggests the influence of that river over many centuries has been to carve out and entrench channels for subsequent thought that are so deeply embedded in our cultural and intellectual history, that Aristotle could not but fail to remain relevant. Perhaps in an alternative universe, human culture and intellectual history could have developed in such a way that the origins of disciplines we know of as biology and politics were markedly different. Perhaps there is another earth where the most influential thinker in a civilization saw his own race not as one kind of animal, but in some way as separate, maybe as descended from Gods or born of the stars. Or, perhaps there is an alternative earth where a figure like Aristotle was a strident theist whose writings faded in or out of favour according to the tenets of rival religious regimes, rather than – strikingly – having been embraced by Greek, Latin, Christian, Islamic and Judaic thinkers.

When we consider problems relating to organization, society and politics, Aristotle's practical philosophy is valuable because we can trace an astonishing intellectual legacy back to these texts. The legacy is at times unavoidable even if we are unaware that this is how our thoughts and culture are structured, or how fundamental problems are framed. If we are lost on our way to understanding public good, ethical decision making, political argument, and wisdom, it is helpful to know what our starting position is.

References

Abbott, A. (2007). 'Notes on replication'. *Sociological Methods & Research*, 36(2): 210–19.

Abrahamson, E. and Fairchild, G. (1999). 'Management fashion: lifecycles, triggers, and collective learning processes'. *Administrative Science Quarterly*, 44(4): 708–40.

Adams, J. S. (1965). 'Injustice in social exchange', in L. Berkowitz (ed.) *Advances in Experimental Social Psychology*. Vol. 2, Academic Press: New York: 267–99.

Akbar, Z. and Venkatraman, N. (1995). 'Relational governance as an interorganizational strategy: an empirical test'. *Strategic Management Journal*, 16(5): 373–92.

Alderfer C. P. (1972). *Existence, Relatedness and Growth*. Free Press: New York.

Allen C. (2003). 'Desperately seeking fusion: on "joined-up thinking", "holistic practice" and the new economy of welfare professional power'. *British Journal of Sociology*, 54(2): 287–306.

Allmark, P. (2008). 'An Aristotelian account of autonomy'. *The Journal of Value Inquiry*, 42(1): 41–53.

Alvesson, M. and Karreman, D. (2000). 'Varieties of discourse: on the study of organizations through discourse analysis'. *Human Relations*, 53(9): 1125–49.

Alvesson, M. and Sveningsson, S. (2003). 'Good visions, bad micro-management and ugly ambiguity: contradictions of non-leadership in a knowledge-intensive organization'. *Organization Studies*, 24(6): 961–88.

Ambler, W. H. (1985). 'Aristotle's understanding of the naturalness of the city'. *Review of Politics*, 47(2): 163–85.

Amir, Y. and Sharon, I. (1991). 'Replication research: a must for the scientific advancement of psychology', in J. Neuliep (ed.) *Replication Research in the Social Sciences*. Thousand Oaks, CA: Sage: 51–69.

Annas, J. (1996). 'Aristotle on human nature and political virtue'. *Review of Metaphysics*, 49(4): 731–53.

Any, C. (1990). 'Boris Eikhenbaum in OPOIAZ: testing the limits of the work-centered poetics'. *Slavic Studies*, 49(3): 409–26.

Argyle, N. J. (2002). 'Developing a foundation: administration in the polis'. *Public Administration Quarterly*, 26(3): 346–72.

Aristotle. *Nicomachean Ethics*. (Translated by D. Ross), Hazell Books: Aylesbury, 1980.

Aristotle. *Poetics*. (Translated by S. Butcher), Dover Publications Inc: New York, 1997.

Aristotle. *Politics*. (Translated by E. Barker, R. F. Stalley ed.), Oxford University Press: Oxford, 2009.

Aristotle. *Rhetoric* (Translated by W. Rhys-Roberts) available on http://www.public.iastate.edu/~honeyl/Rhetoric/ retrieved 7 July 2009.

Aristotle. *The Complete Works of Aristotle*. The revised Oxford translation, 6th printing with corrections, J. Barnes (ed.). Princeton University Press: Princeton, New Jersey, 1995.

Arjoon, S. (2008). 'Reconciling situational social psychology with virtue ethics'. *International Journal of Management Reviews*, 10(3): 221–43.

Arnhart, L. (1983). 'Statesmanship as magnanimity: classical, christian & modern author(s)'. *Polity*, 16(2): 263–83.

Arnhart, L. (1994). 'The Darwinian biology of Aristotle's political animals'. *American Journal of Political Science*, 38(2): 464–85.

Arnhart, L. (1995). 'The new Darwinian naturalism in political theory'. *The American Political Science Review*, 89(2): 389–400.

Arnold, D. G., Audi, R. and Zwolinski, M. (2010). 'Recent work in ethical theory and its implications for business ethics'. *Business Ethics Quarterly*, 20(4): 559–81.

Arnson, C. J. (ed.) (1999). *Comparative Peace Processes in Latin America*. Stanford University Press: New York.

Aronoff, M. and Rees-Miller, J. (eds) (2001). *The Handbook Of Linguistics*. Blackwell: Oxford.

Arrow, K. J. (1997). 'Invaluable goods'. *Journal of Economic Literature*, 35(2): 757–65.

Asia News (2010). 'Suicide among young Chinese workers' available on http://www.asianews.it/news-en/Suicide-among-young-Chinese-workers-18305.html last accessed 29 August 2011.

Astley, W. G. and Zammuto, R. (1992). 'Organization science, managers, and language games'. *Organization Science*, 3(4): 443–60.

Atkinson, J. M. (1984). *Our Masters' Voices: The Language and Body Language of Politics*. Methuen: London.

Atkinson, J. M. (1985). 'Refusing invited applause: preliminary observations from a case study of charismatic oratory', in T. A. van Dijk (ed.) *Handbook of Discourse Analysis*. Vol. 3, Academic Press: London: 161–81.

Auchter, C. W. (1996). 'The democratic problematic in central America and the surprising case of Nicaragua', *Butler University Discussion Paper no. 89*.

Austin, J. (2003). 'Editorial'. *Journal of Organizational Behavior Management*, 22(3): 1–2.

Awamleh, R. and Gardner, W. L. (1999). 'Perceptions of leader charisma and effectiveness: the effects of vision content, delivery, and organizational performance'. *Leadership Quarterly*, 10: 345–73.

Ayers, M. R. (1981). 'Locke versus Aristotle on natural kinds'. *Journal of Philosophy*, 78(5): 247–72.

Bache, I. (2003). 'Governing through governance: education policy control under new labour'. *Political Studies*, 51(2): 300–14.

Ball, T. (2004). 'History and the interpretation of texts', in G. F. Gaus and C. Kukathas (eds) *Handbook of Political Theory*. Sage: London: 18–30.

Ballas, A. A. and Tsoukas, H. (2004). 'Measuring nothing: the case of the greek national health system'. *Human Relations*, 57(6): 661–90.

Bandura, A. (1977). *Social Learning Theory*. Prentice Hall: New Jersey.

Barabashev, A. and Straussman, J. D. (2007). 'Public service reform in Russia, 1991–2006'. *Public Administration Review*, 67(3): 373–82.

Barnes, J. (1995). *The Cambridge Companion to Aristotle*. Cambridge University Press: Cambridge.

Barry, D. and Elmes, M. (1997). 'Strategy retold: toward a narrative view of strategic discourse'. *Academy of Management Review*, 22(2): 429–52.

Bartel, C. A. and Garud, R. (2009). 'The role of narratives in sustaining organizational innovation'. *Organization Science*, 20(1): 107–17.

Bartky, E. (1992). 'Plato and the politics of Aristotle's "poetics"'. *The Review of Politics*, 54(4): 589–619.

Bartky, E. (2002). 'Aristotle and the politics of Herodotus's "history"'. *The Review of Politics*, 64(3): 445–68.

Bartlett, R. C. (1994a). 'The "realism" of classical political science'. *American Journal of Political Science*, 38(2): 381–402.

Bartlett, R. C. (1994b). 'Aristotle's science of the best regime'. *The American Political Science Review*, 88(1): 143–55.

Bartlett, R. C. (2008). 'Aristotle's introduction to the problem of happiness: on book I of the *Nicomachean Ethics*'. *American Journal of Political Science*. 52(3): 677–87.

Battleship Potemkin (Bronenosets Potemkin) (1925). Directed by Sergei Eisenstein. Available via Delta Expedition USA (2004).

Bauer, J. J., McAdams, D. P. and Pals, J. L. (2008). 'Narrative identity and eudaimonic well-being'. *Journal of Happiness Studies*, 9(1): 81–104.

Beach, L. R. (1990). *Image Theory: Decision Making in Personal and Organisational Contexts*. Wiley: Chichester.

Beach, L. R. (ed.) (1998). *Image Theory: Theoretical and Empirical Foundations*. Wiley: Chichester.

Beach, L. R. and Mitchell T. R. (1998). 'The Basics of image theory', in L. R. Beach (ed.) *Image Theory: Theoretical and Empirical Foundations*. Wiley: Chichester: 3–18.

Beach, L. R. and Strom, E. (1989). 'A toadstool among the mushrooms: screening decisions and image theory's compatibility test'. *Acta Psychologica*, 72(1): 1–12.

Belfiore, E. S. (1992). *Tragic Pleasures: Aristotle on Plot and Emotion*. Princeton University Press: Princeton.

Bell, E. (2008). *Reading Management and Organization in Film*. Palgrave: London.

Benjamin, O. and Goclaw, R. (2005). 'Narrating the power of non-standard employment: the case of the Israeli public sector'. *Journal of Management Studies*, 42(4): 737–59.

Bentham, J. (1781/2006). *An Introduction to the Principles of Morals and Legislation*. Full text available on www.utilitarianism.com accessed 25 September 2006.

Benz, M. and Frey, B. (2007). 'Corporate governance: what can we learn from public governance?'. *Academy of Management Review*, 32(1): 92–104.

Bergman, J. Z., Westerman, J. W. and Daly, J. P. (2010). 'Narcissism in management education'. *Academy of Management Learning & Education*, 9(1): 119–31.

Berkman, M. B. and Plutzer, E. (2005). *Ten Thousand Democracies: Politics and Public Opinion in America's School Districts*. Georgetown University Press: Washington.

Betz, J. (1998). 'Business ethics and politics'. *Business Ethics Quarterly*, 8(4): 693–702.

Bevir, M. (2003). 'Narrating the British state: an interpretive critique of New Labour's institutionalism'. *Review of International Political Economy*, 10(3): 455–80.

Bevir, M., Rhodes, R. A. W. and Weller, P. (2003). 'Traditions of governance: interpreting the changing role of the public sector'. *Public Administration*, 81(1): 1–17.

Bhuyan, N. (2007). 'The role of character in ethical decision-making'. *The Journal of Value Inquiry*, 41: 45–57.

Billig, M. (1987). *Arguing and Thinking: A Rhetorical Approach to Social Psychology*. Cambridge University Press: Cambridge.

Billy Elliot (2000). Directed by Stephen Daldry. Available via Universal Studios Home Video USA.

Biondi, C. (2010). 'Lenn E. Goodman and Robert B. Talisse, eds., *Aristotle's politics today*' (Albany, NY: State University of New York Press, 2007). *Journal of Value Inquiry*, 44: 93–8.

Blackmore, S. (1996). 'Memes, Minds and Selves'. Lecture given at the London School of Economics, Thursday 28 November 1996, in the series 'About Biology' available on http://www.susanblackmore.co.uk/memetics/LSE%20 lecture%201996.htm#_edn17 last accessed 12 August 2011.

Blackmore, S. (1999). *The Meme Machine*. Oxford University Press: Oxford.

Blair, T. (1999). Speech to the Labour Party Conference. Available in full on http://news.bbc.co.uk/1/hi/uk_politics/460009.stm last accessed 6 December 2011.

Bligh, M. C., Kohles, J. C. and Meindl, J. R. (2004). 'Charisma under crisis: Presidential leadership, rhetoric, and media responses before and after the September 11th terrorist attacks'. *Leadership Quarterly*, 15(2): 211–39.

Boatright, J. R. (1995). 'Aristotle meets Wall Street: the case for virtue ethics in business'. *Business Ethics Quarterly*, 5(2): 353–9.

Bobonich, C. (2006). 'Aristotle's ethical treatises', in R. Kraut (ed.) *The Blackwell Guide to Aristotle's Nicomachean Ethics*. Oxford: Blackwell: 12–36.

Bocatto, E. and de Toledo, E. P. (2008). 'A democratic story: collaboration in the use of public budget'. *International Journal of Sociology and Social Policy*, 28(1/2): 20–31.

Boje, D. M. (1991). 'The storytelling organization: a study of story performance'. *Administrative Science Quarterly*, 36(1): 106–26.

Booth, W. J. (1994). 'On the idea of the moral economy'. *The American Political Science Review*, 88(3): 653–67.

Booth, J. E., Budd, J. W., Munday, K. M. (2010). 'Never say never? uncovering the never-unionized in the United States'. *British Journal of Industrial Relations*, 48(1): 26–52.

Botley, P. (2004). *Latin Translation in the Renaissance: The Theory and Practice of Leonardo Bruni, Giannozzo Manetti, and Desiderius Erasmus*. Cambridge University Press: Cambridge.

Bourdieu, P. (1993). *The Field of Cultural Production*. Polity Press: Cambridge.

Bozeman, B. (2002). 'Public value failure and market failure'. *Public Administration Review*, 62(2): 145–61.

Bozeman, B. (2007). *Public Values and Public Interest: Counterbalancing Economic Individualism*. Georgetown University Press: Washington.

Bradley, H., Erickson, M., Stephenson, C. and Williams, S. (2000). *Myths at Work*. Polity Press: London.

Bragues, G. (2006). 'Seek the good life, not money: The Aristotelian approach to business ethics'. *Journal of Business Ethics*, 67(4): 341–57.

Bratton, J., Callinan, M., Forshaw, C. and Sawchuk, P. (2007). *Work and Organizational Behaviour*. Palgrave: London.

Brewer, T. (2005). 'Virtues we can share: friendship and Aristotelian ethical theory'. *Ethics*, 115(4): 721–58.

Brinkerhoff, D. W. and Brinkerhoff, J. M. (2002). 'Governance reforms and failed states: challenges and implications'. *International Review Of Administrative Sciences*, 68(4): 511–31.

Brooks, A. C. (2003). 'Public goods and posterity: an empirical test of intergenerational altruism'. *Journal of Public Administration Research and Theory*, 13(2): 165–75.

Camerer, C. and Knez, M. (1997). 'Co-ordination in organisations: A game-theoretic perspective', in Z. Shapira (ed.) *Organisational Decision Making*. Cambridge University Press: Cambridge: 158–90.

Campbell, J., Hollingsworth, R. and Lindberg, L. (1991). *Governance of the American Economy*. Cambridge University Press: Cambridge.

Cannadine, D. (ed.) (1990). *Blood, Toil, Tears and Sweat: Winston Churchill's Famous Speeches*. Cassell Publishers Limited: London.

Carcello, J. V. (2009). 'Governance and the common good'. *Journal of Business Ethics*, 89(1): 11–18.

Cardoso, E. and Helwege, A. (1992). *Latin America's Economy: Diversity, Trends, and Conflicts*. MIT Press: Cambridge, Massachusetts.

Carter Center (1995). *Nicaraguan Property Disputes*. Available on http://www.cartercenter.org/news/publications/peace/americas_reports.html last accessed 18 September 2009.

Cartledge, P. (2009). *Ancient Greece: A History in Eleven Cities*. Oxford University Press: Oxford.

Chakrabortty, A. (2011): 'More modern and more open, but the posh are back in charge: Meritocracy is their mantra – though it's an elite version'. *The Guardian*, Tuesday 1 February 2011, (the figure for ex-Eton ministers was amended in the Guardian's Corrections and clarifications column, 3 February 2011) available on http://www.guardian.co.uk/commentisfree/2011/feb/01/posh-back-in-charge.

Charles, D. (2005). 'Aristotle', in T. Honderich (ed.) *The Oxford Companion to Philosophy*. Oxford University Press: Oxford: 54–8.

Chaudhuri, A., Graziano, S. and Maitra, P. (2006). 'Social learning and norms in a public goods experiment with inter-generational advice'. *The Review of Economic Studies*, 73(2): 357–80.

Chell, E. (2004). 'Critical incident technique', in C. Cassell and G. Symon (eds), *Essential Guide to Qualitative Methods in Organisational Research*. Sage: Thousand Oaks, CA: 45–60.

Chia, R. and Holt, R. (2008). 'The nature of knowledge in business schools'. *Academy of Management Learning & Education*, 7(4): 471–86.

Chreim, S. (2005). 'The continuity change duality in narrative texts of organizational identity'. *Journal of Management Studies*, 42(3): 567–93.

Christensen, R. K. and Wise, C. R. (2009). 'The "efficient" public administrator: Pareto and a well-rounded approach to public administration'. *Public Administration Review*, 69(5): 920–31.

Church Urban Fund (2011). Interview with the Archbishop of Canterbury, July 2009, available on http://www.cuf.org.uk/about last accessed 21 August 2011.

Churchill, W. S. (1939). *Step by Step: 1936–1939*. Thornton Butterworth: London.

Churchill, W. S. (1941). 'Blood, toil, tears and sweat' speech to parliament, full text available online at the Churchill Centre, http://www.winstonchurchill. org last accessed on 14 November 2011.

CID/Gallup (2005). *Encuesta de Opinion Publica en Nicaragua*. Consultoria Interdisplinaria en Desarrollo: Managua, Nicaragua.

Clark, C. M. A. (2010). 'Practical wisdom and understanding the economy'. *Journal of Management Development*, 29(7/8): 678–85.

Clayman, S. E. (1993). 'Booing: The anatomy of a disaffiliative response'. *American Sociological Review*, 58(1): 110–30.

Clayman, S. E. (1995). 'Defining moments, presidential debates and the dynamics of quotability'. *Journal of Communication*, 45(3): 118–32.

Clayton, E. W. (2004). 'The audience for Aristotle's Rhetoric'. *Rhetorica*, XXII(2): 183–203.

Clegg, S. (1989a). *Frameworks of Power*. Sage: London.

Clegg, S. (1989b). 'Radical revisions: power, discipline and organizations'. *Organization Studies*, 10(1): 97–115.

Clegg, S. (2003). 'Strange fruit hanging from the knowledge tree: or, carrying on carping1,2,3'. *Management Learning*, 34(3): 375–78.

Clegg, S. (2010). 'The state, power, and agency: missing in action in institutional theory?'. *Journal of Management Inquiry*, 19(4): 4–13.

Collins, D. (1987). 'Aristotle and business'. *Journal of Business Ethics*, 6(7): 567–72.

Collins, S. D. (2006). *Aristotle and the Rediscovery of Citizenship*. Cambridge University Press: New York.

Collinson, D. (2005). 'Dialectics of leadership'. *Human Relations*, 58(11): 1419–42.

Comte, A. (1853). *The Positive Philosophy of Auguste Comte*. Chapman: London.

Confucius (5th Century BCE). *The Analects*. (Translated by A. Waley). Wordsworth Classics: London, 1996.

Conger, J. A. (1991). 'Inspiring others: the language of leadership'. *Academy of Management Executive*, 5(1): 31–45.

Connolly, T. and Beach, L. R. (1998). 'The theory of image theory: an examination of the central conceptual structure', in L. Beach (ed.) *Image Theory: Theoretical and Empirical Foundations*. Wiley: Chichester: 249–60.

Connolly, T. and Koput, K. (1997). 'Naturalistic decision making and the new organisational context', in Z. Shapira (ed.), *Organisational Decision Making*. Cambridge University Press: Cambridge: 285–303.

Conservative Party (2010). *Invitation to Join the Government of Britain: The Conservative Manifesto*. Pureprint Group: East Sussex.

Cooke, B. (2003). 'The denial of slavery in management studies'. *Journal of Management Studies*, 40(8): 1889–913.

Cooke, B. (2008). 'If critical management studies is your problem ...'. *Organization*, 15(6): 912–14.

Coomber, S. (2007). 'Creating public value – strategic management in government'. *In View*, 15 October, http://www.executive.modern.nhs.uk/inview/ issue.aspx?id=33 last accessed on 10 March 2008.

Cooper, R. (1990). 'Organization/disorganization', in J. Hassard and D. Pym (eds), *The Theory and Philosophy of Organization*. Routledge: London: 167–97.

Cooper, C. and Taylor, P. (2005). 'Independently verified reductionism: prison privatization in Scotland'. *Human Relations*, 58(4): 497–522.

Copp, D. and Sobel, D. (2004). 'Morality and virtue: an assessment of some recent work in virtue ethics'. *Ethics*, 114(3): 514–54.

Corrigan, T. J. (2007). *A Short Guide to Writing about Film*. Pearson: London.

Crabtree, J. (2004). 'The revolution that started in a library'. *New Statesman*, September, available on http://www.newstatesman.com/200409270026 last accessed on 10 March 2008.

Crocker, D. A. (1992). 'Functioning and capability: the foundations of Sen's and Nussbaum's development ethic'. *Political Theory*, 20(4): 584–612.

Crossley, N. and Roberts, J. M. (eds) (2004). *After Habermas: New Perspectives on the Public Sphere*. 1st edition. Blackwell: Malden MA.

Crouch, C. (2006). *Capitalist Diversity and Change: Recombinant Governance and Institutional Entrepreneur*. Oxford University Press: Oxford.

Curran, A. (2001). 'Brecht's criticisms of Aristotle's aesthetics of tragedy'. *The Journal of Aesthetics and Art Criticism*, 59(2): 167–84.

Dadlez, E. M. (2005). 'Spectacularly bad: Hume and Aristotle on tragic spectacle'. *The Journal of Aesthetics and Art Criticism*, 63(4): 351–8.

Daily, C. M., Dalton, D. R. and Cannella, A. A. (2003). 'Introduction to special topic forum corporate governance: decades of dialogue and data'. *Academy of Management Review*, 28(3), 371–82.

Daly, M. (2003). 'Governance and social policy'. *Journal of Social Policy*, 32(1): 113–28.

Dawkins, R. (1976). *The Selfish Gene*. Oxford University Press: Oxford. (Revised edition 1989).

Davies, J. S. (2007). 'The limits of partnership: an exit-action strategy for local democratic inclusion'. *Political Studies*, 55(4): 779–800.

Davis, E. (2005a). *Memories of State: Politics, History, and Collective Identity in Modern Iraq*. University of California Press: Berkeley and Los Angeles.

Davis, F. (2005b). 'No more tax and spend'. *The Tablet*, January, available on http://www.youngfoundation.org/node/265 last accessed on 10 March 2008.

Davis, M. (1999). 'Aphorisms and clichés: the generation and dissipation of conceptual charisma'. *Annual Review of Sociology*, 25: 245–69.

De Haas, F. A. J. (2001). 'Did Plotinus and Porphyry disagree on Aristotle's "Categories"?'. *Phronesis*, 46(4): 492–526.

de Soto, H. (2003). *The Mystery of Capital: Why Capitalism Triumphs in the West and Fails Everywhere Else*. Basic Books: New York.

Deakin, S. and Konzelmann, S. J. (2003). 'After Enron: an age of enlightenment?' *Organization*, 10(3): 583–87.

Dehler, G. (2009). 'Prospects and possibilities of critical management education: critical beings and a pedagogy of critical action'. *Management Learning*, 40(1): 31–49.

Del Caro, A. (2004). 'Nietzsche's Rhetoric on the grounds of philology and hermeneutics'. *Philosophy and Rhetoric*, 37(2): 101–22.

Delbridge, R. and Ezzamel, M. (2005). 'The strength of difference: contemporary conceptions of control'. *Organization*, 12(5): 603–18.

Deleuze, G. (2003). *Desert Islands and Other Texts (1953 – 1974)*. Translated by M. Taormina. Semiotext(e): New York.

Deleuze, G. (2004). *The Logic of Sense*. Translated by M. Lester and C. Stivale. Continuum: London.

Den Hartog, D. N. and Verburg, R. M. (1997). 'Charisma and Rhetoric: the communicative techniques of international business leaders'. *Leadership Quarterly*, 8(4): 355–91.

Denhardt, J. V. and Denhardt, R. B. (2007). *The New Public Service: Serving, Not Steering*. M. E. Sharpe: New York.

Derrida, J. (2009). *The Beast & The Sovereign*. University of Chicago Press: Chicago.

Deslauriers, M. (2006). 'The argument of Aristotle's "Politics"'. *Phoenix*, 60(1/2): 48–69.

DH (2004). 'Choosing health: making healthier choices easier'. HMSO: London.

Dierksmeier, C. and Pirson, M. (2009). 'Oikonomia versus Chrematistike: learning from Aristotle about the future orientation of business management'. *Journal of Business Ethics*, 88(3): 417–30.

Dillman, D. L. (2008). 'Whither the common good?'. *Public Administration Review*, 68(1): 184–87.

Dobbs, D. (1994). 'Natural right and the problem of Aristotle's defense of slavery'. *The Journal Of Politics*, 56(1): 69–94.

Dobbs, D. (1996). 'Family matters: Aristotle's appreciation of women and the plural structure of society'. *The American Political Science Review*, 90(1): 74.

Dobson, J. (2009). 'Alasdair Macintyre's Aristotelian business ethics: a critique'. *Journal of Business Ethics*, 86(1): 43–50.

Donaldson, L. (2005). 'For positive management theories while retaining science: reply to ghoshal'. *Academy of Management Learning and Education*, 4(1): 109–13.

Dorrien, G. (ed.) (2008). *Social Ethics in the Making: Interpreting an American Tradition*. Wiley-Blackwell, New York.

Dryzek, J. S. (2010). 'Rhetoric in democracy: a systemic appreciation'. *Political Theory*, 38(3): 319–39.

Du Gay, P. (2000). *In Praise of Bureacracy – Weber, Organization, Ethics*. Sage: London.

Dunegan, K. J. (1995). 'Image theory: Testing the role of image compatibility in progress decisions'. *Organizational Behavior and Human Decision Processes*, 62(1): 79–86.

Duska, R. F. (1993). 'Aristotle: a pre-modern post-modern? implications for business ethics'. *Business Ethics Quarterly*, 3(3): 227–49.

Dyck, E. (2002). 'Topos and Enthymeme'. *Rhetorica*, 20(2): 105–17.

Eden, D. (2002). 'Replication, meta-analysis, scientific progress and *AMJ*s publication policy'. *Academy of Management Journal*, 45(5): 841–6.

Edwards, P., Collinson, D. and Della Rocca, D. (1995). 'Workplace resistance in western Europe: a preliminary overview and a research agenda'. *European Journal of Industrial Relations*, 1(3): 283–316.

Eikeland, O. (2008). *The Ways of Aristotle. Aristotelian Phrónêsis, Aristotelian Philosophy of Dialogue, and Action Research*. Peter Lang: Bern.

Emirbayer, M. and Mische, A. (1998). 'What is agency?' *American Journal of Sociology*, 103(4): 962–1023.

Erlich, V. (1980). *Russian Formalism: History – Doctrine*. 4th edition. Mouton: New York.

Espeland, W. N. and Stevens, M. L. (1998). 'Commensuration as a social process'. *Annual Review of Sociology*, 24: 313–43.

Eton College (2011) Fees information available on http://www.etoncollege.com/ currentfees.aspx last accessed 29 August 2011.

Everingham, M. (2001). 'Agricultural property rights and political change in Nicaragua'. *Latin American Politics and Society*, 43(3): 61–93.

Ezzamel, M. (2001). 'A difficult act to balance: political costs and economic costs in the public sector'. *Accounting, Accountability and Performance*, 7(1): 31–49.

Ezzamel, M. and Burns, J. (2005). 'Professional competition, economic value added and management control strategies'. *Organization Studies*, 26(5): 755–77.

Fairclough, N. (1995). *Critical Discourse Analysis*. Longman: London.

Fairclough, N. (2000). *New Labour, New Language?* Routledge: London.

Feeney, M. K. and Bozeman, B. (2009). 'Stakeholder red tape: comparing perceptions of public managers and their private consultants'. *Public Administration Review* 69(4): 710–26.

Ferrari, G. R. F. (1999). 'Aristotle's literary aesthetics'. *Phronesis*, 44(3) : 181–98.

Ferraro, F., Pfeffer, J. and Sutton, R. I. (2005). 'Economics language and assumptions: how theories can become self-fulfilling'. *Academy of Management Review*, 30(1): 8–24.

Ferraro, F., Pfeffer, J. and Sutton, R. I. (2009). 'How and why theories matter: a comment on Felin and Foss (2009)'. *Organization Science*, 20(3): 669–75.

Firebaugh, G. (2007). 'Replication data sets and favored-hypothesis bias: comment on Freese (2007) and King (2007)'. *Sociological Methods & Research*, 36(2): 200–10.

Fives, A. J. (2008). 'Human flourishing: the grounds of moral judgment'. *The Journal of Value Inquiry*, 42(2): 167–85.

Fleming, P. and Sewell, G. (2002). 'Looking for the good soldier, Svejk: alternative modalities of resistance in the contemporary workplace'. *Sociology* 36(4): 857–73.

Fleming, P. and Spicer, A. (2003). 'Working at a cynical distance: implications for power, subjectivity and resistance'. *Organization*, 10(1): 157–79.

Flores Silva, M. (2005). *Proyecto de Analisis Politico y Escenarios Prospectivos: Los escenarios posibles y la evolucion probable de las ciudadanías*. Informe de Avance: Managua.

Flynn, G. (2008). 'The virtuous manager: a vision for leadership in business'. *Journal of Business Ethics*, 78(3): 359–72.

Flyvbjerg, B. (2001). *Making Social Science Matter*. Cambridge University Press: Cambridge

Forster, E. M. (2010). *Howards End*. Hodder and Stoughton: London.

Foucault, M. (1991). *Discipline and Punish: The Birth of the Prison*. Translated by A. Sheridan. Penguin: New York.

Foucault, M. (2002). *The Archaeology of Knowledge*. Translated by A. Sheridan Smith. Routledge: London.

Foucault, M. and Gordon, C. (1980). *Power/knowledge: Selected Interviews and Other Writings, 1972–1977*. Pantheon: New York.

Fortenbaugh, W. W. (2005). 'Cicero as a reporter of Aristotelian and Theophrastean rhetorical doctrine'. *Rhetorica*, 23(1): 37–64.

Frank, J. (2004). 'Citizens, slaves, and foreigners: Aristotle on human nature'. *The American Political Science Review*, 98(1): 91–104.

Francis, A. (2010). 'From higher aims to hired hands: the social transformation of American business schools and the unfulfilled promise of management as a profession' review by Rakesh Khurana. *British Journal of Industrial Relations*, 48(1): 211–14.

Frank, J. (2004). 'Citizens, slaves, and foreigners: Aristotle on human nature'. *The American Political Science Review*, 98(1): 91–104.

Frank, R. H. (1988). *Passions within Reason: The Strategic Role of the Emotions*. Norton: New York.

Friedman, M. (1970). 'The social responsibility of business is to increase its profits'. *The New York Magazine*, 13 September 1993 in G. Chryssides and J. Kaler (eds), 249–254.

Fritz, K. von and Kapp, E. (1974). *Aristotle's Constitution of Athens*. Hafner: New York.

Frederickson, H. G. (1990). 'Public administration and social equity'. *Public Administration Review*, 50(2): 228–37.

Frederickson, H. G. (1991). 'Toward a theory of the public for public administration'. *Administration and Society*, 22(4): 395–417.

Frederickson, H. G. (1994). 'Can public officials correctly be said to have obligation to future generations?' *Public Administration Review*, 54(5): 457–64.

Frederickson, H. G. and Hart, David K. (1985). 'The public service and the patriotism of benevolence'. *Public Administration Review*, 45 (5): 547–53.

Frege, C. M. (1996). 'Union membership in post-socialist East Germany: who participates in collective action?'. *British Journal of Industrial Relations*, 34(3): 387–413.

French, J. R. P. and Raven, B. (1959). 'The bases of social power', in D. Cartwright (ed.) *Studies in Social Power*. University of Michigan Press: Ann Arbor, Michigan: 150–67.

Gabriel, Y. (1999). 'Beyond happy families: a critical re-evaluation of the control–resistance–identity triangle'. *Human Relations*, 52(2): 179–203.

Gabriel, Y. (2005). 'MBA and the education of leaders: the new playing fields of Eton?' *Leadership*, 1(2): 147–63.

Gallagher, P. (2009). 'The grounding of forgiveness: Martha Nussbaum on compassion and mercy'. *American Journal of Economics and Sociology*, 68(1): 231–52.

Gándara, L. (2004). '"They that sow the wind..."': proverbs and sayings in argumentation', *Discourse and Society*, 15(2–3): 345–59.

Garland, H. (1990). 'Throwing good money after bad: the effect of sunk costs on the decision to escalate commitment to an ongoing project'. *Journal of Applied Psychology*, 75(6): 728–31.

Gaskill, D. (2002). 'Raiders of the lost art: a review of two explorations into pre-Aristotelian techne'. *Technical Communication Quarterly*, 11(2): 207–09.

Gaudin, J. (1998). 'Modern governance, yesterday and today: some clarifications to be gained from French government policies'. *International Social Science Journal*, 50(1): 47–56.

Gaus, G. F. and Kukathas, C. (eds) (2004). *Handbook of Political Theory*. Sage: London.

Genette, G. (1982). 'Frontiers of narrative', in A. Sheridan (trans.) *Figures of Literary Discourse*, Introduced by Marie-Rose Logan. Columbia University Press: New York: 127–144.

Ghoshal, S. (2005). 'Bad management theories are destroying good management practices'. *Academy of Management Learning and Education*, 4(1): 75–91.

Gibbons, M., Limoges, C., Nowotny, H., Schwartsman, S., Scott, P. and Trow, M. (1994). *The New Production of Knowledge*. Sage: London.

Gibran, K. (1923). *The Prophet*. Wordsworth Classics: London, 1996.

Giddens, A. (1984). *The Constitution of Society*. Polity Press: Cambridge.

Gioia, D. A. (1986). 'Symbols, scripts and sensemaking: creating meaning in the organizational experience', in H. Sims and D. A. Gioia (eds) *The Thinking Organization*. Jossey Bass: San Francisco: 49–74.

Gioia, D. A. and Poole, P. P. (1984). 'Scripts in organizational behavior'. *Academy of Management Review*, 9(3): 449–59.

Goffman, E. (1969). *The Presentation of Self in Everyday Life*. Penguin: London.

Goldstein, L. F. (2001). 'Aristotle's theory of revolution: looking at the lockean side'.
Political Research Quarterly, 54(2): 311–31.

Goodman, L. E. and Talisse, R. B. (eds) (2007). *Aristotle's Politics Today*. State University of New York Press: Albany, New York.

Graafland, J. J. (2010). 'Do markets crowd out virtues? an Aristotelian framework'. *Journal of Business Ethics*, 91(1): 1–19.

Gracián, B. (1637). *The Art of Worldly Wisdom*. Translated by C. Maurer. Mandarin: London, 1994.

Graff, R. (2001). 'Reading and the "written style" in Aristotle's "Rhetoric"'. *Rhetoric Society Quarterly*, 31(4): 19–44.

Gramsci, A. (1971). *Selections from the Prison Notebooks*. International Publishers: New York.

Grandy, C. (2009). 'The "efficient" public administrator: Pareto and a well-rounded approach to public administration'. *Public Administration Review*, 69(6): 1115–23.

Greatbatch, D. and Clark, T. (2003). 'Displaying group cohesiveness: humour and laughter in the public lectures of management gurus'. *Human Relations*, 56(12): 1515–44.

Green, S. E. (2004). 'A rhetorical theory of diffusion'. *Academy of Management Review*, 29(4): 653–69.

Greenberg, J. (2011). *Behavior in Organization*. Pearson: London.

Greenfeld, L. (1987). 'Russian formalist sociology of literature: A sociologist's perspective'. *Slavic Studies*, 46(1): 35–58.

Greenfield, S. (2001). *The Private Life of the Brain*. Penguin: London.

Gremler, D. D. (2004). 'The critical incident technique in service research'. *Journal of Service Research*, 7(1): 65–89.

Grey, C. (2005). *A Very Short, Fairly Interesting and Reasonably Cheap Book about Studying Organizations*. Sage: London.

Grindle, M. S. (2000). *Audacious Reforms: Institutional Invention and Democracy in Latin America*. The Johns Hopkins University Press: Baltimore, MD.

Grindle, M. S. (2007). *Going Local: Decentralization, Democratization and the Promise of Good Governance*. Princeton University Press: Princeton.

Grint, K. (2000). *The Arts of Leadership*. Oxford University Press: Oxford.

Grint, K. (2005). 'Problems, problems, problems: the social construction of "leadership"'. *Human Relations*, 58(11): 1467–94.

Grint, K. (2007). 'Learning to lead: can Aristotle help us find the road to wisdom?' *Leadership*, 3(2): 231–46.

Gross, A. G. and Dascal, M. (2001). 'the conceptual unity of Aristotle's Rhetoric'. *Philosophy and Rhetoric*, 34(4): 275–91.

Gunder, M. (2010). 'Making planning theory matter: a Lacanian encounter with Phronesis'. *International Planning Studies*, 15(1): 37–51.

Hadreas, P. (2002). 'Aristotle on the vices and virtue of wealth'. *Journal of Business Ethics*, 39(4): 361–76.

Halliwell, S. (1986). *Aristotle's Poetics*. Chicago University Press: Chicago.

Halverson, R. (2004). 'Accessing, documenting, and communicating practical wisdom: the Phronesis of school leadership practice'. *American Journal of Education*, 111(1): 90–121.

Hamilton, P. M. and Redman, T. (2003). 'The rhetoric of modernization and the labour government's pay agenda'. *Public Money and Management*, 23(4): 223–8.

Harrison, S. and Wood, B. (1999). 'Designing health service organization in the UK, 1968 to 1998: from blueprint to bright idea and "manipulated emergence"'. *Public Administration*, 77(4): 751–68.

Hartman, E. M. (1994). 'The commons and the moral organization'. *Business Ethics Quarterly*, 4(3): 253–69.

Hartman, E. M. (2008). 'Reconciliation in business ethics: some advice from Aristotle'. *Business Ethics Quarterly*, 18(2): 253–65.

Haskins, E. V. (2000). '"Mimesis" between Poetics and Rhetoric: performance culture and civic education in Plato, Isocrates, and Aristotle'. *Rhetoric Society Quarterly*, 30(3): 7–33.

Haskins, E. V. (2004). 'Endoxa, epistemological optimism, and Aristotle's Rhetorical project'. *Philosophy and Rhetoric*, 37(1): 1–20.

Hassard, J. and Kelemen, M. (2002). 'Production and consumption in organizational knowledge'. *Organization*, 9(2): 331–55.

Haugaard, M. and Clegg, S. (2009). 'Introduction: why power is the central concept of the social sciences', in S. Clegg and M. Haugaard (eds) *The Sage Handbook of Power*. Sage: London: 1–25.

Heath, M. (2008). 'Aristotle on natural slavery'. *Phronesis*, 53(3): 243–70.

Hechter, M. and Kanazawa, S. (1997). 'Sociological rational choice theory'. *Annual Review of Sociology*, 23: 191–214.

Heery, E. and Frege, C. (2006). 'New actors in industrial relations'. *British Journal of Industrial Relations*, 44(4): 601–4.

Hendrick, C. (1991). 'Replications, strict replications, and conceptual replications: are they important?', in J. W. Neuliep (ed.) *Replication Research in the Social Sciences*. Sage: Thousand Oaks, CA: 41–9.

Hendrix, S. (1996/1997). 'Pride of ownership: land tenure and conflict resolution'. *Harvard International Review*, 19(1): 40–3.

Herzberg, F. (1966). *Work and the Nature of Man*. World Publishing Company: Chicago.

HMSO (2003). *Health and Social Care Community Health and Standards Act 2003: Explanatory Notes*. HMSO: London.

Hobbes, T. (1771/1973). *Leviathan*. Dent and Sons: London.

Hogget, P. (2006). 'Conflict, ambivalence and the contested purpose of public organizations'. *Human Relations*, 59(2): 175–94.

Hollenbach, D. S. J. (2002). *The Common Good and Christian Ethics*. Cambridge University Press: New York.

Hollingsworth, J. R. and Boyer, R. (eds) (1997). *Contemporary Capitalism: The Embeddedness of Institution*. Cambridge University Press: Cambridge.

Hollingsworth, J. R., Schmitter, P., Streeck, W. (eds) (1994). *Governing Capitalist Economies: Performance and Control of Economic Sectors*. Oxford University Press: Oxford.

Hogarth, R. M. and Reder, M. W. (eds) (1986). *Rational Choice*. University of Chicago Press: London.

Holt, R. (2006). 'Principals and practice: Rhetoric and the moral character of managers'. *Human Relations*, 59(12): 1659–80.

Hood, C. (1991). 'A public management for all seasons'. *Public Administration*, 69(1): 3–19.

Hosking, G. (1992). *A History of the Soviet Union 1917–1991*. Fontana Press: London.

Howland, J. (2002). 'Aristotle's great-souled man'. *The Review of Politics*, 64(1): 27–56.

Huisman, M. (2001). 'Decision-making in meetings as talk-in-interaction'. *International Studies in Management and Organization*, 31(3): 69–90.

Huczynski, A. and Buchanan, D. A. (2007). *Organizational Behaviour: An Introductory Text*. Prentice Hall: London.

Hudson, J. and Jones, P. (2005). '"Public goods": an exercise in calibration'. *Public Choice*, 124(3): 267–82.

Hughes, J. (2005). 'Bringing emotion to work: emotional intelligence, employee resistance and the reinvention of character'. *Work, Employment & Society*, 19(3): 603–25.

Hyde, P. and Davies, H. T. O. (2004). 'Service design, culture and performance: collusion and co-production in health care'. *Human Relations*, 57(11): 1407–26.

Hyden, G. and Bratton, M. (eds) (1992). *Governance and Politics in Africa*. Lynne Rienner: Colorado, Boulder.

Instituto de Estudios Nicaraguenses (1999). *Proyecto trianual por el fortelecimiento de la gobernabildad democratica de Nicaragua*. IEN: Managua.

Instituto Nacional de Estadisticas y Censos (2001). As listed on http://www.procig.org/ing/resources-censuses.htm last accessed 13 September 2009.

Jackson, N. and Carter, P. (1995). 'Organizational chiaroscuro: throwing light on the concept of corporate governance'. *Human Relations*, 48(8): 875–89.

Jann, W. (2003). 'State, administration and governance in Germany: competing traditions and dominant narratives'. *Public Administration*, 81(1): 95–118.

Jenkins, R. (2002). *Churchill*. Pan: London.

Jessop, B. (1998). 'The rise of governance and the risks of failure: the case of economic development'. *International Social Science Journal*, 50(1): 29–45.

Jones, C., Hesterly, W. S. and Borgatti, S. P. (1997). 'A general theory of network governance: exchange conditions and social mechanisms'. *Academy of Management Review*, 22(4): 911–45.

Jones, C., Parker, M. and ten Bos, R. (2005). *For Business Ethics*. Routledge: London.

Jones, T. M. and Goldberg, L. D. (1982). 'Governing the large corporation: more arguments for public directors'. *Academy of Management Review*, 7(4): 603–11.

Kanter, R. M. (1979). 'Power failure in management circuits'. *Harvard Business Review*, 57(4): 65–75.

Karllson, S. (2000). *Multilayered Governance: Pesticides in the South – Environmental Concerns in a Globalised World*. Linköping University: Linköping.

Kaufmann, D., Kraay, A. and Mastruzzi, M. (2006). 'Governance matters V: aggregate and individual governance indicators for 1996–2005' on http://siteresources.worldbank.org/ last accessed 13 September 2009.

Kazancigil, A. (1998). 'Governance and science: market-like modes of managing society and producing knowledge'. *International Social Science Journal*, 50(155): 69–79.

Kelman, S. (2005). 'Public management needs help!'. *Academy of Management Journal*, 48(6): 967–69.

Kemal, S. (2001). 'Aristotle's poetics, the poetic syllogism, and philosophical truth in Averroes commentary'. *Journal of Value Inquiry*, 35(3): 391–412.

Kenny, A. (1973). *Wittgenstein*. Penguin: London.

Kenko (14th Century). *Essays in Idleness*. Translated by G. Sansom. Wordsworth Classics: London, 1998.

Kiernan, M. (1990). 'Making films politically: marxism in Eisenstein and Godard'. *Alif: Journal of Comparative Poetics*, 10(1): 93–113.

Kim, P. S., Halligan, J., Cho, N., Oh, C. H. and Eikenberry, A. M. (2005). 'Toward participatory and transparent governance: report on the sixth global forum on reinventing government'. *Public Administration Review*, 65(6): 646–54.

Kincaid, J. (1997). 'Review of *Creating Public Value: Strategic Management in Government*' by M. H. Moore, *Journal of Politics*, 59(1): 257–8.

King, G. (1995). 'Replication, replication'. *Political Science and Politics*, 28(3): 444–52.

Klingner, D. E. (2006). 'Building global public management governance capacity: the road not taken'. *Public Administration Review*, 66(5): 775–9.

Knight, K. (2007). *Aristotelian Philosophy: Ethics and Politics from Aristotle to MacIntyre*. Polity Press: Cambridge.

Knight, K. (in press). 'Alasdair MacIntrye's revisionary Aristotelianism: Pragmatism opposed, marxism outmoded, thomism transformed', in F. O'Rourke (ed.) *Moral Philosophy in the Twentieth Century*. University of Notre Dame Press: Notre Dame.

Knights, D. and McCabe, D. (1999). '"Are there no limits to authority": TQM and organizational power'. *Organization Studies*, 20(2): 197–224.

Kniss, J. (1998). 'Juggling organizational goals'. *Journal of Public Administration Research and Theory*, 8(2): 282–90.

Kocher, C., Kumar, K. and Subramanian, R. (1998). 'Physician-hospital integration strategies: impact on physician involvement in hospital governance'. *Health Care Management Review*, 23(3): 38–47.

Koehn, D. (1995). 'A role for virtue ethics in the analysis of business practice'. *Business*

Ethics Quarterly, 5(3): 533–9.

Koehn, D. (1998). 'Virtue ethics, the firm and moral psychology'. *Business Ethics Quarterly*, 8(3): 497–513.

Kohli, Atul (2004). *State-Directed Development: Political Power and Industrialization in the Global Periphery*. Cambridge University Press: Cambridge.

Kohn, M. (2000). 'Language, power, and persuasion: toward a critique of deliberative democracy'. *Constellations*, 7(3): 408–29.

Konstan, D. (2006). *The Emotions of the Ancient Greeks: Studies in Aristotle and Classical Literature*. University of Toronto Press: Toronto.

Konzelmann, S., Conway, N., Trenberth, L. and Wilkinson, F. (2006). 'Corporate governance and human resource management'. *British Journal of Industrial Relations*, 44(3): 541–67.

Kooiman, J. (ed.) (1993). *Modern Governance: New Government-Society Interactions*. Sage: London.

Kraut, R. (1996). 'Are there natural rights in Aristotle?'. *Review of Metaphysics*, 49(4): 755–74.

Kraut, R. (2002). *Aristotle: Political Philosophy*. Oxford University Press: Oxford.

Kraut, R. (ed.) (2006). *The Blackwell Guide to Aristotle's Nicomachean Ethics*. Blackwell: Oxford.

Kraut, R. (2006). 'Introduction' in *The Blackwell Guide to Aristotle's Nicomachean Ethics*. Blackwell: Oxford: 1–11.

Kuhn, T. S. (1970). *The Structure of Scientific Revolutions*. 2nd edition. The University of Chicago Press: Chicago.

Lacayo Oyanguren, A. (2005). *La Difícil Transición Nicaraguense en el Gobierno con Doña Violeta*. Fundación UNO: Managua.

Lancioni, J. (2006). 'Cinderella Dances *Swan Lake*: Reading *Billy Elliot* as Fairytale'. *The Journal of Popular Culture*, 39(5): 709–28.

Langworth, R. M. (2005). '"Blood, Toil, Tears and Sweat": Evolution of a Phrase'. *Finest Hour*, 128: 33.

Lara, A. (2008). 'Virtue theory and moral facts'. *The Journal of Value Inquiry*, 42(3): 331–52.

La Rochefoucauld, F. (1665). *Maxims*. Translated by L. Tancock, Penguin: London, 1959.

Latour, B. (2007). *Reassembling the Social: An Introduction to Actor Network Theory*. Oxford University Press: Oxford.

Lawrence, T. B., Mauws M. K., Dyck B. and Kleysen, R. F. (2005). 'The politics of organizational learning: integrating power into the 4I framework'. *Academy of Management Review*, 30(1): 180–91.

Lee, T. W. and Mitchell, T. R. (1994). 'An alternative approach: the unfolding model of voluntary employee turnover'. *Academy of Management Review*, 19(1): 51–89.

Leftwich, A. (1994). 'Governance, the state and the politics of development'. *Development and Change*, 25(2): 363–86.

Legge, K. (1995). *Human Resource Management: Rhetoric and Realities*. MacMillan: London.

Letiche, H. (2010). 'Polyphony and its other'. *Organization Studies*, 31(3): 261–77.

Levy, H. L. (1990). 'Does Aristotle exclude women from politics?'. *The Review of Politics*, 52(3): 397–416.

Levy, J. (2005). 'Reflections on how the theatre teaches'. *Journal of Aesthetic Education*, 39(4): 20–30.

Lewis, C. (2006). 'In pursuit of the public interest'. *Public Administration Review*, 66(5): 694–701.

Lewis, M. and Kelemen, M. (2002). 'Multiparadigm inquiry: exploring pluralism and paradoxes of contemporary organizational life'. *Human Relations*, 55(2): 251–75.

Lindsay, T. K. (1992). 'Aristotle's qualified defense of democracy through "political mixing"'. *The Journal of Politics*, 54(1): 101–19.

Lindsay, T. K. (1994). 'Was Aristotle racist, sexist, and anti-democratic?'. *The Review of Politics*, 56(1): 127–51.

Lindsay, T. K. (2000). 'Aristotle's appraisal of manly spirit: political and philosophic implications'. *American Journal of Political Science*, 44(3): 433–48.

Linstead, S., Fulop, L. and Lilley, S. (2009). *Management and Organization: A Critical Text*. 2nd edition. Palgrave: London.

Lister, E. D. and Herzog, A. (2000). 'From advocacy to ambassadorship: physician participation in healthcare governance'. *Journal of Healthcare Management*, 45(2): 108–16.

Locke, S. (2001). 'Sociology and the public understanding of science: from rationalization to rhetoric'. *British Journal of Sociology*, 52(1): 1–18.

Long, R. T. (1996). 'Aristotle's conception of freedom'. *Review of Metaphysics*, 49(4): 775–802.

Lowe, G. and Rastin, S. (2000). 'Organizing the next generation: influences on young workers' willingness to join unions in Canada'. *British Journal of Industrial Relations*, 38(2): 203–22.

Lukács, G. (1971). *History and Class Consciousness: Studies in Marxist Dialectics*. Translated by R. Livingstone. Merlin Press: London.

Lukes, S. (2005). *Power: A Radical View*. 2nd edition. Macmillan: London.

Lynch, M. (1992). *Reaction and Revolutions: Russia 1881–1924*. Hodder and Stoughton: London.

Lynn, L. E., Heinrich, C.J. and Hill, C. J. (2001). *Improving Governance: A New Logic for Empirical Research*. Georgetown University Press: Washington.

Lyotard, J-F. (1984). *The Postmodern Condition: A Report on Knowledge*. Manchester University Press: Manchester.

Macchiavelli, N. (1532). *The Prince*. Translated by T. Parks. Penguin: London, 2011.

MacIntyre, A. (1979). 'Corporate modernity and moral judgement: are they mutually exclusive?', in K. E. Goodpaster and K. M. Sayre (eds) *Ethics and Problems of the 21st Century*. University of Notre Dame Press: Notre Dame: 122–33.

MacIntyre, A. (1982). 'Why are the problems of business ethics insoluble', in B. Baumrin and B. Friedman (eds) *Moral Responsibility and the Professions*. Haven Publishing: New York: 350–9.

MacIntyre, A. (1984a). *After Virtue*. 2nd edition. Duckworth: London.

MacIntyre, A. (1984b). 'Does applied ethics rest on a mistake?'. *The Monist*, 67(4): 498–513.

MacIntyre, A. (1988). *Whose Justice? Which Rationality?* Duckworth: London.

MacIntyre A. (1999a). *Dependent Rational Animals: Why Human Beings Need the Virtues*. Open Court: Chicago.

MacIntyre, A. (1999b). 'Social structures and their threats to moral agency.' *Philosophy*, 74: 311–29.

Maheshwari, S. R. (2005). *Public Administration in India: The Higher Civil Service.* Oxford University Press: New Delhi.

Mallette, P. and Hogler, R. L. (1995). 'Board composition, stock ownership and the exemption of directors from liability'. *Journal of Management*, 21(5): 861–78.

March J. G. (1997). 'Understanding how decisions happen in organisations', in Z. Shapira (ed.) *Organisational Decision Making.* Cambridge University Press: Cambridge: 9–34.

Marquand, D. (2004). *Decline of the Public.* Polity Press: Cambridge.

Marr, A. (2007). *A History of Modern Britain.* MacMillan: London.

Maslow, A. (1954). *Motivation and Personality.* Harper and Row: New York.

Masters, R. D. (1990). 'Evolutionary biology and political theory'. *The American Political Science Review*, 84(1): 195–210.

Mathias, N. and Teresa, H. R. (2006). 'A hermeneutic of Amartya Sen's concept of capability'. *International Journal of Social Economics*, 33(10): 710–22.

Mauws, M. K. and Phillips, N. (1995). 'Understanding language games'. *Organization Science*, 6(3): 322–33.

Mayers, D., Shivdasani, A. and Smith, C. W. (1997). 'Board composition in the life insurance industry'. *Journal of Business*, 70(1): 33–63.

McClelland, D. C. (1965). 'Toward a theory of motive acquisition'. *American Psychologist*, 20(5): 321–33.

McLaughlin, J. (2001). 'Evidence based medicine and risk: rhetorical resources in the articulation of professional identity'. *Journal of Management in Medicine*, 15(5): 352–63.

Mellahi K., Morrell, K. and Wood, G. (2010). *The Ethical Business.* 2nd edition. Palgrave: London.

Mellers, B. A., Schwartz, A. and Cooke, A. D. J. (1999). 'Judgment and decision making'. *Annual Review of Psychology*, 49: 447–77.

Mengistu, B. and Vogel, E. (2006). 'Bureaucratic neutrality among competing bureaucratic values in an ethnic federalism: the case of Ethiopia'. *Public Administration Review* 66(2): 205–16.

Mercer, D. (ed.) (1989). *Chronicle of the Twentieth Century.* Longman: London.

Merrow, K. (2003). '"The meaning of every style": Nietzsche, Demosthenes, Rhetoric'. *Rhetorica*, XXI(4): 285–307.

Merton, R. K. (1948). 'The Self-fulfilling Prophecy'. *Antioch Review*, 8: 193–210.

Mill, J. S. (1859). *On Liberty.* Penguin Classics: London, 1985.

Miller, M. H. (1986). 'Behavioral rationality in finance: the case of dividends'. *Journal of Business*, 59(4): S451–S468.

Miller, C. C., Cardinal, L. B. and Glick, W. H. (1997). 'Retrospective reports in organizational research'. *Academy of Management Journal*, 40(1): 189–204

Mintzberg, H. (1973). *The Nature of Managerial Work.* Harper & Row: New York.

Mok, K. (2002). 'Policy of decentralization and changing governance of higher education in post-Mao China'. *Public Administration and Development*, 22(3): 261–73.

Molina, A. D. and Spicer, M. W. (2004). 'Aristotelian rhetoric, pluralism, and public administration'. *Administration & Society*, 36(3): 282–305.

Moore, G. (2005). 'Corporate character: modern virtue ethics and the virtuous corporation', *Business Ethics Quarterly*, 15(4): 659–85.

Moore, M. H. (1995). *Creating Public Value: Strategic Management in Government*. Harvard Business School Press: Harvard.

Moore, G. and Beadle, R. (2006). 'In search of organizational virtue in business: agents, goods, practices, institutions and environments'. *Organization Studies*, 27(3): 369–89.

Morgan, G. (1997). *Images of Organization*. Sage: London.

Morrell, K. (2004a). 'Decision making and business ethics: the implications of using image theory in preference to rational choice'. *Journal of Business Ethics*, 50: 239–52.

Morrell, K. (2004b). 'Enhancing effective careers thinking: scripts and Socrates'. *British Journal of Guidance and Counselling*, 32: 547–58.

Morrell, K. (2006a). 'Policy as narrative: new labour's reform of the national health service'. *Public Administration*, 84(2): 367–85.

Morrell, K. (2006b). 'Governance, ethics and the NHS'. *Public Money and Management*, 26(1): 55–62.

Morrell, K. (2006c). 'Aphorisms and leaders' rhetoric'. *Leadership*, 2(3): 367–82.

Morrell, K. (2007). 'Aesthetics and Learning in Aristotle'. *Leadership*, 3(4): 497–500.

Morrell, K. (2008). 'The Narrative of evidence based management: a polemic'. *Journal of Management Studies*, 45: 613–35.

Morrell, K. (2009). 'Governance and the public good'. *Public Administration*, 87(3): 538–56.

Morrell, K. (in press). 'Evidence-Based dialectics' forthcoming in *Organization* available by Sage online early DOI: 10.1177/1350508411414229.

Morrell, K. and Clark, I. (2010). 'Private equity and the public good'. *Journal of Business Ethics*, 96(2): 249–63.

Morrell, K. and Harrington-Buhay, N. (forthcoming) 'What is in the 'public interest'? The case of the 1995 property forum in post conflict Nicaragua', forthcoming in *Public Administration*.

Morrell, K. and Hartley, J. (2006). 'A Model of political leadership'. *Human Relations*, 59(4): 483–504.

Morrell, K. and Jayawardhena, J. (2010) 'Fair trade, ethical decision making and the narrative of gender difference. *Business Ethics*, 19(4): 393–407.

Moulton, S. (2009). 'Putting together the publicness puzzle: a framework for realized publicness'. *Public Administration Review* 69(5): 889–900.

Moynahan, B. (1997). *The Russian Century*. Pimlico: London.

Moynihan, D. P. and Pandey, S. K. (2007). 'The role of organizations in fostering public service motivation'. *Public Administration Review*, 67(1): 40–53.

Mrotek, D. D. (2001). The drama of dysfunction: value conflict in US managed care. *Human Relations*, 54(2): 147–72.

Mueller, F. and Carter, C. (2005). 'The scripting of total quality management within its organizational biography'. *Organization Studies*, 26: 221–47.

Neuliep, J. W. (ed.) (1991). *Replication Research in the Social Sciences*. Sage: Thousand Oaks, CA.

Neuliep, J. W. and Crandall, R. (1991). 'Editorial bias against replication research', in J. W. Neuliep (ed.) *Replication Research in the Social Sciences*. Sage: Thousand Oaks, CA: 85–90.

New York Times (2008). Transcript of Barack Obama's Acceptance Speech, 28 August 2008 available on http://www.nytimes.com/2008/08/28/us/politics/28text-obama.html?pagewanted=1&_r=1 last accessed 29 August 2011.

Nichols, M. P. (1992). *Citizens and Statesmen: A Study of Aristotle's Politics*. Rowman & Littlefield: Savage, MA.

Nietzsche, F. (1886). *Beyond Good and Evil*. Translated by W. Kaufmann. Penguin Classics: London, 1973.

Nietzsche, F. (1989). *On the Genealogy of Morals*. Translated by W. Kaufmann, Vintage Books: New York.

Nozick, R. (1974). *Anarchy, State, and Utopia*. Basic Books: New York.

Nussbaum, M. C. (1976). 'The Text of Aristotle's De Motu Animalium'. *Harvard Studies in Classical Philology*, 80: 111–59.

Nussbaum, M. C. (1988). 'Nature, function, and capability: Aristotle on political distribution'. *Oxford Studies in Ancient Philosophy*, 6 (supplementary volume): 145–84.

Nussbaum, M. C. (1999). 'Women and equality: the capabilities approach'. *International Labour Review*, 138(3): 227–49.

Nussbaum, M. C. (2001a). *The Fragility of Goodness*. Revised edition. Cambridge University Press: Cambridge.

Nussbaum, M. (2001b). *Upheavals of Thought: The Intelligence of Emotions*. Cambridge University Press: New York.

O'Brien, T. W. (2009). 'Reconsidering the common good in a business context'. *Journal of Business Ethics*, 85(1): 25–37.

O'Leary, M. and Chia, R. (2007). 'Epistemes and structures of sensemaking in organizational life'. *Journal of Management Inquiry*, 16(4): 392–406.

O'Neill, J. (1998). 'Rhetoric, science, and philosophy'. *Philosophy of the Social Sciences*, 28(2): 205–25.

O'Neill, J. (2002). ' The rhetoric of deliberation: some problems in Kantian theories of deliberative democracy'. *Res Publica*, 8(3): 249–68.

Okamoto, D. G. and Smith-Lovin, L. (2001). 'Changing the subject: gender, status, and the dynamics of topic change', *American Sociological Review*, 66(6): 852–73.

Olshewsky, T. M. (1976). 'On the relations of soul to body in Plato and Aristotle'. *Journal of the History of Philosophy*, 14(4): 391–404.

Onega, S. and Landa, J. A. G. (eds) (1996). *Narratology*. Longman: Harlow.

Oswick, C., Keenoy, T. W. and Grant, D. (2000). 'Discourse, organizations and organizing: concepts, objects and subjects'. *Human Relations*, 53: 1115–23.

Parker, M. (ed.) (1998). *Ethics and Organization*. Sage: London.

Parker, M. (2003). 'Ethics, politics and organizing'. *Organization*, 10(2): 187–203.

Parker, M. (2010). 'Inter, neo, trans: editorial'. *Organization*, 17(1): 5–8.

Patashnik, E. (2003). 'After the public interest prevails: the political sustainability of policy reform'. *Governance*, 16(2): 203–34.

Pellegrin, P. (1986). *Aristotle's classification of Animals: Biology and the Conceptual Unity of the Aristotelian Corpus*. University of California Press: London.

Perelman, C. and Olbrechts-Tyteca, L. (1969). *The New Rhetoric: A Treatise on Argumentation*.

Perry, J. L. and Rainey, H. G. (1988). 'The public-private distinction in organization theory: a critique and research strategy'. *Academy of Management Review*, 13(2): 182–201.

Pettigrew, A. M. (2005). 'The character and significance of management research on the public services'. *Academy of Management Journal*, 48(6): 973–77.

Pettigrew, A. M. and McNulty, T. (1995). 'Power and influence in and around the boardroom'. *Human Relations*, 48: 845–73.

Pfeffer, J. (1993). 'Barriers to the advance of organizational science: paradigm development as a dependent variable'. *Academy of Management Review*, 18(4): 599–620.

Pfeffer, J. (1997). 'Mortality, reproducibility, and the persistence of styles of theory'. *Organization Science*, 6(4): 681–6.

Pfeffer, J. and Lawler, J. (1980). 'Effects of job alternatives, extrinsic rewards and behavioral commitment on attitude toward the organisation: a field test of the insufficient justification paradigm'. *Administrative Science Quarterly*, 25: 38–56.

Pickhardt, M. (2005). 'Some remarks on self-interest, the historical schools and the evolution of the theory of public goods'. *Journal of Economic Studies*, 32: 275–93.

Pierre, J. (1998). *Partnerships in Urban Governance: European and American Experience*. Macmillan: Basingstoke, Hampshire.

Pierre, J. and Peters, B. G. (2000). *Governance, Politics and the State*. Macmillan: Basingstoke, Hampshire.

PNUD (*Programa de las Naciones Unidas para el Desarollo*) (2006). *La Democracia en America Latina* .Aguilar, Buenos Aires.

Podrabsky, J. E., Lopez, J. P., Fan, T. W. M., Higashi, R. and Somero, G. N. (2007). 'Extreme anoxia tolerance in embryos of the annual killifish *Austrofundulus limnaeus*: insights from a metabolomics analysis'. *Journal of Experimental Biology*, 210: 2253–66.

Polanyi, K. (1957). *The Great Transformation*. Beacon: Boston.

Pollitt, C. and Bouckaert, G. (2000). *Public Management Reform: A Comparative Analysis*. Oxford University Press: Oxford.

Popper, K. R. (1959). *The Logic of Scientific Discovery*. Basic Books: New York.

Popper, K. R. (1962). *Conjectures and Refutations*. Basic Books: New York.

Poppo, L. and Zenger, T. (2002). 'Do formal contracts and relational governance function as substitutes or complements?'. *Strategic Management Journal*, 23(8): 707–25.

Porter, H. (2006). 'Blair laid bare: the article that may get you arrested', *The Independent*, 29 June 2006 available on http://news.independent.co.uk/uk/politics/article1129827.ece last accessed on 8 June 2007.

Poste, E. (1850). *The Logic of Science: A Translation of the Posterior Analytics of Aristotle with Notes and an Introduction*. Macpherson: Oxford.

Potter, J. (1996). *Representing Reality: Discourse, Rhetoric and Social Construction*. Sage: London.

Potter, J. and Wetherell, M. (1987). *Discourse and Social Psychology*. Sage: London.

Prichard, C. (2009). 'Three moves for engaging students in critical management studies'. *Management Learning*, 40(1): 51–68.

Proctor, S., Papasolomou-Dukakis, I. and Proctor, T. (2002). 'What are television advertisements really trying to tell us? A postmodern perspective'. *Journal of Consumer Behaviour*, 1(3): 246–55.

Purnima, K. (2005). *Deepening Democracy: Challenges of Governance and Globalization in India/Madhu.* Oxford University Press: New Delhi.

Rasmussen, D. M. (1993). 'Business ethics and postmodernism: a response'. *Business Ethics Quarterly,* 3(3): 271–7.

Rawls, J. (1971). *A Theory of Justice.* Harvard University Press: Cambridge, Mass.

Rawls, J. (1999). *A Theory of Justice.* Revised edition. Harvard University Press: Harvard.

Reeve, C. D. C. (1998). 'Aristotelian education', in A. O. Rorty (ed.) *Philosophers on Education. New Historical Perspectives.* Routledge: London: 49–63.

Reeve, C. D. C. (2006). 'Aristotle on the virtues of thought', in R. Kraut (ed.) *Blackwell Guide to Aristotle's Ethics.* Blackwell: Oxford: 198–217.

Reeve, C. D. C. (forthcoming) *Aristotle on Practical Wisdom: Nicomachean Ethics VI.* Translated with an Introduction, Analysis, and Commentary by C. D. C. Reeve. Harvard University Press: Harvard.

Reeve, C. D. C. (2012) *Action, Contemplation, and Happiness: An Essay on Aristotle.* Harvard University Press: Harvard.

Reps, P. (1991). *Zen Flesh, Zen Bones,* Penguin: London.

Rettinger, D. A. and Hastie, R. (2001). 'Content effects on decision making'. *Organisational Behaviour and Decision Processes,* 85(2): 336–59.

Rhodes, R. (2000). 'The Governance narrative: key findings and lessons from the ESRC's whitehall programme'. *Public Administration,* 78(2): 345–63.

Rhodes, R. A. W. (1997). *Understanding Governance: Policy Networks, Governance, Reflexity and Accountability.* Bristol: Open University Press.

Rhodes, R. A. W. (2005). 'Everyday life in a ministry: public administration as anthropology'. *American Review of Public Administration,* XX(1): 1 – 23.

Rhodes, R. and Wanna, J. (2009). 'Bringing the politics back in: public value in Westminster parliamentary government'. *Public Administration,* 87(2): 161–83.

Richards, P. (2004). *Pobladoras, Indígenas, and the State: Conflicts over Women's Rights in Chile.* Rutgers University Press: New Brunswick, NJ.

Robbins, S. P. and Judge, T. A. (2007). *Organizational Behaviour.* 12th edition. Prentice Hall: Englewood Cliffs, NJ.

Roberts, J. (2001). 'Trust and control in Anglo-American systems of corporate governance: the individualizing and socializing effects of processes of accountability'. *Human Relations,* 54(12): 1547–72.

Robinson, A. (2006). *The Last Man Who Knew Everything: Thomas Young, the Anonymous Polymath Who Proved Newton Wrong, Explained How We See, Cured the Sick and Deciphered the Rosetta Stone.* Pi Press: New York.

Rosenau, J. N. and Czempiel, E. O. (eds) (1992). *Governance without Government: Order and Change in World Politics,* Cambridge University Press: Cambridge.

Ross, W. D. (1980). Aristotle, *The Nicomachean ethics.* Hazell Books: Aylesbury.

Ross, W. D. (1991). 'Introduction', in W. D. Ross (ed.) *The Nicomachean Ethics.* Oxford University Press: Oxford. v–xxiv.

Rousseau, J-J. (1755/1984). *A Discourse on Inequality.* Translated by M. Cranston. Penguin: London.

Roxbee Cox, J. W. (1973). 'The appeal to the public interest'. *British Journal of Political Science,* 3(2): 229–41.

Rubenstein, R. (2003). *Aristotle's Children: How Christians, Muslims, and Jews Rediscovered Ancient Wisdom and Illuminated the Dark Ages.* Harcourt: Orlando.

Rudrum, D. (2005). 'From narrative representation to narrative use: towards the limits of definition'. *Narrative*, 13(2): 195–204.

Russell, B. (2010). *Freedom and Organisation*. Routledge: London.

Russell, B. (1984). *A History of Western Philosophy*. Unwin: London.

Russell, D. A. and Winterbottom, M. (1989). *Classical Literary Criticis*. Oxford University Press: Oxford.

Ryan, J. J. (2004). 'Decentralization and democratic instability: the case of Costa Rica'. *Public Administration Review*, 64(1): 81–91.

Sackett, D. L., Rosenberg, W. M., Gray, J. A. M., Haynes, R. B. and Richardson, W. S. (1996). 'Evidence based medicine: what it is and what it isn't'. *British Medical Journal*, 312: 71–2.

Salancik, G. R. and Brindle, M. C. (1997). 'The social ideologies of power in organizational decisions', in Z. Shapira (ed.) *Organisational Decision Making*. Cambridge University Press: Cambridge: 111–32.

Saleh, S. S., Vaughn, T., Rohrer, J. E. and Linden, T. (2002). 'The effect of governing board composition on rural hospitals' involvement in Provider-Sponsored Managed Care Organizations'. *Journal of Healthcare Management*, 47(5): 321–33.

Samuelson, P. A. (1954). 'The pure theory of public expenditure'. *Review of Economics and Statistics*, 36: 387–9.

Saxonhouse, A. W. (1982) 'Family, polity and unity: Aristotle on socrates' community of wives'. *Polity*, 15(2): 202–19.

Sayer A. (1992). *Method in Social Science: A Realist Approach*. Routledge: London.

Sayer A. (2011). *Why Things Matter to People: Social Science, Values and Ethical Life*. Cambridge University Press: Cambridge.

Sbragia, A. M. (2000). 'Governance, the state, and the market: what is going on?', *Governance*, 13(2): 243–50.

Schank, R. C. and Abelson, R. P. (1977). *Scripts, Plans, Goals and Understanding: An Inquiry into Human Knowledge Structures*. Lawrence Erblaum Associates: New Jersey.

Scherer, A. G. and Palazzo, G. (2007). 'Toward a political conception of corporate responsibility: business and society seen from a Habermasian perspective'. *Academy of Management Review*, 32(4): 1096–1120.

Scherer, A. G. and Palazzo, G. (2008). *Handbook of Research on Global Corporate Citizenship*. Edward Elgar Publishing: Northampton MA.

Schofield, M. (2006). 'Aristotle's political ethics', in R. Kraut (ed.) *The Blackwell Guide to Aristotle's Nicomachean Ethic*. Blackwell: Oxford: 305–22.

Schofield, J. and Sausman, C. (2004). 'Symposium on implementing public policy: learning from theory and practice'. *Public Administration*, 82(2): 235–48.

Scholes, R. (1981). 'Language, narrative, and anti-narrative', in W. J. T. Mitchell (ed.) *On Narrative*. University of Chicago Press: Chicago: 200–8.

Schubert, G. (1962). *The Public Interest*. Free Press: Glencoe IL.

Sen, A. K. (1985). *Commodities and Capabilities*. North Holland: Amsterdam.

Sen, A. K. (1992). *Inequality Reexamined*. Harvard University Press: Cambridge, MA.

Sen, A. K. (1999). *Development as Freedom*. Oxford University Press: Oxford.

Senarclens, P. (1998). 'Governance and the crisis in the international mechanisms of regulation'. *International Social Science Journal*, 50(1): 91–104.

Sewell, G. (2004). 'Yabba-Dabba-Doo! evolutionary psychology and the rise of flintstone psychological thinking in organization and management studies'. *Human Relations*, 57(8): 923–55.

Shakespeare, W. (1599). 'Julius Ceasar', in W. J. Craig (ed.) *The Complete Works of William Shakespeare*. Oxford University Press: Oxford, 1962.

Shamir, B., Arthur, M. and House, R. (1994). 'The Rhetoric of Charismatic Leadership: A Theoretical Extension, a Case Study, and Implications for Research'. *Leadership Quarterly*, 5(x): 25–42.

Shapira, Z. (ed.) (1997). *Organisational Decision Making*. Cambridge University Press: Cambridge.

Shapiro, D. L. and Rynes, S. L. (2005). 'The role of management scholarship in the public sector'. *Academy of Management Journal*, 48(6): 989–97.

Sharp, H., Woodman, M. and Hovenden, F. (2005). 'Using metaphor to analyse qualitative data: Vulcans and Humans in software development', *Empirical Software Engineering*, 10(3): 343–65.

Shaw, E. (2008). *Losing Labour's Soul? New Labour and the Blair Government 1997–2007*. Routledge: UK.

Sheaff, R. and West, M. (1997). 'Marketization, managers and moral strain: chairmen, directors and public service ethos in the national health service'. *Public Administration*, 75(2): 189–206.

Shergold, P. (1997). 'The colour purple: perceptions of accountability across the Tasman'. *Public Administration and Development*, 17(3): 293–306.

Shillabeer, A., Buss, T. F. and Rousseau, D. M. (2011). *Evidence-Based Public Management: Practices, Issues, and Prospects*, M. E. Sharpe: New York.

Shulsky, A. (1991). 'The 'infrastructure' of Aristotle's politics: Aristotle on economics and politics', in C. Lord and D. K. O'Connor (eds) *Essays on the Foundations of Aristotelian Political Science*. University of California Press: Berkeley: 74–111.

Simo, G. and Bies, A. L. (2007). 'The role of nonprofits in disaster response: an expanded model of cross-sector collaboration'. *Public Administration Review*, 67(2): 125–42.

Simon, H. A. (1983). *Models of Bounded Rationality*. MIT press: Mass.

Sinclair, A. (2007). 'Teaching leadership critically to MBAs: experiences form heaven and hell'. *Management Learning*, 38(4): 458–71.

Sison, A. J. G. (2003). *The Moral Capital of Leaders: Why Virtue Matters*. Edward Elgar: Cheltenham.

Sison, A. J. G. (2008). *Corporate Governance and Ethics: An Aristotelian Perspective*. Edward Elgar: Cheltenham.

Skinner, B. F. (1953). *Science and Human Behaviour*. Macmillan: New York.

Snyder, R. and Mahoney, J. (1999). 'The missing variable: institutions and the study of regime change'. *Comparative Politics*, 32(1): 103–22.

Solomon, R. C. (1993). *Ethics and Excellence*. Oxford University Press: New York.

Solomon, R. C. (1994). 'The corporation as community a reply to Ed Hartman'. *Business Ethics Quarterly*, 4(3): 271–85.

Solomon, R. C. (1998). 'The moral psychology of business: care and compassion in the corporation'. *Business Ethics Quarterly*, 8(3): 515–33.

Spender, J. C. and Grinyer, P. H. (1995). 'Organizational renewal: top management's role in a loosely coupled system'. *Human Relations*, 48(8): 909–26.

Spies, K., Hesse, F. and Loesch, K. (1997). 'Store atmosphere, mood and purchasing behavior'. *International Journal of Research in Marketing*, 14(1): 1–17.

Spivak, G. C. (1999). *A Critique of Postcolonial Reason: Toward a History of the Vanishing Present*. Harvard University Press: Cambridge, MA.

Stalley, R. F. (2009). 'Introduction' in Aristotle (2009). *Politics*. Translated by E. Barker, R. F. Stalley (eds) Oxford University Press: Oxford: vii–xlvii.

Starbuck, W. H. (2003). 'Shouldn't organization theory emerge from adolescence?'. *Organization*, 10(3): 439–52.

Starkey, K. (1995). 'Opening up corporate governance'. *Human Relations*, 48(8): 837–44.

Staw, B. (1997). 'The escalation of commitment: an update and appraisal', in Z. Shapira (ed.) *Organisational Decision Making*. Cambridge University Press: Cambridge: 191–215.

Steiner, P. (1984). *Russian Formalism: A Metapoetics*. Cornell: London.

Stoker, G. (2006). 'Public value management a new narrative for networked governance?'. *The American Review of Public Administration*, 36(1): 41–57.

Strike (1925). Directed by Sergei Eisenstein. Available via Image Entertainment USA (2000).

Stubbs, M. (1983). *Discourse Analysis: The Sociolinguistic Analysis of Natural Language*. Blackwell: Oxford.

Sturdy, A. and Fineman, S. (2001). 'Struggles for the control of affect – resistance as politics *and* emotion', in A. Sturdy, I. Grugulis and H. Willmott (eds) *Customer Service: Empowerment and Entrapment*. Critical Perspectives on Work and Organizations Series. Palgrave: Basingstoke: 135–56.

Sun, W., Stewart, J. and Pollard, D. (2012). *Corporate Governance and the Global Financial Crisis: International Perspective*. Cambridge University Press: Cambridge.

Sun Tzu (4th Century BCE). *The Art of War*. Translated by S. Griffith. Oxford University Press: Oxford 1971.

Sundaramurthy, C. and Lewis, M. (2003). 'Control and collaboration: paradoxes of governance'. *Academy of Management Review*, 28(3): 397–415.

Suppe, F. (2001). 'Definitions', in W. Newton-Smith (ed.) *A Companion to the Philosophy of Science*. Blackwell: London: 76–8.

Swanson, J. A. (1992). *The Public and the Private in Aristotle's Political Philosophy*. Cornell University Press: Ithaca and London.

Swift, J. (2004). *A Tale of a Tub*. Penguin: London.

Symons, C. S. and Johnson, B. T. (1997). 'The self-reference effect in memory: a meta-analysis'. *Psychological Bulletin*, 121(3): 371–94.

Taras, D. and Steel, P. (2007). 'We provoked business students to unionize: using deception to prove an IR point'. *British Journal of Industrial Relations*, 45(1): 179–98.

Thompson, P. and McHugh, D. (2002). *Work Organisations*. 3rd edition. Palgrave: London.

Thorpe, C. (2001). 'Science against modernism: the relevance of the social theory of Michael Polanyi'. *British Journal of Sociology*, 52(1): 19–35.

Timmerman, D. M. (2002). 'The Aristotelian fix: fourth century B.C. Perspectives on political deliberation'. *Rhetoric Society Quarterly*, 32(3): 77–98.

Timmins, N. (1995). *The Five Giants: A Biography of the Welfare State*. HarperCollins: London.

Tindale, C. W. (2006). 'Perelman, informal logic and the historicity of reason'. *Informal Logic*, 26(3): 341–57.

Tullock, G. (1984). 'A (partial) rehabilitation of the public interest theory'. *Public Choice*, 42(1): 89–99.

Tversky, A. and Kahnemann, D. (1981). 'The framing of decisions and the psychology of choice'. *Science*, 211: 453–58.

UN Economic and Social Commission for Asia and the Pacific (UNESCAP) *What is Good Governance* available on http://www.unescap.org/pdd/prs/ ProjectActivities/Ongoing/gg/ last accessed 12 May 2009.

UN General Assembly (UNGA) (1994). *International assistance for the rehabilitation and reconstruction of Nicaragua: aftermath of the war and natural disasters: G.A. Resolution 49/16*. United Nations: New York.

UNGA (2000). *United Nations Millennium Declaration*. United Nations: New York.

United Nations Development Programme (UNDP) (2002). *Deepening democracy in a fragmented world*. Oxford University Press: Oxford.

van Blijswijk, J. A. M., van Breukelen, R. C. J., Franklin, A. L., Raadschelders, J. C. and Slump, N. P. (2004). 'Beyond ethical codes: the management of integrity in the Netherlands tax and customs administration'. *Public Administration Review*, 64(6): 718–27.

Van Maanen, J. (1995). 'Style as theory'. *Organization Science*, 6(1): 133–43.

Van Staveren, I. (2001). *The Values of Economics. An Aristotelian Perspective*. Routledge: London.

Vecchio. R. P. (2001). *Organizational Behavior*. 4th edition. Dryden: New York.

Velasquez, M. G. (2001). *Business Ethics: Concepts and Cases*. 5th edition. Prentice Hall: London

Veltman, A. (2004). 'Aristotle and Kant on self-disclosure in friendship'. *The Journal of Value Inquiry*, 38(2): 225–39.

Vigoda-Gadot, E. and Meisler, G. (2010). 'Emotions in management and the management of emotions: the impact of emotional intelligence and organizational politics on public sector employees'. *Public Administration Review*, 70(1): 72–86.

Vroom, V. H. (1964). *Work and Motivation*. Wiley: New York.

Wagner, J. A. and Hollenbeck, J. R. (2010). *Organizational Behaviour: Securing Competitive Advantage*. Routledge: London.

Walsh, J. P., Weber, K. and Margolis, J. D. (2003). 'Social issues and management: Our lost cause found'. *Journal of Management*, 29(6): 859–81.

Walton, C. C. (1993). 'Business ethics and postmodernism: a dangerous dalliance'. *Business Ethics Quarterly*, 3(3): 285–305.

Watson, T. J. (1995). 'Rhetoric, discourse and argument in organizational sense making: a reflexive tale'. *Organizational Studies*, 16(5): 805–21.

Watson, T. J. (1996). 'Motivation: that's maslow, isn't it?'. *Management Learning*, 27(4): 447–64.

Watson, T. J. (2006). *Organising and Managing Work*. 2nd edition. Prentice Hall: London.

Weick, K. E. (1995). *Sensemaking in Organizations*. Sage: London.

Weick, K. E. (1999). 'Theory construction as disciplined reflexivity: tradeoffs in the 90s'. *Academy of Management Review*, 24(4): 797–806.

Weidhorn, M. (1972). 'Churchill the phrase forger'. *Quarterly Journal of Speech*, 58(2): 161–74.

Weidhorn, M. (1975). 'Blood, toil, tears, and 8,000,000 words: Churchill writing'. *The Columbia Forum*, 4(1): 19–23.

Wheeler, M. A., Stuss D. T. and Tulving E. (1997). 'Toward a theory of episodic memory: the frontal lobes and autonoetic consciousness'. *Psychological Bulletin*, 121(3): 331–54.

Wilson, F. (2010). *Organizational Behaviour and Work: A Critical Introduction*. 3rd edition. Oxford University Press: Oxford.

Wittgenstein, L. (1921). *Tractatus Logico-Philosophicus*. Routledge: London, 2001.

Wittgenstein, L. (1953). *Philosophical Investigations*. Translated by G. Anscombe. Blackwell: Oxford.

Worth, S. E. (2000). 'Aristotle, thought, and mimesis: our responses to fiction'. *The Journal of Aesthetics and Art Criticism*, 58(4): 333–9.

Wright Mills, C. (1959). *The Sociological Imagination*. Oxford University Press: New York.

Yin, R. K. (2004). *Case Study Research: Design and Methods*. Sage: Thousand Oaks, CA.

Young, C. (2006). 'Aristotle's justice', in R. Kraut (ed.) *Blackwell Guide to Aristotle's Ethics*. Blackwell: Oxford: 179–97.

Zajac, E. J. and Westphal, J. D. (1997). 'Managerial incentives in organisations: Economic, political and symbolic perspectives', in Z. Shapira (ed.), *Organisational Decision Making*. Cambridge University Press: Cambridge: 133–57.

Zey, M. (ed.) (1992). *Decision Making: Alternatives to Rational Choice Models*. Sage: London.

Žižek, S. (2002). 'A plea for Leninist intolerance'. *Critical Inquiry*, 28(2): 542–66.

Index